# REWIRING THE REAL

Religion, Culture, and Public Life

# RELIGION, CULTURE, AND PUBLIC LIFE

Series Editors: Alfred Stepan and Mark C. Taylor

The resurgence of religion calls for careful analysis and constructive criticism of new forms of intolerance, as well as new approaches to tolerance, respect, mutual understanding, and accommodation. In order to promote serious scholarship and informed debate, the Institute for Religion, Culture, and Public Life and Columbia University Press are sponsoring a book series devoted to the investigation of the role of religion in society and culture today. This series includes works by scholars in religious studies, political science, history, cultural anthropology, economics, social psychology, and other allied fields whose work sustains multidisciplinary and comparative as well as transnational analyses of historical and contemporary issues. The series focuses on issues related to questions of difference, identity, and practice within local, national, and international contexts. Special attention is paid to the ways in which religious traditions encourage conflict, violence, and intolerance and also support human rights, ecumenical values, and mutual understanding. By mediating alternative methodologies and different religious, social, and cultural traditions, books published in this series will open channels of communication that facilitate critical analysis.

*After Pluralism: Reimagining Religious Engagement*, edited by Courtney Bender and Pamela E. Klassen

*Religion and International Relations Theory*, edited by Jack Snyder

*Religion in America: A Political History*, Denis Lacorne

*Democracy, Islam, and Secularism in Turkey*, edited by Ahmet T. Kuru and Alfred Stepan

*Refiguring the Spiritual: Beuys, Barney, Turrell, Goldsworthy*, Mark C. Taylor

*Tolerance, Democracy, and Sufis in Senegal*, edited by Mamadou Diouf

MARK C. TAYLOR

# REWIRING THE REAL

IN CONVERSATION WITH

WILLIAM GADDIS, RICHARD POWERS,
MARK DANIELEWSKI, AND DON DELILLO

Columbia

University

Press

*New York*

Columbia University Press

*Publishers Since 1893*

New York    Chichester, West Sussex

cup.columbia.edu

Library of Congress Cataloging-in-Publication Data

Taylor, Mark C., 1945–

Rewiring the real : in conversation with William Gaddis, Richard Power, Mark Danielwski, and Don DeLillo / Mark C. Taylor.

p. cm. — (Religion, culture, and public life)

Includes bibliographical references and index.

ISBN 978-0-231-16040-7 (cloth : alk. paper)—ISBN 978-0-231-53164-1 (e-book)

1. Technology in literature. 2. American literature—20th century—History and criticism. 3. American literature—21st century—History and criticism. 4. Gaddis, William, 1922–1998. Recognitions. 5. Powers, Richard, 1957– Plowing the dark. 6. Danielewski, Mark Z. House of leaves. 7. DeLillo, Don. Underworld. 8. Technological innovations—Religious aspects. 9. Theology in literature. 10. Spirituality in literature. I. Title.

PS228. T42T39  2012

810.9'356—dc23

Columbia University Press books are printed on permanent and durable acid-free paper. This book is printed on paper with recycled content.

Printed in the United States of America

c 10 9 8 7 6 5 4 3 2 1

Cover image: © 2012 Bruce Nauman / Artists Rights Society (ARS), New York Digital image © The Museum of Modern Art/Licenced by SCALA/Art Resource, NY

Cover design: Lisa Hamm

> After one has abandoned a belief in god, poetry is that essence which takes its place as life's redemption.
>
> —Wallace Stevens

*modernist*

*save for end*

*Some good commentary on novels,*

*esp. of* *recognitions*

*But deconstructive frame quickly becomes tedious. And Taylor fails to adequately destroy postmodern*

*between modernism + postmodern + so fails to recognize how modern his music is*

Too much autobiography, most of which could have been deleted. Example of choosing to read Richard Powers & DeLillo. References to his own school and background) including a picture of Taylor in his short - Analysis of DeLillo truncated because interspersed w/ autobio. narrative.

# CONTENTS

## 5. CONCLUDING UNSCIENTIFIC POSTSCRIPT: TWO STYLES OF THE PHILOSOPHY OF RELIGION  250

# ILLUSTRATIONS

# REWIRING THE REAL

# ne𝝌us

**REWIRING THE REAL**: *In Conversation with William Gaddis, Richard Powers, Mark Danielewski, and Don DeLillo* complements and completes *Refiguring the Spiritual.* In the previous book, I examine four artists, one dead and three living (Joseph Beuys, Matthew Barney, James Turrell, and Andy Goldsworthy); in this book, I explore four writers, one dead and three living. I consider these artists and writers to be among the most important cultural figures of our era.

Like everything else in my life, this book and the interests it represents began at the knees of my parents. Thelma Kathryn Cooper (1910–1988) taught literature and was an amateur painter; Noel Alexander Taylor (1907–1992) taught biology and physics and was a semiprofessional photographer. When I was very young, my mother asked a friend to teach me how to paint, and my father taught me how to take, develop, and print photographs. They both instilled in me the conviction that teaching, writing, and art are neither

*autobiographica*   *parents*

careers nor jobs but vocations. Though I was raised in a churchgoing family, it was always clear to me that the most important scripture was literature and that the most sacred icons were artistic. I did not realize it at the time, but I was also learning that religion is most interesting where it is least obvious. Over the years, I have continued to take photographs, returned to painting from time to time, created sculptures, and undertaken big projects that fall somewhere between gardens and earthworks. I have written books about art and published elaborately designed works that border on art. I have even been fortunate to have had an exhibition at the Massachusetts Museum of Contemporary Art.[1]

My professional life took me in what I thought was a different direction. Having become interested in religion and philosophy while an under-graduate, I eventually completed an American doctorate in religion and a Danish doctorate in philosophy. For reasons I still find mysterious, I was initially drawn to philosophy and theology by reading the works of Søren Kierkegaard. Kierkegaard borrows lines from Lichtenberg for the epigram to his book *Stages on Life's Way*. "Such works are mirrors: when an ape looks in, no apostle can look out."[2] When I first read Kierkegaard's pseudonymous writings as an undergraduate, it was, indeed, like looking in a mirror—in his writings I saw my own life reflected. Only gradually did I begin to under-stand how unusual a "philosopher" Kierkegaard is; indeed, I discovered that many who fashion themselves philosophers refuse to admit him to their club. This made his work even more interesting to me. In the first course I took on Kierkegaard, I learned that he described his most important works as his "aesthetic authorship." Ever since that time I have been convinced that no clear line separates art, religion, and theology. *Rewiring the Real* would not have been possible without the lessons his writings taught me.

Over the years I have come to realize that Kierkegaard is not only the greatest writer Denmark has ever produced but also one of the greatest styl-ists in the history of philosophy and theology. Kierkegaard's preoccupation with aesthetics and, by extension, style was, in large measure, a reaction to Hegel's insistence that philosophy is scientific—*wissenschaftlich*. For Hegel, art is, in his infamous words, "a thing of the past." He did not, of course, mean that art is no longer produced but rather that philosophical conceptions have replaced religious representations and artistic images as the locus of truth. The task of philosophy in Hegel's scientific system is to translate religious and artistic *Vorstellungen* (representations) into philosophical *Begriffe* (concepts). Though the meaning of "scientific" has changed over the years, Kierkegaard and Hegel still pose very different alternatives for philosophical and theological reflection: on the one hand, art, and, on the other, science. I have always been torn between Hegel and Kierkegaard but have never doubted that on this crucial question, Kierkegaard is right—far from being a thing of the past, art creates the opening through which the future approaches.

As I studied the background and context for Kierkegaard's and Hegel's thought, my conviction about the importance of art for philosophy and theology deepened. The decisive period for the emergence of modernism and postmodernism was the decade of the 1790s, and the most important place was the small duchy of Jena, in what is now Germany. The nineteenth century effectively begins in 1790, with the publication of Kant's *Critique of Judgment*. In this work, Kant frames most of the philosophical, theological, and artistic issues that continue to be important today.[3] In the course of his analysis of aesthetic judgment, he develops the distinction between fine art and craft, or high art and low art, that became normative for modernists and the target of attack for postmodernists. Artists and writers found new possibilities for creative production in Kant's work.

At the same time, important changes were occurring in theology and religion. Throughout the eighteenth century, philosophers had attempted to defend religious belief on rational grounds by developing arguments to prove the existence of God. While the approaches on the continent and in the United Kingdom differed, over the course of the century, deists borrowed empirical methods from the natural sciences to argue for the existence of God. Far from being a vestige of primitive mentality or lingering superstition, religious faith, many argued, can be rationally justified on the basis of empirical evidence. Basing their arguments on the principle of causality, defenders of the cosmological argument argued from the existence of the world the creator God, who is its necessary cause, and proponents of the teleological argument argued from the design and purpose of the world to God as the ground of order. This line of argument finally collapsed when Hume carried empirical epistemology to its logical conclusion. Since all knowledge is based upon sense experience, he argued, causality must be understood as a subjective habit rather than as an objective fact. If belief were to be considered rational, another justification for it would have to be found.

Kant tried to salvage the sinking ship of rational theism by shifting the basis for religious belief from theory to practice. Moral activity, he argues in the *Critique of Practical Reason* (1788), presupposes belief in a moral God, human freedom, and immortality. Acting morally makes no sense if a moral god does not govern the world, and human beings do not have the freedom to accept or reject the moral law. For many of the artists, writers, poets, and philosophers who gathered in Jena in the 1790s, Kant's ethical defense of religion exacerbated the personal fragmentation and social alienation they sought to overcome. Schleiermacher, Schiller, the Schleger brothers, Hölderlin, Novalis, and others turned away from the stern dictates of the moral conscience and turned toward art as the source of religious and spiritual insight and inspiration. Friedrich Schlegel spoke for many of his fellow artists and writers when he wrote, "Whoever has religion will speak in poetry. But to seek and find religion, you need the instrument of philosophy."[4] The vision of the interplay of art, philosophy, and religion developed by the Jena romantics eventually spread to England by way of Samuel Taylor Coleridge and William Wordsworth and then to the United States, where American transcendentalists like Ralph Waldo Emerson and Henry David Thoreau fell under its sway. A century later, this trajectory led to the poetry of Wallace Stevens, whose work realizes Schiller's dream of "the aesthetic education of man." "God and the imagination," Stevens insists, "are one," and the world is, in effect, a work of art. In these writers, poets, and artists, the transcendent creator dies and is reborn as creative activity immanent in human life and the natural world.

There is, however, another romanticism that casts the lingering shadow of a different God. Within religious traditions West and East, God, the gods, and the sacred do not always bring light, certainty, and security; all too often they disrupt, disturb, and dislocate human life in ways that are profoundly unsettling. In the modern and postmodern West, the heirs of these gods are, inter alia, Schopenhauer, Kierkegaard, Freud, Poe, Melville, Blanchot, Jabès, and Derrida. For these philosophers and writers, the real, however it is conceived, is other, wholly other, or, in Kierkegaard's words that continue to echo, "infinitely and qualitatively different." If the real is radically other, it remains irreducibly obscure and cannot be rationally comprehended, scientifically analyzed, or directly communicated; rather, it must be approached indirectly in works that artfully figure what eludes precise language, clear concepts, and transparent images. Through a long and circuitous course, Kierkegaardian aestheticism eventually reappears in Derridean *ècriture* to form what Jean-Luc Nancy and Philippe Lacoue-Labarthe aptly label "the literary absolute."[5]

*Rewiring the Real* explores the complex interrelation of religion, literature, and philosophy by focusing on single works by four American writers. With one exception, these writers are not concerned with or directly influenced by European philosophy. However, just as religion is most interesting where it is least obvious, so philosophy often is important even when it is not recognized or acknowledged. The work of Gaddis, Powers, Danielewski, and DeLillo would have been impossible without the issues Kant framed and his followers elaborated. The point of this study is not to trace historical influences but to explore pressing contemporary issues that the nexus of religion, literature, and technology illuminates. In a world plagued by the literalism of both belief and unbelief, these four authors present writerly counterparts to the figurative inquiries of Beuys, Barney, Turrell, and Goldsworthy. They solicit a return of the repressed underside of our cultural unconscious in works designed to enable people to see, think, and perhaps even live otherwise.

While Gaddis, Powers, Danielewski, and DeLillo are different writers, they all share a recognition of the ways in which new media, communications, and information technologies transformed life during the latter half of the twentieth century and continue to shape our world in predictable and unpredictable ways. Neither simply utopian nor dystopian, they acknowledge that these developments both change the conditions of cultural production and pose unprecedented artistic challenges. Paradoxically, these new technologies provoke some to reject traditional orthodoxies and others to return to fundamental beliefs that have long seemed passé. At the same time, though rarely recognized, technological innovation expresses desires and aspirations once deemed religious. In the lingering twilight between belief and unbelief, technologies designed to redeem life and renew the world often turn destructive. By recasting ancient questions in new language, Gaddis, Powers, Danielewski, and DeLillo reveal new gods and demons we ignore at our own peril.

William Gaddis is arguably the most underappreciated major twentieth-century novelist. One of the reasons for this is that his most important works—*The Recognitions* and *JR*—are long and difficult. While *The Recognitions* was almost completely ignored when it was published in 1955, *JR* (1975) received the National Book Award but remains little read and rarely discussed. Gaddis is a writer's writer who asks big questions and tackles tough problems; his works are as complicated as the issues they probe. Always ahead of the times, he saw things coming long before others even suspected important changes were on the horizon. *The Recognitions* is, in my judgment, one of the two most important theological novels ever written (the other is *Moby-Dick*). This work bridges past and future by showing the relationship between traditional religious beliefs and practices and contemporary social, economic, and technological developments. Gaddis draws on ancient christological controversies and discussions of both the Christian Eucharist and Mithraic rites to illuminate psychological and social conflicts inherent in modern skepticism and secularism created by rapid technological change. This trenchant analysis anticipates what Guy Debord later labeled "the society of the spectacle" and Baudrillard described as "the culture of simulacra."

Having had a day job in an advertising agency in the 1950s, Gaddis foresaw the contemporary world of global media, where images become real and reality become imaginary. Just as the transcendent God empties (*kenosis*) himself into the figure of Jesus to render the profane sacred and the sacred profane, so the real (i.e., the signified) empties itself into the image or representation (i.e., signifier) to create a world in which signs are always signs of other signs. In the society of the spectacle and the culture of simulacra, it is impossible to be sure what is real and what is fake—everything appears to be counterfeit or, even worse, a counterfeit of a counterfeit. The primary concern of *The Recognitions* is postwar American consumer culture, where advertising keeps the economy running by creating desire where there is no need. In *JR*, the focus shifts from consumer to financial capitalism. As I have argued in *Confidence Games: Money and Markets in a World Without Redemption*, *JR* is an astonishing anticipation of the global financial capitalism that emerged at the end of the twentieth century and continues to dominate the world today. Just as signs become signs of other signs in postmodern art, architecture, and literature, so money becomes nothing more than figures of other figures coded in algorithms that govern the global flow of currencies. The world Gaddis foresees in these two novels is the world Powers, Danielewski, and DeLillo know as their own. Each of these writers asks in a different way whether art has any role to play in a world where change occurs faster than our ability to comprehend it.

All of Richard Powers's novels take as their point of departure a scientific theory or technological innovation. Powers immerses himself in scientific literature and keeps himself informed about the current state of technology: he is the rare novelist who actually understands the science and technology about which he writes. *Plowing the Dark* presents a provocative exploration of the unexpected interplay of art and religion through an account of virtual reality technology. The narrative weaves together two stories that unfold on opposite sides of the world—a VR lab in Seattle and a terrorist cell in Lebanon. West and East meet in Hagia Sophia, where Byzantine mosaics are transformed by the Web browser Mosaic. Powers sees connections where others see oppositions. Religion, art, and technology, he suggests, all express the human longing for some kind of transcendence. The question that lingers after the end of the book is whether technology has displaced art, which previously had displaced religion, as the most telling manifestation of contemporary spiritual aspiration. If so, what are the tenets and practical implications of this belief?

Mark Danielewski's style is always indirect—in the world his work portrays nothing is ever certain, and everything is subject to endless revision. Dennis Potter's *Singing Detective* might well have been describing *House of Leaves* when he repeats again and again, "All clues, no solutions." Danielewski leaves clues—countless clues—and as his tale unfolds the canny detective begins to suspect that the labyrinthian *House of Leaves* is, incongruously, the World Wide Web, which, in turn, is nothing less than the current house of God. While all four novels considered in *Rewiring the Real* erase any clear distinction between style and substance by devising stylistic innovations to convey elusive ideas, *House of Leaves* is an ingenious performative work that is graphically designed to resemble the networks it explores. The central trope of the novel is a haunted house that is bigger on the inside than on the outside. *House of Leaves* is, among other things, a book that cannot be contained between its covers—the work exceeds the bounds of the traditional novel. It begins before the beginning and continues after the end, on the World Wide Web. Far from style for style's sake, this carefully designed work communicates by doing rather than merely describing; Danielewski is as savvy about literary theory as Powers is about scientific theory. More than any other novelist now writing, he recognizes the inseparable relation of poststructural theory and postmodern art to what I have described elsewhere as "network culture."[6] Furthermore, he realizes that the intersection of art, literary theory, and technology has something to do with religion. If *The Recognitions* is the most important theological novel to have been written in the twentieth century, *House of Leaves* might be described as the most suggestive a/theological novel that has yet appeared.

DeLillo picks up where Gaddis leaves off. By the last decade of the twentieth century, counterfeits of counterfeits have become the currency of the realm, and JR has grown up to become a confidence man trading virtual securities that are anything but secure. In the course of telling the story of life in America from the beginning of the Cold War to the end of the Soviet Union, *Underworld* presents a sustained analysis and critique of both consumer and financial capitalism. I begin my discussion of the novel by writing a postscript to DeLillo's *Point Omega*, which forms a bridge between the conclusion of *Underworld*, *Das Kapital*, and his account of hypercapitalism in *Cosmopolis*.

The interplay of technology, literature, art, and, less obvious but no less important, religion lies at the heart of all these works. DeLillo has always been suspicious of technology but realizes that the tape of history cannot be rewound. For a generation raised with air-raid drills and bomb shelters, the collapse of the Berlin Wall represented the failure of communism and the triumph of capitalism. However, where others saw triumph and opportunity, DeLillo sees failure and danger. The world of global capitalism, he insists, is considerably less stable and secure than the world of the Cold War. Power no longer is divided between two superpowers that can be identified and whose boundaries can be clearly defined. Decentralization and deregulation have created a world of flows in which maintaining a semblance of order has become increasingly difficult, if not completely impossible. One of the most important factors contributing to global instability is the accelerating rate of technological change. The most important line in the novel identifies the necessary condition for so-called creative destruction in network culture: "Everything is connected." As connectivity expands, volatility increases and creates economic, social, political, and psychological instability. The danger, according to DeLillo, is not that capitalism will fail but that it will succeed all too well. Constantly searching for new markets and greater market share, capitalism is driven to excesses that prove to be its own undoing. From the nuclear bomb and environmental disaster to political upheaval and financial collapse, "an apocalyptic tone" runs throughout *Underworld*.[7] What this end portends is not at all clear.

I conclude with an essay that explains the philosophical, theological, and artistic presuppositions that lie behind both *Rewiring the Real* and *Refiguring the Spiritual*—"Concluding Unscientific Postscript: Two Styles of the Philosophy of Religion." Ever since my undergraduate days, I have returned again and again to Paul Tillich's seminal essay, "Two Types of Philosophy of Religion," in which he contrasts Augustinian and Thomistic approaches to philosophy and theology.[8] In the former, labeled the ontological type, the relation to God (or the real) is implicit though unrecognized; in the latter, labeled the cosmological type, the relation to God (or the real) is external and must be established from without.[9] While the terms of debate have changed over the years, the current distinction between continental and analytic philosophy corresponds to Tillich's distinction between the onto-logical and cosmological types. It is important to stress that the continental/analytic distinction is a twentieth-century invention. With the revival of Hegelianism in the early 1900s, British philosophy established its identity by creating its own other, over against which it defined itself. Though rarely noted, the ghost of religion haunts the machine of analytic, linguistic, and positivistic philosophy. Each of these trajectories can be traced to the late medieval nominalism of William of Ockham, who, it is important to note, spent his most productive years at Oxford. Continental philosophy, by con-trast, has no single source or origin—it is more rhizomatic than arboreal. Far from a coherent tradition, continental philosophy is a loose aggregation of movements as different as idealism, phenomenology, existentialism, herme-neutics, and, more recently, deconstruction and poststructuralism. The con-trast between continental and analytic philosophy has been useful, but its ceaseless repetition has led to a familiarity that obscures more than it clari-fies. It is time to recast the distinction in a way that opens new possibilities for creative reflection. It is more fruitful, I suggest, to think of two contrast-ing philosophical *styles*: one that models itself on art and one that models itself on an interpretation of science that is deliberately contrasted to art. This way of posing the issue is intentionally provocative because it suggests that there is nothing outside or beyond style. Furthermore, art and style are inseparable—there is no art without style and no style without art. The choice is not between style and nonstyle but between a style that represses its artistic and aesthetic facets and a style that expresses them stylistically. In order to explore the difference, in the final essay-chapter of this book, I consider alternative philosophical and theological styles through a consid-eration of the work of Martin Heidegger and Rudolph Carnap.

No philosopher since Kierkegaard has insisted on a closer interrelation of art, philosophy, and religion than Heidegger. His turn toward art is a deci-sive turn away from science. Modern science and technology, Heidegger argues, bring to closure the Western philosophical-theological tradition by enacting Nietzsche's will to power in a will to mastery that knows no bounds. Instrumental reason has created weapons of mass destruction that threaten planetary survival. Writing in the shadow of the atomic bomb and what he presciently describes as the cybernetic revolution, Heidegger's response is as unexpected as it is suggestive. He turns to religion by way of art by citing Rilke: "Only a God can save us now."[10]

For Carnap and his many followers, Heidegger's vision of philosophy is not only wrong but actually dangerous. Rather than harboring destruction, modern science and its extension in technology offer our only hope for survival. If philosophy has a role to play in the world today, its language must be as precise and its analyses as rigorous as the scientific method it emulates. Needless obscurantism, Carnap argues, creates confusion and deception that history teaches can be exploited for pernicious purposes. In the years since Carnap and his colleagues issued their manifesto, philosophy has become more and more resistant to philosophy that fashions itself aesthetic and increasingly committed to its version of the scientific method: cognitive science, evolutionary psychology, neurophysiology, machine intelligence, robotics, experimental philosophy . . . For more than a century, mainstream Anglo-American philosophy has become increasingly allergic to any writing or thinking that does not conform to its misguided criteria of rigor. The opposition between science and art is, like all such oppositions, specious and must be undone.

I began *Refiguring the Spiritual* by writing, "Art has lost its way"; I might have begun *Rewiring the Real* by writing, "Philosophy has lost its way." Over the course of the twentieth century, philosophy became more and more about less and less—and less and less about the issues and questions that really matter. This trajectory is neither necessary nor desirable. What if philosophy were to become more artful and art more philosophical? And what if, in so doing, philosophy and art were to create a new opening for the religious imagination? To explore this opening would require stylistic experiments that begin on, migrate from, and return to the page as we have known it in the past.

# 1

## COUNTERFEITING COUNTERFEIT RELIGION

*William Gaddis, The Recognitions*

> *He even said once, that the saints were counterfeits of Christ, and that Christ was a counterfeit of God.*
>
> —William Gaddis

## BETWEEN BELIEF AND UNBELIEF

**WILLIAM GADDIS'S** *The Recognitions* is one of the most theologically sophisticated novels ever written. It is also one of the richest and most difficult works of fiction in any language. Gaddis's ambition is as large as his book: his aim is nothing less than to write the *last* Christian novel. To read this prescient work is to gaze into a mirror and discover ourselves anew. The events recounted in *The Recognitions* take place in the time between belief and unbelief. While modernization and secularization make belief impossible for many erstwhile faithful, the memory of belief and the assurance it brings defer the advent of a thoroughly postmodern age of unbelief. Though never explicitly stated, Gaddis suspends his narrative between a series of polarities:

Pagan/Christian
Devil/Christ
Catholic/Protestant
Europe/America
Completion/Incompletion
Original/Counterfeit
Transcendent/Immanent
Depth/Surface
Negation/Affirmation
*Homoiousian/Homoousian*
Unbelief/Belief
Fake/Real

Gaddis's consistent purpose throughout *The Recognitions* is to subvert such simple oppositions by showing how each term folds into the other to create a nonsynthetic third that joins without precisely uniting differences.

Far from merely dismissing religion, Gaddis recognizes that the convolutions of contemporary society and culture cannot be understood apart from the ancient theological preoccupations from which they have emerged. The title and two prefatory epigrams frame the theological issues the novel explores. Gaddis borrows his title from the fourth-century work mistakenly attributed to Clement, the third bishop of Rome, who is best known for his letter to the church at Corinth (96–97 CE) that established the authority of Rome by formulating the doctrine of apostolic succession. The pseudo-Clementine *Recognitions*, some historians maintain, is the first Christian novel. Uncertainty surrounding the authorship of the original work poses the question of authenticity that preoccupies Gaddis. Quoting this little-known work in an epigram to one of his chapters, he indicates that *The Recognitions* is not only theologically allusive but also philosophically suggestive:

This is as if a drunk man should think himself to be sober, and should act indeed in all respects as a drunk man, and yet think himself to be sober, and should wish to be called so by others. Thus, therefore, are those who do not know what is true, yet hold some appearance of knowledge, and do many evil things as if they were good, and hasten to destruction as if it were salvation.[1]

In what he intends to be the *last* Christian novel, Gaddis returns to the central issues raised in the *first* Christian novel: the problem of the relation between truth and appearance and, by extension, the possibility or impossibility of salvation. The title of the novel is carefully chosen—the word *recognition* marks the intersection of epistemological and ontological questions. On the one hand, if, following Plato and his theological descendents, knowledge involves re-cognition, then truth exists prior to and independent of human knowledge. The transcendence of truth renders worldly appearances faint shadows of a reality that is never totally present. Salvation can be achieved, if at all, only through the flight from or negation of the material world. On the other hand, if, following Nietzsche and his a/theological descendents, knowledge is a human fabrication, then truth is a fiction, which might or might not be re-cognized as such. In the wake of the disappearance of transcendent truth, worldly appearances are the only "reality." Salvation can be achieved, if at all, only through the involvement in and affirmation of the material world in all of its horror and glory.

Between the title and the first chapter, Gaddis inserts an epigram drawn from Irenaeus's *Against Heresies*:

Nihil cavum neque sine signo apud Deum.
With God, nothing is empty of meaning.

Persuaded that Gnosticism posed a serious threat to the early Christian community, Irenaeus developed an extended polemic directed primarily against Valentinus, who had taught in Rome between 135 and 160. According to the conventional view, Valentinus, like other Gnostics, was a radical dualist for whom the world as we know it was created by a lower deity and remains an irredeemable realm of evil and corruption.[2] The only hope for imprisoned humanity is to escape the material realm through secret knowledge (*gnosis*) imparted by an alien divine messenger from the realm of pure light. Since Valentinus denies that the highest god is the creator and does not believe that the redemptive messenger becomes incarnate, Irenaeus argues that Gnostic speculation drains all purpose from worldly existence. For Christians, he maintains, the interrelated doctrines of creation, incarnation, and redemption (i.e., bodily resurrection) confirm the abiding goodness of the created order and thereby render life in this world meaningful. The translation of the line Gaddis selects for his epigram is ambiguous: "With God, nothing is without meaning" means, first, that with God everything is filled with meaning and, second, that with God nothing or, more precisely, nothingness (*Nihil, das Nichts*) is without meaning, i.e., has no meaning. Efforts to the contrary notwithstanding, the affirmation of God cannot completely silence the echo of nothing and the nihilism it harbors. By opening *The Recognitions* with this line from Irenaeus, Gaddis implicitly suggests that without God everything *is* empty of meaning.

To fathom the depthless depths of his world, Gaddis returns to the figure who has come to embody modernity—Faust. Though the roots of the Faust legend can be traced to ancient Gnostic and alchemical myths and rituals, Gaddis identifies the pseudo-Clementine *Recognitions* as its origin.

> The what? *The Recognitions*? No, it's Clement of *Rome*. Mostly talk, talk, talk. The young man's deepest concern is for the immortality of his soul, he goes to Egypt to find the magicians and learn their secrets. It's been referred to as the first Christian novel. What? Yes, it's really the beginning of the whole Faust legend. But one can hardly . . . eh? My, your friend is writing for a rather small audience, isn't he? (373)

To underscore his Faustian ambitions, Gaddis cites Goethe's *Faust* in the epigram to the first chapter.

> *Mephistopheles* (more softly): What's going on?
> *Wagner* (more softly): A man is being made.[3]

These seemingly simple lines signal two themes that are central in the novel: creativity and originality. What Gaddis gives with one hand, he takes away with the other. Layers of citations simultaneously frame his analysis and deliberately call into question its originality. As if to mock his own literary ambitions, Gaddis freely admits that his work is not original but is a copy of a work whose author is a fake. His novel, in other words, is a copy of a copy whose origin is unknown. Just as Faust sold his soul to the devil, so there is something devilish about the games Gaddis is playing in *The Recognitions*. Throughout the Western tradition, the devil is repeatedly associated with mimicry and, by extension, duplicity, deception, and deceit. What makes the conjuring tricks of the devil so disturbing to Christians is the way in which they simultaneously usurp and mock God's creative power. What if the source of creative power were not divine light but darker powers, forces, and energies circulating through human beings? And what if something demonic lurks in God's creative power?

In the romantic period, which effectively begins with Goethe's poetry and Kant's critical philosophy, the creative artist displaces the creator God as the source of transformational change. As the religious prophet gives way to the avant-garde artist, art becomes an elixir that holds the promise of salvation.[4] The scene between Mephistopheles and Faust's assistant, Wagner, which Gaddis cites, takes place in an alchemical laboratory where a homunculus is being produced.[5] The dream of the alchemist is to become God by assuming his creative power. This ambition finds its most explicit expression in the effort to create a simulacrum of a human being. Alchemy, which began in ancient mining and metallurgical rituals intended to produce pure gold from base metals, eventually became what Mircea Eliade aptly describes as "a spiritual technique and soteriology."[6] In this esoteric tradition, gold is valued less for its material worth than for its power in the economy of redemption. By refining base metals into gold, the alchemist seeks to purify both self and world. The goal of alchemy is to become as good as gold—pure gold, which is the most rarefied form of the *prima materia* that forms the true substance of all things. As such, gold is, in effect, God, and to become as good as gold is, indeed, to become as good as God. Alchemists labeled the process by which base metals become gold sublimation. By the twentieth century, this esoteric tradition was transformed into a new psychic therapy. Freud, in effect, rereads alchemical rituals as psychological processes. Sublimation, he argues, transforms base instincts into the highest religious and artistic ideas, ideals, and images. For the psychologist, as for the alchemist, sublimation is therapeutic even if not always salvific. In the era between belief and unbelief, Gaddis asks whether art can redeem life any better than ancient myths and rituals.

By the latter half of the twentieth century, the restless striving of the Faustian subject had, for many artists and critics, led to a sense of exhaustion. Paris, the capital of modernism, which, according to Gaddis, was "synonymous with the word *art*," "lay like a promise accomplished" (73, 63). This accomplishment, however, did not bring completion, satisfaction, or fulfillment. Stanley, the only character who continues to believe in the redemptive power of art, captures the tenor of the time between no longer and not yet: "And yet, well . . . you know I never read Nietzsche, but I did come across something he said somewhere, somewhere where he mentioned, 'the melancholia of things completed'" (599). In the post-age of *The Recognitions*, originality and the new beginnings it brings are distant memories haunting the imagination of sojourners destined to err in a world of forgeries and counterfeits, where images are always recycled and signs are signs of other signs. In this recombinant culture, motions without emotions are symptoms of the indifference and emptiness that accompany the loss of purpose. Unlike the superficial personae of his later novel *JR*, Gaddis is not at home in the culture of fakes he finds around him and is deeply unsettled by something that slips away every time he approaches it or it approaches him. In a conversation with his wife, Wyatt, the main character in *The Recognitions*, confesses:

> —There's always the sense. . . . —the sense of recalling something, of almost reaching it, and holding it . . . She leaned over to him, her hand caught his wrist and the coal of tobacco glowed, burning his fingers. In the darkness she did not notice.
>
> —And then it's . . . escaped again. It's escaped again, and there's only a sense of disappointment, of something irretrievably lost.

He raised his head.

—A cigarette, she said. —Why do you always leave me so quickly afterward? Why do you always want a cigarette right afterward?

—Reality, he answered. (119)

Wyatt's response is as duplicitous as his world. Is reality what is lost forever, or is reality nothing more than a cigarette after a good fuck? In either case, reality remains elusive, and what once was recognized as the ground of being immediately turns to ash.

This sense of something "irretrievably lost" is what drives Gaddis on and on and on for almost a thousand pages, until his narrative becomes overwhelmingly excessive. It seems as though he cannot stop writing. As long as the end does not arrive, the irretrievably lost might be found. The urgency of the search transforms the nature of the work: the narrative repeatedly turns back on itself to create strange loops that never come full circle. Chapter upon chapter, association upon association, allusion upon allusion, the work unravels and becomes hypertextual—click on any name, word, term, idea, or image, and you are led to another node in a seemingly infinite textual web. The threads of this web intersect but are not united in the central character.

Wyatt is the son of a sixth-generation New England Congregational minister who, after the death of his wife, undergoes a crisis of faith. This character is, however, less a person than a persona whose name is a pseudonym or series of pseudonyms. After his parents named him Stephen, in memory of the first Christian martyr, his aunt changed his name to Wyatt, which had been a traditional family name. In the years following his crisis of faith, a sinister counterfeiter with whom he becomes involved gives him the fake name Stephan Asche, which Wyatt eventually transforms back into his "original" name Stephen. The multiplicity of names suggests the slippage of identity among many of the characters in the novel. As seemingly distinct personae fade into one another in a play of shifty masks, it is often difficult to be sure who is speaking; indeed, voices often seem to "come from nowhere" (652). In a rare interview given in 1986, Gaddis described all the characters as "reflecting facets of the central figure, who, for all practical purposes, disappears."[7] Expressing growing frustration with Wyatt's insistent reserve, his wife reflects:

> Moments like this (and they came more often) she had the sense that he did not exist; or, to re-examine him, sitting there looking in another direction, in terms of substance and accident, substance the imperceptible underlying reality, accident the properties inherent in the substance which are perceived by the senses: the substance transformed by consecration, but the accidents remain what they were. (94)

Here, as elsewhere, theology becomes anthropology: the words of the Eucharist prefigure the transformation of the self. In the Christian ritual, God, as if by magic, becomes incarnate in flesh and blood. *Hoc est meum corpus*—hocus-pocus. Through ecclesiastical fiat, substance becomes accident, and, conversely, accident becomes substance. Distraught by her husband's elusiveness, Esther does not realize that transubstantiation renders the accidental substantial, thereby reconciling appearance and reality. Gaddis's artful rewriting of the word extends the incarnational process by revealing the heterodox implications of orthodox theology. If the divine is incarnate, the real can be found in space and time. Accordingly, natural and historical life is no longer tragic but now can be re-cognized as the divine comedy it has always been. Gaddis admits that while his work is "sometimes a heavy-handed satire," he nonetheless "wanted it to be a large comic novel in the great tradition."[8] Indeed, *The Recognitions* can be the last Christian novel *only* if it is a comedy. One of the least important characters expresses one of the most important points: "What's tragedy to you is an anecdote to everybody else. We're comic. We're all comics. We live in a comic time. And the worse it gets the more comic we are" (640). Slipping and sliding between the sublime and the ridiculous, *The Recognitions* becomes a comedy of errors bordering on slapstick.

Yet this often unmanageable novel is also filled with death. Amid the overwhelming plethora of details and digressions, it is possible to discern a structure organized around three deaths: Camilla, Wyatt's mother; Gwyon,

Wyatt's father; and Stanley, Wyatt's friend.[9] Each of these deaths is associated with a pagan festival that has been displaced by a Christian holiday: Samhain—All Saint's Day, the Feast of Sol Invictus—Christmas, and Eostur—Easter. What unites these religious rituals is their common participation in the seasonal cycles of death and renewal. In a culture of seemingly endless counterfeits, Gaddis asks: are renewal and redemption any longer possible?

## SAMHAIN—ALL SAINTS DAY

Originality is first and foremost a *theological* issue. In classical philosophy and orthodox theology, God is the creator who is the origin of the universe. In his influential formulation of what eventually became known as the cosmological argument for God's existence, Aristotle argues from the effects of motion in the world to God as its origin. God is the Unmoved Mover, the first and final cause of all motion necessary for life. This argument rests upon Aristotle's assumption that an infinite regress is impossible because time is not eternal. Since time is inseparable from motion and, therefore, from change, the temporal domain must originate with an unmoved mover that is unchanging and, thus, eternal. Christian theologians translate Aristotle's unmoved mover into the Creator, who brings the world into being and sustains its existence. Though their reasons differ, Christians share Aristotle's rejection of the eternity of creation. Unlike many cosmogonic myths in which the world emerges from the struggle between the timeless forces of chaos and order, which is often embodied in a battle between a goddess and a god, Christianity, in its traditional forms, is an ethical monotheism in which God alone is eternal. Theologians developed the doctrine of creation ex nihilo to express the uniqueness and omnipotence of God. As the *fons et origo* of everything, God inevitably creates out of nothing.

In the modern period, philosophers and artists translate this theology into anthropology to develop an understanding of human creativity that mimics the divine original. Like Aristotle's Unmoved Mover and the Christian creator God, the romantic genius creates out of nothing other than

*Kant on "genius"*

himself. Kant formulates the modern notion of originality in his interpretation of genius, developed in *The Critique of Judgment*:

> From this it may be seen that genius (1) is a *talent* for producing that for which no definite rule can be given: and not an aptitude in the way of cleverness for what can be learned according to some rule; and that consequently *originality* must be its primary property. (2) Since there may also be original nonsense, its products must at the same time be models, i.e., be *exemplary*; and, consequently, though not themselves derived from imitation, they must serve that purpose for others, i.e., as a standard or rule of estimating.

This distinction between original and imitation becomes one of the norms by which fine or high art is distinguished from craft or low art, which eventually becomes known as kitsch. "Imitation," Kant argues, "becomes *aping* when the pupil *copies* everything down to the deformities which the genius only of necessity suffered to remain, because they could hardly be removed without loss of force to the idea."[10] While the original is always new, the copy is already old. So understood, the notion of originality defines a foundational principle of both modernity and modernism. To be modern is to be of the present rather than the past (*modernus*, from *modo*, just now); the modern, therefore, is the new, and the new is original rather than derived. The mantra of the modern artist is: "Make it new!" The new, however, is always already old as soon as it appears and must, therefore, be repeatedly replaced. Far from preaching the gospel of modernism, Gaddis believes this obsession with the new is nothing less than a *plague*.

> On the ceiling grew the graph of Stanley's existence, his central concern: Expendability.
>
> Everything wore out. What was more, he lived in a land where everything was calculated to wear out, made from design to substance with only its wearing out and replacement in view, and that replacement to be replaced. . . . Phonograph needles? Razor blades? Thrown away entire,

when their edges and points were worn out. Automobile batteries? Someone had told him that batteries in European cars lasted for years, but here companies owned those life-long patents, and guarded them while they sold batteries to replace those they had sold a year before. But there was more to it than gross tyranny of business enterprise; and advertising, whose open chancres gaped everywhere, only a symptom of the great disease, this plague of newness."[11]

(319–320)

As Gaddis spins his complex tale, it becomes clear that America is the land of the new where both modernity and modernism come to devastating completion. Dedicated to the new, modernism can become itself only in and through its own *self*-negation. The doctrine of the new, however, eventually becomes old, and, when the new becomes old, the old can return anew. In different terms, modernism harbors postmodernism as a condition of its own becoming. The "originality" of postmodern writers and artists is their avowed unoriginality. Their duplicitous works are self-confessed counterfeits of counterfeits, which no longer mask originals. With nothing new to say, artists recycle the cultural debris left by their predecessors.

*The Recognitions* opens with masquerades, a burial, and the fourteen Stations of the Cross.

Even Camilla had enjoyed masquerades, of the safe sort where the mask may be dropped at the critical moment it presumes itself as reality. But the procession up the foreign hill, bounded by cypress trees, impelled by the monotone chanting of the priest and retarded by hesitations at the fourteen Stations of the Cross (not to speak of the funeral carriage in which she was riding, a white horse-drawn vehicle which resembled a baroque confectionary stand), might have rebuffed the shy countenance of her soul, if it had been discernible.

(3)

Two weeks earlier, Gwyon and Camilla had left their infant son, Stephen, on the "clean Protestant soil of New England" (3) and set sail on the *Purdue Victory* for Catholic Spain.[12] At the midpoint of their voyage, on All Saint's

Day, Camilla is stricken with appendicitis and dies at the hands of the ship's incompetent surgeon. The date—All Saint's Day—will prove significant because of the mistaken identity of an eleven-year-old cross-eyed saint, who plays a crucial role in the extended masquerade that follows.

To appreciate the broader implications of this drama, it is necessary to note that All Saint's Day represents a Christian appropriation of the ancient Celtic festival of Samhain, known elsewhere as Allhallows Eve or Hallow-een. After harvesting the crops and securing the flocks, the Celts marked the end of summer and the beginning of winter with this celebration. They believed that at this time

> a gathering of supernatural forces occurred as during no other period of the year. The eve and day of Samhain were characterized as a time when the barriers between human and supernatural worlds were weakened or even broken. Otherworldly entities, such as the souls of the dead, were able to visit earthly inhabitants, and humans could take the opportunity to pen-etrate the domains of the god and supernatural creatures. Fiery tributes and sacrifices of animals, crops, and possibly human beings were made to appease supernatural powers who controlled the fertility of the land.[13]

When the Celtic roots of Allhallows Eve faded, the custom of adults solic-iting tributes of food and drink while dressed in disguises and masks and imitating the gods persisted well into the Christian era. Today's Halloween obviously harbors traces of these ancient rituals. What makes Samhain so intriguing in this context is the way in which the masquerade confuses the identity of humans and the gods. For those with eyes to see on Allhallows Eve, the whole world becomes a Galilee where God roams in disguise.

The person responsible for Camilla's death turns out not to be a surgeon but a confidence man named Frank Sinisterra.[14]

> The subsequent inquiry discovered that the wretch (who had spent the rest of the voyage curled in a coil of rope reading alternatively the Book of Job and the Siamese National Railway's Guide to Bangkok) was no surgeon

at all. Mr. Sinisterra was a fugitive traveling under what, at the time of his departure, had seemed the most logical of desperate expedients: a set of false papers he had printed himself. (He had done this work with the same artistic attention to detail that he gave his banknotes, even to using Rembrandt's formula for the wax ground on his copper plate.)                    (5)

A fake who traffics in fakes, Sinisterra's game is counterfeiting. He escaped federal agents pursuing him on charges of counterfeiting by assuming the guise of the ship's surgeon. Having set the events of the novel in motion, Sinisterra withdraws until the end of the narrative.

Gwyon refuses to bury Camilla at sea and, much to the dismay of his family and congregation, decides not to return her body to New England but to lay her to rest in the "heathen soil" of Spain. After a prolonged search, he eventually finds a site next to a little girl destined for sainthood in the village of San Zwingli. Ulrich Zwingli (1484–1531) was not, of course, a Catholic saint but the reformer whose protest eventually led to the Congregationalism Gwyon was paid to preach in New England. Camilla's death, however, shook his faith and delayed his return to the States. Needing time to reassess his mission in life, Gwyon withdraws to a monastery whose name suggests it is more a copy than an original: the Royal Monastery of Our Lady of a Second Time. This retreat had been founded by heretical Franciscans who, during the spirited Christological debates in the fourth century, had sided with supporters of the doctrine of *Homoiousios*, rather than what became the orthodox doctrine of *Homoousios*. The details of this obscure theological debate play a crucial role in the novel.

In 325, the Council of Nicea established the doctrine of *Homoousios*, which, after almost six decades of heated controversy, was reconfirmed at the Council of Constantinople in 381. Traces of ancient heresy hung over the monastery like a dark cloud hiding the son. In one of the many theological passages framing the narrative, Gaddis writes:

> *Homoiousian*, or *Homoousian*, that was the question. It had been settled one thousand years before when, at Nicea, the fate of the Christian

church hung on a diphthong. *Homoousian*, the meaning of *one* substance. The brothers in faraway Estremadura had missed the Nicean Creed, busy out of doors as they were, or up to their eyes in cold water, and they had never heard of Arius. They chose *Homoiousian*, of like substance, as a happier word than its tabular alternative (no one gave them a chance at *Heterousian*).[15] (9)

Though turning on an apparently inconsequential iota, this controversy had far-reaching theological and political implications. In theological terms, the issue involves the person of Christ and the possibility of salvation. As Gaddis observes, the difference between *Homoiousios* and *Homoousios* is the difference between similarity and identity. While proponents of the notion of *Homoiousios* claimed that the Son, i.e., Christ, is *like* the Father, those who backed the doctrine of *Homoousios* insisted that the Son is *identical* to the Father. Since the *Homoiousians* believed that God is absolutely transcendent and perfectly immutable, they were convinced that it was impossible for Jesus, who was a temporal and, therefore, mutable human being, to be divine. The most one could claim for Christ is that he is *like* God. For *Homoousians*, by contrast, the belief that Christ is merely like God is a denial of the incarnation. Since Christ cannot redeem what he does not assume, salvation is impossible unless Christ is *fully* God and *fully* man. While not immediately obvious, this seemingly obscure theological doctrine has important implications for the way in which believers understand themselves and relate to the world. If Christ does not become fully incarnate in a human body, life in this world is ultimately irredeemable, and believers must withdraw or flee from it. If, however, Christ does become fully incarnate, nature and history can be redeemed, and believers are drawn ever more deeply into worldly existence.

Plagued by doubt and tempted by a world daring him to embrace it, Gwyon hesitates and finally retreats behind the walls of the Real Monasterio de Nuestra Señora de la Otra Vez to immerse himself in esoteric traditions long deemed heretical. One afternoon, while gazing at "the motionless figures of monarchs" in a Madrid park, he discerns clues to the life he is struggling to leave behind. His devout puritanical relatives, he realizes, "had surrounded him in a cold disjointed disapproval of life. As the statues bore the currents of the seasons his family had lived with rock-like negligence for time's passage, lives conceived in guilt and perpetuated in refusal. They had expected the same of him" (13). But he is no longer convinced that a life of denial is the best way to live. Though his doubts are not resolved by the time he leaves the monastery, he has a feeling of liberation, though "whether it was released from something, or into something, he could not tell" (15). Gwyon returns to New England with a head full of new ideas, a collection of "un-Protestant relics," and, incongruously, a Barbary ape.[16]

When Gwyon arrives home, he discovers that his sister has renamed his four-year-old son Wyatt. An unyielding Calvinist, Aunt May had objected to the trip to Spain, protested Camilla's burial in Catholic soil, and is horrified by the changes in Gwyon revealed in his sermons. In his absence, she had subjected the young Wyatt to a spiritual discipline more severe than anything his father had ever undergone. The childless Aunt May lives "a life bounded by negation, satisfied with its resistance to anything which might have borne fruit." Resolutely devoted to a motto—"NO CROSS NO CROWN"—that underscores the irony of her name, she urges Wyatt to emulate her hero, John Hus (1369–1415), who was a Protestant reformer burned at the stake for his beliefs. Not always a willing student, Wyatt resists his aunt's instruction. Their deepest conflict is provoked by the child's passionate interest in art. A gifted artist from his earliest years, the intriguing images Wyatt discovers in the strange books his father has brought back from Europe enflame his imagination. Aunt May strenuously disapproves of both the father's books and the son's drawing. Accepting Protestantism's deep suspicion of images, she regards art as nothing less than the work of the devil. While destroying one of Wyatt's innocent drawings, she preaches to her errant nephew:

Lucifer was the archangel who refused to serve Our Lord. To sin is to falsify something in the Divine Order, and that is what Lucifer did. His name means Bringer of Light but he was not satisfied to bring the light of Our

*Lucifer*

Lord to man, he tried to steal the power of Our Lord and to bring his own light to man. He tried to become original, she pronounced malignantly, shaping that word round the whole structure of damnation, repeating it, crumpling the drawing of the robin in her hand,—original, to steal Our Lord's authority, to command his own destiny, to bear his own light.     (34)

The original sin, then, is originality; yielding to Satan's temptation, the creative artist attempts to usurp God's creative power. As the romantics had insisted, the original artist enacts the death of the transcendent God and the resurrection of divine power in human creative activity.

Aunt May and Wyatt eventually reach a compromise when she permits him not to draw originals but to copy images he finds in his father's books. Though frustrated by this restriction, her hellfire-and-brimstone rants are sufficiently sobering to make him hesitant to pursue genuinely creative work. As long as Aunt May is around, Wyatt limits his artistic efforts to copying copies of what he believes are original paintings by others. After she dies, however, he begins doing work of his own but remains cautious; as the son of six generations of Calvinist ministers, he cannot help wondering if his aunt might have been right:

> Every week or so he would begin something original. It would last for a few days, but before any lines of completion had been drawn he abandoned it. Still the copies continued to perfection, that perfection to which only counterfeit can attain, reproducing every aspect of inadequacy, every blemish on Perfection in the original. He found a panel of very old wood, nearly paper-thin in places but almost of exact size, and on this he started the Seven Deadly Sins: Superbia, Ira, Luxuria, Avaritia, Invidia . . . one by one they reached completion unbroken by any blemish of their originality. Secrecy was not difficult in that house, and he made his copy in secret.     (55)

Wyatt's unwillingness to complete his original paintings not only is the result of Aunt May's warnings but also represents his anxiety about his artistic abilities. He is not sure whether he can attain the level of mastery he sees in the works of others, and an unfinished painting, like an endless novel, keeps the possibility of perfection open.

One of the paintings Wyatt secretly copies becomes the central object around which questions about originality, forgery, and counterfeiting circulate. Bosch's *Seven Deadly Sins* forms the top of a table Gwyon had brought back from Europe:

> A large low table appeared under the window in the dining room. It was the prize of this incipient collection, priceless, although a price had been settled which Gwyon paid without question to the old Italian grandee who offered it sadly and in secret. This tabletop was the original (though some finagling had been necessary at Italian customs, confirming it a fake to get it out of the country), a painting by Hieronymus Bosch portraying the Seven Deadly Sins in medieval (mededy-evil, the Reverend pronounced it, an unholy light in his eyes) indulgence. Under the glass which covered it, Christ stood with one maimed hand upraised, beneath him in rubrics, *Cave, Cave, Dˢ videdet* [Careful, Careful, God is watching]. (25)

Fascinated by the painting and what it represents, Wyatt presses his father about the originality of the work: "How were you certain it was the original? Suppose . . ." Aunt May interrupts the conversation and Wyatt's question is not directly answered. But Gwyon gives a hint about how he had acquired the painting: "That took some . . . uum . . . conniving, getting it through customs. It's prohibited, you know, taking works of art out of Italy" (39). Gwyon managed to get the work of art through Italian customs by convincing officials that the original was a fake. The question of the originality of Bosch's painting and its significance for Wyatt runs throughout the novel. At a critical turning point, it appears that Gwyon himself might have been duped by another con man, who had actually substituted a forgery for Bosch's original work. With copies and originals confused beyond recognition, it no longer is possible to be sure what is counterfeit and what is not. By lying to the Italian authorities, Gwyon might, in fact, have been telling the truth. This possibility, in turn, suggests a far more troubling prospect: perhaps truth itself is really a lie, and thus the only way to tell the truth might be to lie.

The resistance of his aunt and doubts about his talent do not prevent Wyatt from pursuing his artistic vocation. When he succumbs to a protracted illness, his interest in art becomes obsessive. As the weeks pass, his drawing and painting become more frantic until it seems as though he is seeking a cure through art. But his condition continues to worsen, until Gwyon begins to fear for his son's life. Convinced that serious illness calls for a drastic cure, the pastor decides to sacrifice his beloved ape, whom he has named Hercules, in an effort to save his only son. In a scene bordering on the burlesque, Gwyon takes the ape to the barn, where he kills him in a parodic imitation of the crucifixion. Suffering delirium, Wyatt hears the screams of Hercules while imagining nails being driven into his own hands and feet. When consciousness eventually returns, he remains confused:

> For he woke on the floor with his father beside him, holding him up by the shoulders, his father whom he did not recognize, wild-eyed in that dim light. Then he broke open sobbing at the memory of the pain which had just torn up through his body. —In my feet, he cried, —it was like nails being driven up through my feet, as he was laid back on the bed blood-spotted at the shoulders, by this shaking man who could hardly walk from the room.
>
> A few days later, Wyatt began to recover. He regained the weight of his body by meticulous ounces. That fever had passed; but for the rest of his life it never left his eyes. (51)

This pivotal scene is fraught with ambiguity. Gwyon's sacrifice of the ape is obviously a copy of Christ's original sacrifice, and Wyatt's suffering is clearly a copy of this copy. Since the son recovers, the father's copy seems to be as effective as the original. But Gaddis chooses Gwyon's sacrificial victim carefully. The ape is the figure of imitation, which, we have discovered, Kant contrasts with the originality of artistic genius. How is Gwyon's aping of Christianity's originary sacrifice to be understood? Does his mimetic cure demonstrate the abiding power of the original, or does the efficacy of the imitation displace the need for the original?

Haunted by the sacrifice to which he suspects he owes his life, Wyatt follows in the footsteps of his ancestors by deciding to attend divinity school. But he does not last long and soon succumbs to the siren call of Paris. For the rest of the book, Wyatt drifts between the United States and Europe like the *Flying Dutchman,* "sailing without a steersman around the North Sea condemned never to make port, while he and the Devil played dice for his soul" (816).

Wyatt is not in Paris long before he meets the Devil incarnate—Recktall Brown, whose name obviously suggests the anality with which Protestants, since Luther's provocative scatological writings, have associated the Devil. Avoiding the Left Bank art world, Wyatt settles, significantly, on the Right Bank, near the stock exchange, where he gets a job restoring paintings. His reputation quickly spreads throughout the city and provokes the interest of Brown, whose business is counterfeiting and forgery. During their first encounter, Wyatt and Brown engage in a debate about the redemptive power of art. Though often doubtful, Wyatt nonetheless clings to the possibility that art can bring the salvation religion once promised; for Brown, by contrast, art, like everything else, is all about money.

—We're talking business, Recktall Brown said calmly.
—But . . .
—People work for money, my boy.
—But I . . .
—Money gives significance to anything.
—Yes. People believe that, don't they. People believe that.

Recktall Brown watched patiently, like someone waiting for a child to solve a simple problem to which there is only one answer. . . .

—You know . . . Saint Paul tells us to redeem time.
—Does he? Recktall Brown's tone was gentle, encouraging.
—A work of art redeems time.
—And buying it redeems money, Recktall Brown said.                    (144)

A savvy businessman, Brown recognizes a profitable opportunity when he sees it. He urges Wyatt to cash in on his talents by forging paintings he can market for him. When Brown assures Wyatt that with his talent there is no limit to the money he can make, the bargain proves irresistible.[17]

Here as elsewhere, the issues Gaddis probes surpass the individual characters he creates: Brown is, in effect, Mephistopheles, and Wyatt is Faust. A telling exchange in the 1986 interview underscores the importance of the Faust legend for *The Recognitions* and suggests its far-reaching implications for Gaddis.

> *Interviewer:* Disregarding now the immense symbolic-thematic complexity that the myth itself entails in the novel, I think that the logic of the Faust story lends itself particularly well to the message about the postmodern world, namely, manipulation and forgery. The Faustian pact with the devil is nothing but giving up originality, isn't it? And vice versa, a painter, Wyatt, manipulated into selling his soul, giving up originality, is bound to be Faustian, besides being emblematic of the artist's position in a corrupt, manipulative, counterfeit world. Is this a correct interpretation of Wyatt's central function as a Faust figure?
>
> *Gaddis:* It is, yes, originality also being Satan's "original sin" if you like. I think also, further, I tried to make clear that Wyatt was the very height of a *talent* but not a genius—quite a different thing. Which is why he shrinks from going ahead in, say, works of originality. He shrinks from this and takes refuge in what is already there, which he can handle, manipulate. He *can* do quite perfect forgeries, because the parameters of perfection are already there.[18]

Original sin is the sin of originality. Though Recktall Brown proposes the deal, his associate, Basil Valentine, closes it. Once again, names prove to be decisive. Basil Valentine was the name of a leading alchemist, a Benedictine monk widely regarded as the "Father of Modern Chemistry." Alchemy, as we have seen, is not merely a metallurgical technique but, more importantly, a strategy for salvation. Throughout *The Recognitions*, Gaddis repeatedly associates the artist with the alchemist, thereby suggesting the possibility of art's redemptive power. The latter-day Valentine's art, however, appears to be black magic because he deals in fakes rather than originals. But Valentine's counterfeits are no ordinary fakes; indeed, some of them are highly original. In Wyatt, he sees a special talent with whom he hopes to pull off the perfect scam by creating an original fake.

Never abandoning religious concerns, Wyatt prefers to copy Flemish masters. What intrigues him about these works is their extraordinary attention to detail. He attributes this distinctive characteristic to the then widely held belief that God can be found everywhere and that, thus, nothing is insignificant. In an exchange with Recktall Brown, Wyatt explains that these works from the Age of Faith reveal contemporary realism to be an illusion.

> —This . . . these . . . the art historians and the critics talking about every object and . . . everything having its own form and density and . . . its own character in Flemish painting, but is that all there is to it? Do you know why everything does? Because they found God everywhere. There was nothing God did not watch over, nothing, and so this . . . and so in the painting every detail reflects . . . God's concern with the most insignificant objects in life, with everything, because God did not relax for an instant then, and neither could the painter then. Did you get the perspective in this? he demanded, thrusting the rumpled reproduction before them.
> —There isn't any. There isn't any single perspective, like the camera eye, the one we all look through now and call it realism. (251)

In the modern era, the I is inseparable from the eye; in other words, visual perspective and the centered subject are inseparable. But what if, as Wyatt suggests, perspective is an illusion? What if divine omnipresence decenters the subject? How would one paint the disappearance of the subject, which such omnipresence might imply? Perhaps Irenaeus's criticism of Valentinian Gnosticism suggests an answer. If God is omnipresent and no detail is too insignificant for his attention, then "nothing is without meaning," and if nothing is without meaning, then everything is significant. To capture this significance, it would be necessary to paint something like an endless surface on which nothing is more important than anything else. Far from superficial, such a surface would be infinitely profound. Wyatt does not yet grasp this possibility, but his fascination with the flatness of Flemish paintings anticipates it.

For Valentine, Wyatt's preoccupation with medieval Flemish masters creates the opportunity for a scheme he believes is foolproof. He proposes that Wyatt forge a work by van Eyck—not the well-known Jan but his lesser-known brother, Hubert, whom some art critics and historians doubt ever lived. If Wyatt could create a counterfeit original, Brown predicted, "it might be the art discovery of the century, if it were absolutely perfect, signed and documented" (249). Wyatt's past experience has prepared him for the challenge. While in New York, he works in a downtown studio resembling an alchemist's secret laboratory, where he mixes chemicals and potions for his profitable forgery business. Brown and Valentine have such confidence in Wyatt's ability that they propose taking their game to another level. By creating a copy that, paradoxically, is an original, they believe they are much less likely to be caught than when they create forgeries of known works. A fake original need not be perfect because there is nothing to which to compare it. Valentine predicts that art critics and historians, eager for the publicity, will unwittingly become coconspirators by authenticating Hubert van Eyck's newly discovered work. Furthermore, their strategy creates the prospect of other profitable scams. With Hubert's existence no longer in doubt, it would be reasonable to expect that other "originals" would be discovered and find their way to the market.

While obviously not adverse to forgery, Wyatt nevertheless continues to harbor misgivings about his trade. Anticipating the possibility of one day wanting to reveal the confidence game he is playing, he keeps a fragment of every painting he forges, which he can use to prove the works are fake. When Valentine discovers this secret plan, he dismisses it, insisting that Wyatt inevitably would fail because people actually *want* to be deceived. Art, he insists, has never been about truth and redemption—not even for Wyatt's beloved Flemish masters. What moved medieval artists to create was not faith in the omnipresence of God but vanity, avarice, and, above all, fear. Then, as now, doubt, according to Valentine, rather than certainty produced great art:

> Yes, I remember your little talk, your insane upside-down apology for these pictures, every figure and every object with its own presence, its own consciousness because it was being looked at by God! Do you know what it was? What it really was? that everything was so afraid, so uncertain God saw it, that it insisted its vanity on His eyes? Fear, fear, pessimism and fear and depression everywhere, the way it is today, that's why your pictures are so cluttered with detail, this terror of emptiness, this absolute terror of space. Because maybe God isn't watching. Maybe he doesn't see. (690)

While Irenaeus's *Adversus Haereses* is directed against Valentinian speculation, Valentinus's speculation about the origin of art might be entitled *Adversus Irenaeus*: Without God everything is empty and without meaning.

The argument between Valentine and Wyatt eventually centers on the table Gwyon had brought back from Spain. Visiting the studio to pick up the latest forgery, Valentine plants the seed of doubt about the originality of the painting after which Wyatt had fashioned his work since he was a child. Once raised, doubt continues to fester.

> —That damned table. God's watching? Invidia, I was brought up eating my meals off envy, until today. And it was false all the time! He spoke with more effort than he had yet made to control his voice. —Copying a copy? Is that where I started? All my life I've sworn it was real, year after year, that damned table top floating in the bottom of the tank, I've sworn it was real, and today? A child could tell me it's a copy, he broke off, wrenching the folds of flesh and veins on his hand, and he dared look up. . . .
>
> —Now, if there was no gold? . . . continuing an effort to assemble a pattern from breakage where the features had failed.
>
> —And if what I've been forging, does not exist? And if I . . . if I, I . . . (381)

Three hundred pages later, Valentine explains the mind games he has been playing with Wyatt. Intent on stealing Bosch's painting and sending it "back to Europe where it belongs," Valentine provokes Wyatt by making him defend the originality of the painting. Knowing that Wyatt's spirited defense will reassure Recktall Brown about the work's authenticity regardless of what others might say, Valentine is free to pursue his nefarious plot. But Valentine's strategy depends upon an even more deceitful trick that Wyatt appears to have played on his father. When he was young, Wyatt copied the work his father had brought back from Spain and sold the original. Valentine, however, knew that what Wyatt believed to be the original was actually a copy, which the European owner had already substituted for Bosch's painting. As the scene unfolds, the search for the original begins to resemble Abbot and Costello's well-known comic routine "Who's on first?" Valentine plays the self-assured Abbot and Wyatt the befuddled Costello.

—And you were the boy! Valentine said in a tone gone almost childish with recrimination. —The boy in our story? Whose father owned the original? The boy who copied it, stole the original, and sold it, for "almost nothing" to . . . him.

—To him! How did I know, I didn't know who bought it, I just sold it. The original! I thought . . . do you know what it was like, coming in here years later with him, and seeing it here? Waiting, seeing it here waiting for me? Waiting to burn this brand of final commitment, as though, all of those years, as though it was what I thought, instead of . . . a child could tell, even in this light . . .

—Perhaps you were right all the time, Valentine said quietly, coming closer.

—But this is a copy!

—Of course it is. When the old count sold his collection in secret, this was one of the copies he had made.

—And, the original? All this time . . . ?

—All this time, the original has been right where this one is now. Basil Valentine stood very near him by the table. —Of course it was the original here for so long, the one you sold him. And this, I picked this one up in Rome myself scarcely a year ago. Do you recall when we first met? Right here, across the table? Of course that was the original. I said it was a copy simply to hear you defend it. I knew Brown would trust your judgment. And I knew Brown would be troubled enough to have it gone over again, by "experts." I brought the idea into his mind simply to let him kill it himself, so that once I've exchanged the two, no matter who called this a copy, he'd simply laugh at them. He'd just made absolutely certain, hadn't he? And the original? It's on its way back to Europe where it belongs. I exchanged them quite recently. Do you think he knew the difference? And Valentine laughed, a sound of disdain severed by a gasp of pain at the shock of his lip.

—Yes, thank God! The figure across the table stood up illumined at the edges with the steady glow of the fire. —Thank God there was gold to forge! (688–689)

I have quoted this passage at length because its last line, according to Gaddis, is the key to the entire book. In making this point, Gaddis draws together the themes of alchemy, the currency of art, and the economy of salvation:

My early impression was that the alchemists were simply trying to turn base metals into gold. Later I came to the more involved reading and better understanding of it all—that it was something between religion and magic and that it did not necessarily mean literally lead and gold. So the gold in many of the symbolic senses in alchemy is the perfection, is the sun, is a kind of redemption. When at some despairing moment Wyatt says—when he realizes that the table of the Seven Deadly Sins is the original and not his copy—"Thank God there was gold to forge," that is very much the key line to the whole book.[19]

But this explanation settles nothing. With copies proliferating and the original increasingly obscure, it is not clear how to read this line. Is Valentine telling the truth or playing a confidence game? Was gold ever really real? Is any painting truly original? In a world where counterfeits replicate faster than machines can print, is anything real? Is anything original? If art is latter-day alchemy, it might be nothing more than fool's gold. With these questions racing through his mind, Wyatt stabs Basil Valentine with a knife, smashes the table, and burns the *Seven Deadly Sins* in a confused fit of rage. No longer sure what is real and what is fake, the doubts of the father are visited upon the son. Repeating—perhaps even copying—Gwyon's journey, Wyatt flees to Europe, where he also ends up in the Royal Monastery of Our Lady of a Second Time.

## FEAST OF *SOL INVICTUS*—CHRISTMAS

While *The Recognitions* begins with the death of Wyatt's mother, Camilla, on All Saint's Day, the second major division of Gaddis's tangled narrative opens with the winter solstice in 1949, a few days before the death of Wyatt's father, Gwyon.[20] When Gwyon returns from Spain after his sojourn in the monastery, he is preoccupied with "primitive" myths and rituals. He develops an extensive library with rare books on paganism, Eastern and Western esoteric traditions, and beliefs and practices of heterodox Christian sects. Since it had long been rumored that Camilla's father "had Indian blood," Gwyon is particularly interested in Native American myths and rituals. As his studies progress, he becomes fascinated by the ancient cult of Mithra. Mithraism originated in Persia and, between the first and fourth centuries CE, gradually spread westward, where it became a powerful force in the military during the Roman Empire. At one point in its history, Mithraism posed a serious threat to the primacy of Christianity. Mithra is a solar deity who "shines with his own light and in the morning makes the many forms of the world visible."[21] As each dawn brings forth forms out of darkness, so the winter solstice marks the turning point of the year when the powers of light and order once again gain ascendancy over the powers of darkness and chaos. The cult of Mithra centers on the ritual slaughter of a bull, which is supposed to regenerate life. This ancient rite prefigures a ceremonial banquet, similar to the Christian Eucharist, in which devotees are renewed by eating the body and drinking the blood of the sacred bull. Archaeological evidence suggests that some early Christian basilicas were built above subterranean caverns where the followers of Mithra secretly met.

An early exchange between Gwyon and Aunt May establishes the relation between Christianity and Mithraism as the prototype for the tension between Protestantism and paganism running through the novel. Disgusted by an image in one of the books Gwyon has brought back from Spain, Aunt May leaves little doubt about her attitude toward what she regards as aberrant religious practices.

> —A nice . . . place of worship! The illustration pinioned by her gaze was captioned *Il Tempio di Mitra.* —Look at it! a dirty little underground cave, no place to kneel or even sit down, unless you could call this broken stone bench a pew? She got her breath when he interposed, —But . . . — And the altar! look at it, look at the picture on it, a man . . . god? And it looks like a bull!
> —Yes, a pagan temple, they've excavated and found the basilica of Saint Clement was built right over a temple where worshipers of . . .    (38)

For Gwyon, this discovery is of more than archaeological significance. What makes Mithraism so intriguing is that it establishes the possibility that Christianity is not truly original but is really a copy of an earlier pagan religion. Immersing himself in Sir James Frazer's monumental *The Golden Bough: A Study in Magic and Religion*, Gwyon's doubts about the originality of Christianity become even more profound.[22] Perhaps neither Mithraism nor Christianity is original but both are copies of the even more ancient myth of "the sacrifice of the king's son," which is found in many cultures throughout the world. Just as the alchemist detects the *prima materia* underlying the multiplicity of forms in the world, so Gwyon glimpses a *religio perennis* beneath the rich diversity of world religions. If his suspicion were proven correct, Christianity would be a copy of a copy or, even worse, a counterfeit of a counterfeit.

*Christianity*
*+ paganism*

The relation between Christianity and paganism is not merely an academic matter for Gwyon because he sees in them different forms of life that present alternative existential possibilities. Gwyon increasingly regards the Calvinism he is paid to promote as a world-denying religion devoted to the veneration of needless suffering, and he finds paganism more and more attractive because he believes it is a world-affirming religion that dares to enjoy life. Having become disillusioned with the former, Gwyon turns his sermons into lessons about the latter:

> Like Pliny, retiring to his Laurentine villa when Saturnalia approached, the Reverend Gwyon avoided the bleak festivities of his congregation whenever they occurred, by retiring to his study. But his disinterest was no longer a dark mantle of preoccupation. A sort of hazardous assurance had taken its place. He approached his Sunday sermons with complaisant audacity, introducing, for instance, druidical reverence for the oak tree as divinely favored because so often singled out to be struck by lightning. . . . No soberly tolerated feast day came round, but that Reverend Gwyon managed to herald its grim observation by allusion to some pagan ceremony which sounded uncomfortably like having a good time.     (55–56)

The seeds of pagan religion Gwyon spreads fail to take root in "the clean Protestant soil of New England," and, as his sermons become more heretical, his congregation becomes more baffled.

On December 22, 1949, Wyatt, in a state of confusion and distress, boards a train to return home to confront his father with the question upon which he believes his life depends. The doubts Valentine planted about the originality of *Seven Deadly Sins* raise questions that drive Wyatt to the brink of madness: "Now, if there was no gold? . . . And if what I've been forging, does not exist?" The issue, of course, is not merely artistic but, more importantly, religious. Here, as elsewhere, uncertainty about chronology complicates the narrative. Throughout the book, Gaddis repeats episodes and sequences in ways that confuse the timeline of the work. Since some of the chapters are not in chronological order, it is often difficult or even impossible to detect causal sequences and narrative continuity. The last chapter of part 2 folds back on a pivotal chapter that forms the midpoint of the novel to create loops as strange as the events they narrate. Though separated by three hundred pages, these two chapters actually form a sequence whose temporal dispersion mirrors the fragmentation and disintegration of its characters. Seemingly delusional interior monologues, which might or might not be the thoughts of individual characters who roam across strange theological and philosophical landscapes in search of clarity in a world rapidly sinking in obscurity, proliferate to create a text as mad as the tale it spins.

With a golden bull he has stolen from Valentine under his arm, Wyatt approaches his father's church at dawn just as the sun's rays "caught the weathercock atop the church steeple" (700). The description of dawn's first light might well have been lifted from a Mithraic myth:

> In the daylight's embrace, objects reared to assert their separate identities, as the rising sun rescued villagers from the throbbing harmony of night, and laid the world out where they could get their hands on it to assail it once more on reasonable terms. Shapes recovered their proper distance from one another, becoming distinct in color and extension, withdrawn and self-sufficient, each an entity because it was not, and with daylight could not be confused with, or be a part of anything else. Eyes were opened, things looked at, and, in short, propriety was restored. (700)

But a spectacular snow- and thunderstorm worthy of ancient Druid mythology breaks out, and the sun fades behind forbidding clouds.

Wyatt's reappearance sets off a comedy of errors: Gwyon mistakes him for a priest of Mithra; Camilla's father thinks he is Presbyter John; Janet, Gwyon's assistant, believes he is Christ returned to earth; and Wyatt himself seems to think he is John Hus. Amid the confusion, Wyatt finds the parsonage and church strangely transformed and the village rife with rumors about his father's strange behavior.[23] Gwyon has redesigned the sanctuary to resemble a subterranean retreat for devotees of Mithra. The pure white imageless walls of the Congregational church are gone, and in their place is

*Gwyon replaces Christianity w/ Mithraism*

a forbidding cavern filled with strange figures and forms. A single opening is positioned to capture the sun's rays at the precise moment of the solstice. When Wyatt stops by the local watering hole, the town drunk reports having seen his father slay a large bull and, impossibly, carry it around a meadow on his shoulders.

The purpose of Wyatt's journey home is to meet with his father in the hope of resolving his religious doubts once and for all. In an earlier conversation with his then wife, Esther, Wyatt explains why he dropped out of divinity school. The issue is redemption: if he were to become a minister, he would have to believe that Christ had really died for him. The question driving Wyatt on his endless quest for the truth he could never find turns on the apparently inconsequential iota of ancient Christological debates. Drifting in and out of delusions of being John Hus, Wyatt wonders how he should approach his father: "What was it? What am I supposed to ask? Am I the . . . Homoousian or Homoiousian? Am I the man that . . . What holds me back? . . . for whom . . . for whom . . . What was it? . . ." (420). When the decisive encounter between father and son occurs, Gwyon is preoccupied with the perennial myth of the slain king, and Wyatt is obsessed with the subtleties of Christology.

> The wren had flown, as he turned from the window and approached with burning green eyes fixed on Gwyon. —King, yes, he repeated, —when the king was slain and eaten, there's sacrament. There's sacrament. Then at the side of the table he paused and lowered his head, a closed wrist couched in the back of his neck, mumbling, —Homo . . . homoi . . . what I mean, is, Did He really suffer? And . . . no, that's not it, I mean. . . . He stopped; and clinging to the edge, sank into his chair. (430)

Wyatt's remarks about sacrifice prove disturbingly prophetic.

Unable or unwilling to answer his son, Gwyon's ranting and raving make it clear that he has forsaken Christianity to become a follower of Sol Invictus. The latter part of this fragmented chapter bears an epigram purported to be the despairing words of the dying Roman emperor known as Julian the

Apostate: "Thou hast prevailed, O man of Galilee." Julian's hope for reviving the empire had rested upon his faith in the solar deity Sol Invictus, who, when identified with Mithra, is known as Sol Invictus Mithra. In the cult devoted to the most powerful pagan god, the birthday of Sol Invictus Mithra is December 25. Just as Mithraic caves were hidden beneath Christian churches, so the birth of the sun lies behind the birth of the Son. Preaching the gospel of Mithraism with a passion that suggests Christianity is little more than a pale copy of a more vital original, Gwyon proclaims:

> —No one can teach the Resurrection without first suffering death himself. No one can be reborn without dying. No one can be Mithras' priest without being reborn . . . to teach them to observe Sunday, and keep sacred the twenty-fifth of December as the birthday of the sun. Natalis invicti, the Unconquered Sun, Gwyon finished, turning his face to the window.
> —But I . . . you . . . to worship the sun?
> —Nonsense, said Gwyon, brisk now. —We let them think so, he confided, —those outside the mysteries. But our own votaries know Mithras as the deity superior to it, in fact the power behind the sun. Here, his name you see . . . . Gwyon revealed the marginal notes on the newspaper clipping. —Abraxas and Mithras have the same numerical value, the cycle of the year as the sun's orbit describes it. Abraxas, you know, the resident of the highest Gnostic heaven.[24]                                    (432–433)

While the messenger has changed, Gwyon's message remains much the same. Unable to accept paganism's embrace of the world, he continues to preach a message of renunciation to his son. "—There must be priests strong enough and passionless, able to renounce the things of this world . . . Gwyon reached out and took his wrist, as though to pull him aboard. —To preach Him Who offers rest from sin and hope beyond the grave. Born of the Rock, He comes forth to offer Remission of sins, and Everlasting life" (431). At last Wyatt poses the question upon which he believes his life depends. With thunder booming and lightning striking the local tavern as if in a drudicial ritual, Wyatt confronts his father:

—Father . . . Am I the man for whom Christ died?

Louder than laughter, the crash raised and sundered them in a blinding agony of light in which nothing existed until it was done, and the tab-
lets of darkness betrayed the vivid, motionless, extinct enduring image of
the bull in his stall and Janet bent open beneath him.

Then it seemed full minutes before the cry, pursuing them with its
lashing end, flailed through darkness and stung them to earth. Water fell
between them, from a hole in the roof. The smell of smoke reached them
in the dark. (440)

The apocalyptic scene ends without resolution. Wrapped in veils of madness, the father drifts farther and farther into the fantastic world he imagines, while the son returns to the reality of a world he once thought his own.
His question unanswered and his beliefs reduced to ash, Wyatt returns to
New York more confused than when he had left. As if lightning could strike
twice, he discovers his studio has burned to the ground. With nowhere left
to turn, he flees to Europe.

In the wake of his encounter with his son, Gwyon completely unravels.
Three days and three hundred pages later, he performs the Feast of Sol Invictus—Christmas. In the Mithraic cavern that had once been the Congregational sanctuary he arranges an altar on which he places the stolen golden
bull Wyatt had brought him. The bull, of course, is reminiscent of the golden
calf Moses discovered when he descended from Mount Sinai with the tab-
lets bearing the prohibition of graven images. After positioning the golden
bull to catch the fleeting rays of the rising solstice sun, Gwyon goes to the
field where he keeps his sacred bull and slaughters the animal. When parishioners enter the church, they are not prepared for what they see and hear.
Their once familiar pastor is completely transformed into a strange high
priest of paganism.

—Natalis Inviciti Solis . . .

—The birth of the Unconquered Sun . . . We are gathered here in the
world cave before him born of the Rock, the one Rock hewn without

human hands, in the sight of the shepherds who witnessed his birth, whose name signifies friend, and mediator, who comes with rest from sin and hope beyond the grave . . . and offers the revival of the Sun in promise and pledge of his own . . .                                                    (703)

For the baffled congregation, this is the last straw. They insist that Gwyon be institutionalized and arrange to have him confined to a nearby asylum named Happymount. An interim minister is called in to restore order and offer shaken believers reassurance about the reality of Christ and his resurrection. A few weeks later, a permanent replacement is appointed to help the congregation overcome its dark past. Well schooled in Christianity Lite, Pastor Dick is as superficial and lighthearted as Gwyon is serious and troubled. Instead of hefty tomes of mythology and theology, Dick restricts his intellectual inquiry to *Reader's Digest*. Anticipating the new age Gaddis sees emerging around him, Dick is at ease in the world of televangelism and reality TV, where the erstwhile advertising executive, Ellery, produces shows like *Lives of Saints* and *Let's Get Married*. The formula to Ellery's success is staging fake events as if they were real.[25] The more Dick learns about what Gwyon had done, the more troubled he becomes until he finally addresses the issue directly in a sermon about the mortal dangers of Mithraism. Though his criticisms are many, the most telling charge is that this pagan cult is a counterfeit designed to mislead true Christians. Contrary to his expectations, the sermon does more to disturb than reassure his wavering flock.

> If "Dick's" bonhomie was, as it appeared to be, exaggerated after the service, it was because with his penetrating insight he had sensed something wrong, about halfway through his sermon, a restlessness which commenced with his passage from I Corinthians, and seemed to rise especially among the older faces, as he went on into the contents of the "quaint and curious volumes of forgotten lore," doing his best to show Mithraism in its "true" light, and its most recent propagator, if not demented, certainly misled. Supported by the battery of purloined mercenaries, Justin Martyr and Tertullian, Origen, Arnobis, Firmicus Maternus, Augustine

Bishop of Hippo, Paul of Nola . . . "Dick" could hardly fail in his unnecessary cause. Reading from the ex-Manichee Hippian bishop, he had reached this point when he noticed lips moving here and there, as though minds were already wandering: —"For evil spirits invent for themselves certain counterfeit representations of high degree, that by this means they can deceive the followers of Christ . . . "                                    (719)

Doubts once aroused cannot be easily dismissed, and evil spirits once conjured are slow to disappear. Wary parishioners suspect that "Dick's" easy Christianity is not the real thing. Unable to escape the specter of doubt or flee ghosts of the past, Dick moves out of the parsonage to a bright and cheerful house. While tearing down Gwyon's barn, he unearths the skeleton of the sacrificed ape. When the townspeople hear about this discovery, they leap to the dark conclusion that the skeleton is the remains of the prodigal son, Wyatt.

Happymount turns out to be an unhappy place for Gwyon. His roommate is the delusional Mr. Fairsy (i.e., Pharisee), who claims "to have been appointed by the Congregation of the Sacred Rites, at the Vatican, to investigate early methods of crucifixion" (712). A scientist by training, Fairsy is committed to the latest empirical methods and, in a fit of madness, carries out an experiment by crucifying Gwyon in their room. Gwyon's death only compounds the mystery of his life. Among the papers required for admission to Happymount, officials find instructions Gwyon had left for his body to be cremated. But he had not indicated what to do with his ashes. Since his only remaining relative, Wyatt, is somewhere in Europe, the erstwhile pastor's remains are sent to Reverend Dick, who has no idea what to do with them and puts the urn on a shelf in the study he rarely uses. One night while going through some of the books Gwyon left in the parsonage library, a piece of paper slips from a copy of St. John of the Cross's *The Dark Night of the Soul*. On it Gwyon had written his last will and testament, in which he requested that his ashes be sent to San Zwingli and buried next to Camilla. Since Dick does not know where the cemetery is located, Gwyon's instructions do not solve his dilemma. The befuddled pastor finally stumbles on a solution while preparing to send a care package to the Real Monasterio. Ever since Gwyon had returned from Spain, his New England congregation had regularly sent the monks ingredients for making bread from his family's cereal factory. Displaying characteristic ignorance, Dick assumes Spain could not be all that big and decides that if he sends his predecessor's remains to the Real Monasterio, the Franciscans can find San Zwingli and dispose of the ashes. Squeamish about death and eager to leave the dark chapter of his church's history behind, Dick mails the parcel but not without a final comic twist.

> Remembering the sturdy oatmeal boxes in the upstairs closet, he got one, transferred the ashes from the delicate urn in which they'd been delivered, and clamped the round top in tight, noting as he did that it carried the family name stamped on the tin. This he put into the parcel already bound for Spain, sent it off (by ordinary ship post, since he was paying the charges himself), and only when he sat down to write the covering letter did he realize that he'd forgot to take the name of the monastery where it was bound. In an almanac, he found a prominent monastery located at Montserrat, and so he addressed his letter, in cordial English (on a church letterhead) there, considering that if it were not quite the right one, things would be straightened up at the other end, where they were, after all, all Spanish, and after all, all Catholic. (717–718)

Dick's wager pays off: Reverend Gwyon's ashes finally arrive at the Royal Monastery of Our Lady of a Second Time, where father and son are unexpectedly reconciled.

## EOUSTUR—EASTER

While *Samhain*–All Saint's Day marks the end of the hot season and the beginning of the cold season and the Feast of Sol Invictus–Christmas commemorates the victory of the powers of light over the powers of darkness,

*Eoustur*-Easter celebrates the renewal of fertility, which comes when winter turns to spring. As we have seen, Christian holidays displace but do not completely replace their pagan antecedents. Easter traces its roots not only to the Jewish Passover but also to ancient Scandinavian rituals. The word "Easter derives from *Eoustur*, the Norse word for the spring-season." From the fourth century on, Easter, like the Saturnalia, was a nocturnal festival in which the symbolism of light was very important. "It was customary on the Saturday evening of the Easter vigil to illuminate not only churches but entire towns and villages with lamps and torches; thus the night was called the night of illumination. . . . In Northern European countries use of special lights at Easter coincided with the custom of lighting bonfires on hilltops to celebrate the coming of spring."[26]

Like all proper Christian stories, *The Recognitions* has three parts. The third part begins with an enigmatic epigram whose importance does not become clear until the third chapter of the concluding section: "There are many Manii in Aricia" (723). As threes continue to proliferate, it becomes difficult to ignore Gaddis's trinitarian numerology. In his notes to the novel, Stephen Moore explains that *manii* refers to sacramental loaves made in the shape of men, which the Romans called *maniae*. *Mania*

> was also the name of the Mother or Grandmother of Ghosts, to whom woolen effigies of men and women were dedicated at the festival of the Compitalia. The tradition that the founder of the sacred grove of Aricia was a man named Manius, from whom many Manii were descended, would thus be an etymological myth invented to explain the name of maniae as applied to these sacramental loaves.[27]

Never one to play on merely two registers at once, Gaddis's use of the term *manii* also suggests Mani (b. 527), who was a prophet and founder of Manichaeism, a radically dualistic religion that shared much with Gnosticism. Like Mithraism, Manichaeism envisions the life in terms of the struggle between good and evil enacted in the cosmic conflict between the powers of light and darkness. Earlier in the novel, there is an exchange between Max, a painter turned forger, and an associate of Wyatt named Anselm, who, following in the footsteps of the influential second-century theologian named Origen, took literally the admonition that one must make oneself a eunuch to enter the kingdom of God. Speaking with Max, Anselm anticipates the sinister tale these sacrificial loaves portend.

> —As Frazer says, Max explained indulgently, —the whole history of religion is a continuous attempt to reconcile old custom with new reason, to find sound theory for absurd practice . . .
> —And what does Saint Augustine mean when he talks about the Devil perverting the truth and imitating the sacraments?
> —This sacrament will go the way of all the rest of them, Max smiled.
> —It won't be long before they're sacrificing Christ to God as God's immortal enemy.
> —Hey Anselm, listen to this, Daddy-o-noster. Daddy-o, up in thy way-out pad. You are the coolest, and we dig you like too much . . .
> —The god killed, eaten and resurrected, is the oldest fixture in religion, Max went on suavely. —Finally sacrificed in the form of some sacred animal which is the embodiment of the god. Finally everyone forgets, and the only sense they can make out of the sacrament is that they must be sacrificing the animal to the god because that particular animal is the god's crucial enemy, responsible for the god's death . . .                    (536)

For those who know their history, Daddy-o-noster is not only Our Father but also Dionysus. One of the guises of Dionysus, god of wine, is, of course, the bull. When the bull becomes the sacred animal who embodies the death of God, the Antichrist and Christ finally become one, and the unhappy consciousness of Calvin becomes the gay wisdom of Nietzsche. But this "bacchanalian revel in which no member remains sober"[28] is still hundreds of pages away.

The third chapter of the third part of the novel brings Gaddis's endlessly complex tale full circle. What begins in "The First Turn of the Screw" with Camilla's burial in San Zwingli ends in "The Last Turn of the Screw" with

Wyatt's visit to San Zwingli to find his mother's grave. Upon his arrival, Wyatt discovers the village abuzz with excitement about the impending canonization of the little girl buried next to his mother. The Easter ceremony in Rome marks the culmination of a long and expensive campaign to publicize the canonization, which local officials hope will boost the tourist business and revive the economy. Over the course of the narrative, it becomes clear that Wyatt's trip to Spain was not direct—he took a detour through Algeria, where he met his former homosexual lover, Han, who was serving in the French Foreign Legion. When Han realizes that Wyatt has no intention of reconciling, a fight breaks out, and Wyatt kills him. Having first stabbed Valentine and left him for dead and then killed his erstwhile lover, Wyatt panics and flees to the Real Monasterio "to rest, recuperate and start over." Not merely a sinner but now a murderer, his real concern is more than ever redemption.

The epigram to the concluding chapter, which is not the end of the book, suggests that the masquerade Gaddis imagines in the first sentence finally becomes a reality: "To Love without Knowing Whom [to Love]" (769). Moore points out that this line, which is from a poem by Lope de Vega (1562–1635), "concerns Don Juan's quest for a veiled lady, who turns out to be the sister of his friend Fernando." As the chapter unfolds, veils continue to multiply in masks that mask other masks. In a twist contrived for comic effect, Frank Sinisterra also turns up in San Zwingli masquerading as Yak, a Romanian scholar that yet another disguised character has been paid to assassinate. Sinisterra has also returned to seek redemption of sorts—he is trying to redeem his reputation after one of his counterfeiting schemes has gone awry. This time, the currency of exchange is not money but a mummy (i.e., mommy). Sinisterra decides to cash in his chips by fabricating a fake. In search of a body small enough to have been an ancient Egyptian emperor, he develops a plan to steal the body of the little girl buried next to Camilla in the San Zwingli cemetery. While plotting his strategy, he meets Wyatt, who is visiting his mother's grave. When Sinisterra realizes that this is the son of the woman he inadvertently killed many years ago, he becomes obsessed with reconciling with Wyatt without revealing his true identity—if, indeed, he has one. Wyatt, however, is more interested in losing himself in wine and women than in getting to know this sinister stranger. With Wyatt repeatedly resisting his advances, Sinisterra begins to suspect that Wyatt is fleeing someone or something and attempts to ingratiate himself by offering assistance. A master of deceit, the con man counterfeits for Wyatt a Swiss passport with the pseudonym Stephan Asche. Though Sinisterra does not realize it, the fake name he crafts is actually Wyatt's real name—or almost his real name. As I have noted, Stephen (spelled with an "e" rather than an "a") is the name of the first Christian martyr, and it is the name that Camilla and Gwyon had given their son. "Asche" is no less significant than Stephan. *Asche* is the German word for ash, which suggests both the past Wyatt is attempting to flee and the future toward which he is unknowingly moving. Whether in the form of the world ash tree of Nordic mythology (Yggdrasil), the ashes from which the phoenix rises, or the ash of Ash Wednesday, ashes are overdetermined in many religious symbols and myths. When Wyatt declines Sinisterra's offer, the irrepressible con man explains the value of a counterfeit passport by parodying the rebirth of the Son of his victim has always been seeking. "What do you say now? This is no joke, I can fix you up with this passport. This is what you want to do, see? Like putting off the old man, you know what I mean, see? . . . like it says in the Bible, that's it, see? . . . that's what you want to do, put on the new man, like it says in the Bible. What do you say? . . . All right, listen. Shall I leave you here then? . . . " (785). Sinisterra reassures Wyatt that if he wears the mask long enough, it will become real: "All right, I'll call you Stephan, all right? That will help you get used to it, see? See, Stephan? See? . . . you're getting used to it already, see? See Stephan? After a while you think of yourself as Yak, as Mr. Yak, see?" (785–786). When the mask becomes real, it no longer can be dropped.

The question of identity, it seems, does not end with death. Persistent to the point of obsession, Sinisterra eventually draws Wyatt into his scheme to create a fake mummy. Town officials mistakenly exhume Camilla's body instead of the little girl's and send it to Rome for canonization. Though Wyatt does not realize it, his mother turns out almost literally to be a saint. While agreeing to accompany Sinisterra to San Zwingli in the dead of the night, Wyatt remains wary of the scam. When he hears rumors that police are searching for a team of body snatchers, Wyatt panics and splits from Sinisterra. A few weeks later, he reads an article in the newspaper reporting that authorities have found the body of someone named Yak, who apparently had committed suicide. The reality, of course, is different; Sinisterra had been mistaken for Yak and was assassinated. His advice to Wyatt proved prophetic: the mask *does* become reality.

More distraught than ever, Wyatt retreats behind the walls of the Real Monasterio. During the days he visits the Prado, where he studies his beloved Flemish masters and El Greco, for whom he has a growing appreciation. At night, he contributes to the monastery by using his painterly skill to restore their treasured El Grecos. The longer Wyatt studies El Greco, the more he comes to suspect that far from representing an ideal world, the works of the Flemish masters actually anticipate all that is wrong with modernity. The separation and isolation of people as well as things in the medieval paintings foreshadow the fragmentation plaguing life in what Gaddis dubs "the Age of Publicity." "Separateness," Wyatt muses, "that's what went wrong, you'll understand . . . or, —Everything withholding itself from everything else . . ." (874) Though a modern plague, the roots of this fragmentation are buried in puritanical Protestantism. Hundred of pages earlier and a continent away, one of Wyatt's forlorn friends reflects:

> "LONELY? 25¢ brings magazine containing pictures, descriptions of lonely sincere members everywhere, seeking friendship, companionship, marriage . . . " —What better reason is there to get out of this stupid white Protestant country, for Christ's sake. At least Catholic countries take sin as part of human nature, they don't blow their guts when they find you've gone to bed with a woman. (526)

In the paintings by El Greco, Wyatt sees a creative alternative to Protestant individualism, separation, isolation, and fragmentation.

> With a painter like El Greco, somebody called him a visceral painter, do you see what I mean? And when you get so much of his work hung

together, it . . . the forms stifle each other, it's too much. Down where they have the Flemish painters hung together, it's different, because they're all separate . . . the compositions are separate, and the . . . the Bosch and Breugel and Patinir and even Dürer, they don't disturb each other because the . . . because every composition is made up of separations, or rather . . . I mean . . . do you see what I mean? But the harmony in one canvas of El Greco is all one . . . one . . . (807)

For Wyatt, the vision of unity El Greco offers is nothing less than sacred. Since he had been raised to believe in a transcendent God and, correlatively, isolated subjectivity, the prospect of this all-encompassing unity is not only attractive but also terrifying. To become one with this reality would truly be to lose oneself in God.

Having lost faith in traditional religion, Wyatt realizes his only possibility of salvation lies in art. If he is to find redemption in art, however, he can no longer merely copy the works of others or even restore the paintings of past masters but must actually *become* El Greco. Paradoxically, by becoming an other, Wyatt becomes himself. But the other he becomes is not just any other—it is *El Greco*, an artist whose originality he deeply admires. When the mask of El Greco becomes Wyatt's "own" face, his copies become original, and he becomes the artist he has always really been. This is the recognition toward which *The Recognitions* has been circuitously moving. At this critical moment, Wyatt becomes Stephen—not Sinisterra's Stephan but his parents' Stephen, the person he originally was. When Stephen leaves the old man behind and takes on the new, which is, of course, really old, his restorations become creative.

As he struggles to make himself anew, Wyatt discovers that it is not easy to leave the old behind. Not even the walls of the Real Monasterio can protect him from the world of fakes and counterfeiting in which he has lived so long. Strapped for cash, the Franciscan brothers earn a modest income by providing food and lodging for tourists. During Stephen's stay, the quiet of the retreat is broken by an American family straight out of Chevy Chase's *European Vacation*. The father has a business that manufactures and sells plastic religious relics, and the wife and kids would prefer being back in the 'burbs to roaming around Italy. The husband of another couple staying in the monastery had studied food chemistry at Yale and now works for a firm named Necrostyle. To escape the boisterous chatter of the tourists, Wyatt befriends a well-known novelist named Ludy (i.e., ludic), who has been commissioned to write an article on spiritual life for a popular magazine. Believing he had discovered a fellow artist, Wyatt is disappointed to learn that Ludy is a fake who fabricates experiences as well as interviews and then represents them as real. Ludy and Wyatt are actually inverse images of the other. Like Ludy, Wyatt's career in forgery and counterfeiting involved passing off fakes as real. After his conversion, however, Stephen hides his work as a creative artist behind the mask of a master restorer. While Ludy passes off a fake as real, Wyatt disguises his original art as works of restoration. Watching Wyatt at work, Ludy suddenly realizes what he is really doing.

For almost a minute, there was nothing but the rapid scraping of the blade, and Ludy came forward further and further until he almost went off balance. —But . . . he finally broke out, —the foot here, it's almost gone. You . . . why are you taking it away, it . . . this whole part of the picture here, it's not damaged.

—Yes . . . Stephen whispered, —it's very delicate work. Why you can change a line without touching it. Yes . . . "all art requires a closed space," ha! remember Homunculus?

—But wait, stop! What are you doing? Ludy brought a hand up as though he were going to interpose. —You can't . . . But you can't . . . Ludy protested weakly.

—That El Greco up in the Capilla de los Tres . . .

—Yes . . . ?

—I'm going to restore it next.

—But you . . . there's nothing wrong with it at all, it's . . . it's in fine condition, that painting.

—Yes, he studied with Titian. That's where El Greco learned, that's where he learned to simply, Stephen went on, speaking more rapidly,

> —that's where he learned not to be afraid of spaces, not to get lost in
> details and clutter, and separate everything. (872)

Wyatt, of course, is not restoring but creating—by faking. For Wyatt to become El Greco, he must erase the line separating the copy and the original.

By transforming himself into El Greco, Wyatt becomes the artist his parents originally had named Stephen. Stephen, in turn, can become himself only through the reunion with his father, Gwyon. This reconciliation between father and son is brought about through a parodic repetition of the Eucharist. While restoring the paintings, Stephen, like all the other members of the monastic community, eats bread resembling the sacramental loafs called *manii*. One day the bread is unusually dry and specked with red. The puzzled monks ask the wife of the Necrostyle food chemist what she thinks might be wrong. She shows the bread to her husband and, while reporting what the monks had told her to other visitors, expresses her bewilderment:

> —because it's real hard to get flour over here, especially if you're poor like
> monks, they have to get it off the black market. That isn't exactly the way
> he put it, she amended when his silence unleashed her full confusion.
> —He says they even get food packages from America, like there was this
> Protestant minister who came here on a visit about thirty years ago and he
> always sends them these packages of food, they just got one lately. This is
> where I get sort of mixed up, she confessed, while the figure at the head
> of the table watched her querulously. —I think it's something he wants
> me to explain to him, because in this last food package they just got there
> was some kind of powdery stuff in a tin box they mixed up with the flour
> when they made this bread, and it came out funny. . . . She sighed, looking
> almost wistfully at the scrap of bread by her husband's hand on the table,
> hard crust, crumbled fine gray texture flecked with spots "like blood."
> —Home, she repeated. —Now it's almost Easter. (884)

We do not need the expert from Necrostyle to tell us that the powder is the cremated body of Gwyon and that the red spots are traces of his blood.

Wyatt finally becomes Stephen when he consumes Gwyon. By eating the sacred loaves, the son embodies the father in the ritual resurrection *Eostur*-Easter celebrates.

But is the renewal real? Is the death of the forger and counterfeiter named Wyatt the birth of the artist named Stephen? Or does Wyatt assume another counterfeit identity by becoming quite literally Stephan Asche? Rather than recovering his original identity, Stephen/Wyatt/Stephan/Stephen's identities continue to proliferate. He now confesses that he is the father of a little girl in the village, and, with no further explanation, leaves the Royal Monastery of Our Lady of a Second Time to find her and, in the words of Thoreau, "live deliberately." Precisely what this means remains a mystery.

The novel, however, does not end with the last chapter. Like the young Wyatt, Gaddis has trouble finishing what he starts. An unconcluding epilogue recounts the fates of most of the more or less minor characters who appear throughout the novel. With all of Wyatt's New York friends heading to Europe, everything appears reversed—the anxiety of influence gives way to the fascination with simulacra. The land of the original—Europe—is now copying the land of the copy—the United States. Anticipating his upcoming trip, Stanley, who is the most important character in the epilogue, observes: "—And I mean Chrahst, everybody's leaving, everybody's going abroad. I haven't been in Paris since I was seven years old, Chrahst to go there now! I mean to Saint Germain de Pres where they're imitating Greenwich Village and here we are in Greenwich Village still imitating Montmartre" (746). From the beginning of the novel, Stanley has been working on a Requiem Mass that he simply cannot complete. After the death of his mother, he resolves to finish the work and travel to Europe to play it in Rome on Easter Sunday. This is the same day that Camilla's body is going to Rome for her mistaken canonization. Upon his arrival, Stanley solicits the help of the wealthy mother of one of his New York friends, whose name, Agnes Deigh, suggests the term for the Lamb of God—*Agnus Dei*. When Mrs. Deigh was young, peasant children, seeing her swimming naked off the coast of Portugal, had mistaken her for the Virgin Mary. Through Agnes's intervention, Stanley gets an audience with Father Martin. In pleading for permission to play in the church at Fenestrula, Stanley appeals to the abiding importance of original art, which, he insists, can provoke "authentic experience." Though obviously unconvinced, Father Martin, eager to please his wealthy patron, nonetheless grants him permission in words that leave Stanley puzzled:

> We live in a world where first-hand experience is daily more difficult to reach, and if you reach it through your work, perhaps you are not fortunate the way most people would be fortunate. But there are things I shall not try to tell you. You will learn them for yourself if you go on, and I may help you. He arranged things for Fenestrula immediately, and Stanley left with the assurance to steady the bewilderment of his heart at everything else, a bewilderment exactly doubled as Fenestrula became the only possible position left when Father Martin was shot and killed in broad daylight, later in the day. (952)

It is impossible to be sure whether the murder is intentional, a case of random violence, or the result of mistaken identity.

Shaken yet undaunted, Stanley dons his best suit on Easter Sunday and heads to Fenestrula. He has finally finished the work but does not experience the elation he had expected because in a moment of sudden recognition, he realizes what his work had cost him as well as others. Like so many characters in the novel, Stanley suffers Nietzsche's "melancholia of things completed." To make matters worse, he now recognizes that his lifelong devotion to art had taken him away from those closest to him:

> He looked at it [his work] with sudden malignity, as though in that moment it had come through at the expense of everything and everyone else, and most terribly, of each of those three souls: but there was this about him, standing, running a hand through his short hair, pulling up his belt, and staring at that work, which since it was done, he could no longer call his own: even now, it was the expense of those three he thought of, not his own. (955)

As he enters the church, his Italian is not adequate to understand the instructions and warning the priest offers. Caught up in the enthusiasm of the moment, Stanley pulls out all the stops as he raises a joyful noise unto the Lord:

> The music soared around him, from the corner of his eye he caught the glitter of his wrist watch, and even as he read the music before him, and saw his thumb and last finger come down time after time with the three black keys between them, wringing out fourths, the work he had copied coming over on the *Conte di Brescia*, wringing that chord of the devil's interval[29] from the full length of the thirty-foot bass pipes, he did not stop. The walls quivered, still he did not hesitate. Everything moved, and even falling, soared in atonement. (956)

Everything, that is, but Stanley, who lies buried in the rubble of the fallen church. For the only character who clings to the belief in art's redemptive power, art brings death and not life. The end, however, is comic rather than tragic. With references to Dante circulating through the final lines, the lingering question is whether the comedy staged in "the last Christian novel" is divine.

## COUNTERFEITING COUNTERFEITS

> —Now, if there was no gold? . . . continuing an effort to assemble a pattern from breakage where the features had failed. —And if what I've been forging does not exist? And if I. . . . if I, I . . . (381)

In the final analysis—if there can be a final analysis—art is *about* religion and religion is *about* art.[30] Nietzsche haunts *The Recognitions* as the unspoken presence who sets everything in motion. In portraying Stanley trying to explain to Agnes why he cannot finish his work, Gaddis explicitly invokes Nietzsche for the only time in the novel:

> — . . . And yet, well . . . you know I never read Nietzsche, but I did come across something he said somewhere, where he mentioned "the melancholia of things completed." Do you know . . . well that's what he meant. I don't know, but somehow you get used to living among palimpsests. Somehow that's what happens, double and triple palimpsests pile up and you keep erasing, and altering, and adding, always trying to account for this accumulation, to order it, to locate every particle in its place in the whole . . .
>
> —But Stanley, couldn't you just . . . I don't know what a palimpsest is, but couldn't you just finish off this thing you are working on now, and then go on and write another? . . . —No, that . . . you see, that's the trouble, Agnes, he said. —It's as though this one thing must contain it all, all in one piece of work, because, well it's as though finishing it strikes it dead, do you understand? And that's frightening, it's easy enough to understand why, killing the one thing you . . . love. I understand it, and I'll explain it to you but that, you see, that's what's frightening, and you anticipate that, you feel it all the time you're working and that's why the palimpsests pile up, because you can still make changes and the possibility of perfection is still there, but the first note that goes on the final score is . . . well that's what Nietzsche . . . —All I know about Nietzsche is that he's decadent, that's what they say.
>
> Stanley withdrew his hand, and it hung in the air for a moment, like an object suddenly unfamiliar, which he did not know how to dispose of. —He was, because of . . . well that's the reason right there, because of negation. That is the work of Antichrist. That is the word of Satan. No, the Eternal No, Stanley said, and put his hand in his pocket.                    (599)

Stanley's understanding of Nietzsche is misleading because it is incomplete. The son of three generations of Protestant pastors, Nietzsche declared Christ to be the Antichrist and Christianity the work of Satan. Since the time of

Saint Paul, Nietzsche argues, Christians have worshipped pain and suffering and preached a resentful gospel of world negation. For the Christian believer, God is transcendent and redemption otherworldly. To love this God is to hate the world.

The disease of Protestantism plagues not only Stanley but also Wyatt/Stephan/Stephen. Esther makes this point when she says to her husband: "you never will let yourself be happy. . . . There are things like joy in the world, there are, there are wonderful things, and there is goodness and kindness, and you shrug your shoulders" (590). Wyatt's obsession with redemption creates his preoccupation with the person of Christ. If Christ were not truly God, he believes, redemption would be impossible. This issue is of more than Christological significance. If Christ were, as the monks of the Real Monasterio had believed, merely *like* God and not *identical* to God, the world would remain fallen and could never be redeemed. The only salvation, then, would be to retreat from or even escape the world. Though not immediately apparent, this pivotal theological doctrine also carries important implications for art. If the finite cannot hold the infinite, things in this world are penultimate and hence are signs pointing to a transcendent reality, which is never here but always elsewhere. If, however, the infinite can be embodied in the finite, signs implode because *there is nothing beyond*, and the finite, therefore, is in some sense infinite. Far from being the shadows of an otherworldly realm, the real is or can become immanent in space and time. Esme, a poet as well as Wyatt's model and sometimes lover, seems to have found what Wyatt is searching for.[31] Though she, like everyone else, "lives in fragments," Esme recognizes that beyond chaos

> lay simplicity, unmeasurable, residence of perfection, where nothing was created, where originality did not exist: because it was origin; where once she was there work and thought in casual and stumbling sequence did not exist, but only transcription: where the poem she knew but could not write existed, ready-formed, awaiting recovery in that moment when the writing down of it was impossible: because she was the poem. (299–300)

But Esme has trouble communicating her vision to Wyatt and finally decides to write what she cannot say directly. She leaves her lover a letter.

> *To recognize, not to* establish *but to* intervene. *A remarkable illusion? Painting, a sign whose reality is actuality, I, never to be abandoned, a painting is myself, ever attentive to me, mimicking what I never changed, modified, or compromised. Whether I, myself, am object or image, they at once, are both, real or fancied, they are both, concrete or abstract, they are both, exactly and in proportion to this disproportionate I, being knowingly or unknowingly neither one nor the other, yet to be capable of creating it, welded as one, perhaps not even welded but actually from the beginning one, am also both and what I must, without changing, modifying, or compromising, be.*

(472)

*Recognitions.* To become oneself, Esme incongruously insists, *one must become a painting.* A painting is the unity of object and image, the concrete and the abstract, the actual and the fancied, and, most important, sign and reality. If sign and the real are one, the sign is not the shadow of a reality that lies elsewhere but is reality itself. To become a painting is to transform life into a work of art; far from an illusion with no future, such an artful life is the only reality there is.

The obscurities of ancient theological debates turn out to be surprisingly relevant for life in postmodern worlds. The truth of the incarnation is *Homoousios,* identity, rather than *Homoiousios,* likeness. If Jesus *is* God, appearance *is* reality. The *imago,* then, is not merely a pale reflection of a transcendent reality but is nothing less than *Deus ipse.* The good news that the real is present *here and now* marks the end of the regime of representation. In the words of the contemporary painter Frank Stella, "What you see is what you see." Though the Christology is orthodox, the message is not; to the contrary, this is the gospel of the Antichrist. But this Antichrist turns out not to be Satan but Jesus, who, as Nietzsche maintains, denies "everything that today is called Christian."[32] In his manifesto entitled *The*

*Antichrist*, Nietzsche proclaims: "Jesus had abolished the very concept of 'guilt'—he had denied any cleavage between God and man; he *lived* this unity of God and man as his 'glad tidings.' And *not* as a prerogative!"[33] From the time of Saint Paul, Christians have reversed Jesus' glad tidings by changing his Yes to a No. As the Antichrist, Jesus says "Yes" by saying "No" to No—the Eternal No that Aunt May imposes and Wyatt struggles to escape. The other name of this Antichrist is Dionysus, who becomes incarnate in the bull.[34] This is the bull Mithra slays, the bull Gwyon sacrifices, the bull whose body and blood Stephan/Stephen eats in the sacrificial loaves. When the father and son become one, salvation is no longer deferred but now is at hand. This salvation, which is the work of man and not the gift of the gods, is the end toward which Stephen's voyage has been circuitously moving: "I told you, there was, a moment in travel when love and necessity become the same thing. And now, if the gods themselves cannot recall their gifts, we must live them through, and redeem them" (898). Nietzsche calls this love *amor fati*, which embraces and affirms the world in all its complex richness and horror. To say "Yes" to this reality is to confess that nothing lies beyond—absolutely nothing. Yet, Gaddis insists, hope is still possible.

> Many reviewers and critics draw attention to all my books as being hopeless, that no good is going to come of anything, that everything is winding down in the entire entropic concept. But Wyatt's line, I think late in the book, says that one must simply live through the corruption, even become part of it. As Esme, the model, is a quite corrupted person but still innocent in some way. Well, Wyatt has been part of the corruption, but at the end he says we must simply live it through and make a fresh start. I mean you could almost say—though the way the phrase is used now is *not* what I mean—that it is a notion of being born again in *this* life, with no reference to our "born again" Christians, and the next one.[35]

This is the deliberate life Stephen begins when he leaves the cloister of the heretical Franciscans.

*from modern to postmodern* *simulacra*

To follow Stephen into *this* life is to leave behind not only the Age of Faith but also the world of modernity and to dare to enter a thoroughly postmodern world where sign and reality, copy and original are one. *The Recognitions* begins with a safe masquerade "where the mask may be dropped at the crucial moment it presumes itself as reality" (3). By the end of the novel, a very different masquerade emerges, in which masks, when dropped, reveal not the face but other masks.

> . . . real no longer opposed to factitious nor, as in law, opposed to personal, nor as in philosophy distinguished from ideal, nor the real number of mathematics having no imaginary part, but real filled out to embrace those opponents which made its definition possible and so, once defined, capable of resolving the paradox in the moment when the mask and the face become one, the eternal moment of the Cartesian God, Who can will a circle to be square. (561)

When the real fills out to embrace the opponents that made its definition possible, the real itself disappears by emptying itself into appearance. In theological terms, through the process of *kenosis*, God (i.e., the real) empties himself by becoming thoroughly incarnate in Jesus (i.e., image or appearance). The death of the real is the disappearance of the origin and, thus, the end of originality. In the absence of the original, the copy is always a copy of a copy. But the simulacrum is no longer second best. If, as Gaddis suggests, the saints were counterfeits of Christ and Christ a counterfeit of God, then to imitate Christ would be to counterfeit a counterfeit. A counterfeit counterfeit, however, is not simply a fake. In a world where the real turns out to be fake, fakes can be recognized as real. To accept this reality is to be born again in *this* life for the first time.

# 2
## MOSAICS

Richard Powers, *Plowing the Dark*

> *You turn in the entranceway of illusion, gaping down the airplane aisle, and you make it out. For God's sake, call it God. That's what we've called it forever, and it's so cheap, so self-promoting, to invent new vocabulary for every goddamned thing, at this late a date. The place where you've been unfolds inside you. A space in your heart so large it will surely kill you, by never giving you the chance to earn it.*
>
> —Richard Powers

*God*

## MISRECOGNITIONS

**I FIRST** encountered Richard Powers indirectly—through his image rather than in the flesh. In the pre-Amazon days, when I still had leisure time to browse in bookstores, I stumbled on his arresting novel *Galatea 2.2*. I had heard of neither Powers nor this book, but I scanned the jacket description, and his work seemed interesting. At the time, I was reading about the recent advances in neuroscience and cognitive science that had grown out of the appropriation of models of complex adaptive systems for understanding mental processes. While long avoided by both philosophers and scientists, the problem of consciousness suddenly had become a hot topic. One of the critical issues in these debates was the question of whether the brain functions like a computational machine to which all mental activity can be reduced and, if so, whether it is an analog or digital device. Scientists who were convinced that mind emerges from digital processes in the brain were developing artificial intelligence programs and machines that simulate cognitive functions to prove their point. With these thoughts circulating through my own neural networks, Powers's translation of the Pygmalion story into an account of an artificial intelligence program named Helen that apparently passes the Turing test was particularly intriguing. It was not, however, the substance of the novel but the author's photograph that really caught my attention. When I saw the image of the young Powers, with his riveting eyes, it was clear to me that he knew things others do not and that he's only going to let you in on his secrets gradually. I immediately said to myself, "I know this person—I have met him somewhere before." As I pondered this experience, the only word adequate to describe it was "uncanny." Though I could not place him for sure, I managed to convince myself that he once had been my student. That was enough to make me buy the book.

When I returned home, I began the novel and quickly was captivated. *Galatea 2.2* tells the tale of a young writer by the name of "Richard Powers" who returns to the United States after living abroad for several years to become the humanist-in-residence at the Center for the Study of Advanced Studies, which recently had been established at his Midwestern alma mater. One of the fellows at the center was conducting cutting-edge research in artificial intelligence. In an effort to demonstrate that the brain is nothing more than an information-processing machine whose operations can be reduced to a few simple algorithms, Philip Lentz, a leading cognitive neurologist, enlists "Powers" to create an elaborate Turing test for his AI program. "Powers" is charged with tutoring the machine, Helen, in the Western literary canon. The culmination of the experiment is a contest between Helen and a twenty-two-year-old master's student that tests their knowledge of the history of literature.

The more deeply "Powers" is drawn into Lentz's labyrinthine machinations, the more uneasy he becomes about the implications of the experiment. Having already published four novels at a young age, "Powers" is a recognized writer of some accomplishment. Unlike so many artists and humanists who cannot bridge the chasm separating C. P. Snow's two cultures, his interest in science runs deep. After graduating from high school, he attended the university to study the natural sciences but switched direction after a life-changing freshman literature seminar. Struggling to reacclimate to life in the United States and readjust to a university that has changed in their absence, "Powers" and his partner, C., gladly accept a dinner invitation from his erstwhile professor, whom he credited with "ruining a promising scientific career." Though looking forward to catching up on old times and the most recent faculty gossip, he is more interested in discussing some of the philosophical questions and ethical dilemmas posed by his deepening involvement with Helen. Having thought I recognized Powers as one of my former students, imagine my surprise when I read the fictional account of his reunion with his college professor:

> After my mother, the man had taught me how to read. Taylor *was* reading for me. Through Taylor, I discovered how a book both mirrored and elicited the mind's real ability to turn inward upon itself. He changed my life. He changed what I thought life was. But I'd never done more than revere him from a distance, forever the eighteen-year-old student. Now, to my astonishment, we became friends.[1]

My surprise doubled, and I became even more curious about Powers. Who was imitating whom? Another Taylor had first taught me how to read—my mother was a high school literature teacher, and her favorite poet was Emily Dickinson. When I began reading *Galatea 2.2*, I discovered that the epigram to Powers's story about "Powers," Helen, and Taylor is a poem by Emily Dickinson:

> The brain is wider than the sky,
>     For, put them side by side,
> The one the other will contain
>     With ease and you beside.

The brain is deeper than the sea,
  For, hold them, blue to blue,
The one the other will absorb,
  As sponges, buckets do.

The brain is just the weight of God,
  For, heft them, pound for pound,
And they will differ, if they do,
  As syllable and sound.

If the brain is wider than the sky, deeper than the sea, and just the weight of God, Helen will never be able to contain it. Nor will any machine be designed to program thinking.

But my astonishment did not stop with the poem by Emily Dickinson. The syllabus for "Powers's" freshman seminar could have been from a course he had taken with me. In preparation for the dinner party, his partner, C., quizzes "Powers" about Taylor's course:

> "What did you read?" C. wanted to know.
> "He started us out on Freud's *Introductory Lectures*. Then we applied the dream work to fairy tales and lyric poetry. After a while, we went on to longer stuff—short stories, plays, novels."  (142)

Once again, the uncanny. More convinced than ever that Powers had been one of my students, I called the college alumni office and asked if Richard Powers had graduated from Williams College and, if so, what year. A few hours later, the director of alumni relations called to say there was no such name in his files. When he asked why I had asked, I hesitated to tell him the real reason.

Though Richard Powers never took a course from me, he might as well have been one of my students. During their dinner with the Taylors, "Powers" and C. learn that his teacher is dying of cancer. Before leaving town a few months later, "Powers" visits his mentor and gives him the first bound galley of his new book, *Prisoner's Dilemma*, which was, in fact, written by Richard

Powers. "'I don't know how to say good bye,' I told Taylor. The book was my goodbye, because symbols are all that become of the real. They change us. They make us over, alter our bodies as we receive and remake them. The symbols a life forms along its way work back out of the recorder's office where they wait, and, in time, they themselves go palpable. Lived" (204).

A year or so after I read *Galatea 2.2*, a former student, one whom I had actually taught, José Márquez, and I were invited to give a presentation on art and technology at Hofstra University. I had recently published *Hiding*, in which I analyze the complex circuits joining art, religion, and technology. In an effort to integrate word and image, I developed an elaborate visual design for the book. In *Hiding*, I pushed the book as far in the direction of multimedia hypertext as I could at the time. José and I then translated the argument into an electronic format by creating a CD-rom named *Motel Réal: Las Vegas, Nevada*, which is a video game built around the interface of a slot machine. Each of the hotel's fifty-two rooms has a narrative that probes questions raised in *Hiding*. Players navigate through *Motel Réal* by inserting tokens in the slot machine. The game presents an account of late twentieth-century media culture through an interpretation of Las Vegas. Vegas is where the real becomes virtual and the virtual becomes real. Though I have never said so directly, *Hiding* and *Motel Réal* are two parts of a single work. Our presentation had lots of bells and whistles and was very heavy on graphics. After our talk, Richard Powers introduced himself to me and said that he had been thinking about many of the same questions. This brief exchange began a conversation that has continued intermittently over the years. There was no way I could have known that afternoon when we first met that Richard was working on the novel that one day would lead me to write this essay.

## RECOVERY

It is, of course, Freud who has taught us more about the uncanny than any other writer. In his seminal essay entitled simply "The 'Uncanny,'" he suggests that the word *unheimlich* harbors clues to the meaning of this

*Freud.*
*Uncanny*

primordial psychological condition. Exploring the multiple dimensions of *unheimlich*, Freud identifies two seemingly unrelated meanings of *heimlich*. First, *heimlich, heimlig*, which derives from *Heim* (home), means belonging "to the house, not strange, familiar, tame, intimate, friendly, etc." *Heimlich*, by extension, suggests "intimate, friendly, comfortable; the enjoyment of quiet content, etc., arousing a sense of agreeable restfulness and security as in one within the four walls of his house." The second meaning of *heimlich* is "concealed, kept from sight, so that others do not get to know of or about it, withheld from others." The prefix *un-*, Freud explains, carries the negative connotation of "eerie, weird, arousing gruesome fear." *Unheimlich*, then, is un-homelike—something strange that can engender fear or even dread. What makes the word *unheimlich* so rich is an ambiguity that borders on a contradiction:

> among its different shades of meaning the word "*heimlich*" exhibits one which is identical with its opposite "*unheimlich*." . . . On the one hand it means what is familiar and agreeable, and on the other, what is concealed and kept out of sight. "*Unheimlich*" is customarily used . . . as the contrary of the first signification of "*heimlich*," and not of the second. . . . On the other hand, we notice that Schelling says that something throws quite a new light on the concept of the *Unheimlich*, for which we were certainly not prepared. According to him, everything is *unheimlich* that ought to have remained hidden but come to light.

Homelike and unhomelike, familiar and strange, reassuring and disconcerting, hidden and exposed, attractive and repulsive—what is the secret of the uncanny?

While the details of Freud's argument need not concern us here, two closely related points are important for the interpretation of Powers's fiction. First, Freud argues that the uncanny is inseparable from repetition, which is integral to the déjà-vu experience. What was so strange about first seeing the photograph of Richard Powers was my firm conviction that I had seen this person before. Unable to persuade myself that this belief was an illusion,

I attempted to reconnect image and person by tracing the representation to its origin. Second, drawing on his psychoanalytic experience, Freud associates the experience of the uncanny with the mother.

> It often happens that neurotic men declare that often they feel there is something uncanny about the female genital organs. This *unheimlich* place, however, is the entrance to the former *Heim* of all human beings, to the place where each of us has lived once upon a time and in the beginning. There is a joking saying that "Love is home-sickness" and whenever a man dreams of a place or a country and says to himself, while he is still dreaming: "this place is familiar to me, I've been here before," we may interpret this place as being his mother's genitals or her body.[2]

In Freud's developmental theory, life is an archaeoteleological process in which the goal of life is to return to the origin that gave us birth. The mother represents the home from which we come and to which we both long and dread to return. Simultaneously womb and tomb, the mother is the primal origin we profoundly desire yet cannot bear. Life begins with loss and becomes a circuitous route to a recovery that is repeatedly deferred. In the absence of what we most desire, we are left with substitutes for the real that always leave us wanting. This story, which is cosmological, theological, and psychological, is as old as creation itself.

The far-reaching implications of Freud's analysis of the uncanny become apparent in his late work, *Civilization and Its Discontents*, written in the shadow of World War I, when cancer was devouring his body. The argument begins with an account of religion that is reminiscent of Freud's earlier interpretation of the longing to return to the mother's body. He notes that his comments on religion are a "response to a call" from a friend who was responding to *The Future of an Illusion*: "I had sent him my small book that treats religion as an illusion, and he answered that he entirely agreed with my judgment upon religion, but that he was sorry I had not properly appreciated the true source of religious sentiments. . . . It is a feeling that he would like to call a sensation of 'eternity,' a feeling as of something limitless, unbounded—as it were, 'oceanic.'"[3] Describing this oceanic sense as "a feeling of an indissoluble bond of being at one with the external world as a whole," Freud traces its source to the original unity of the ego and the world. In the prelapsarian condition of plenitude, all desires are satisfied and every longing is fulfilled; more precisely, neither desire nor need has yet emerged because self and world remain one. For Freud, the source of this archaic satisfaction is, of course, the mother. Once the maternal bond is broken, life becomes a ceaseless effort to return to a home that forever disappears.

While admitting that the oceanic feeling exists in some people, Freud denies that it is the *fons et origo* of religion. Trying to salvage his argument in *The Future of an Illusion*, he reasserts that religion originates in the infant's sense of helplessness and the longing for a protective father that sense engenders. Having broached the issue of oceanic consciousness, however, Freud is forced to confess that his analysis might be incomplete: "The origin of the religious attitude can be traced back in clear outlines as far as the feeling of infantile helplessness. There may be something further behind that, but for the present it is wrapped in obscurity" (19). Though Freud never quite admits it, what lies behind the father is the mother. The loss of the mother creates desires that can never be fulfilled. In the absence of true satisfaction, a series of supplements inevitably emerges. The four "substitute satisfactions" Freud identifies represent gradual refinements of the method for sublimating base instincts into generally acceptable cultural currency.

If, as Marx insists, religion is an opiate, then opiates are, in a certain sense, religious. By incorporating "intoxicating drugs," Freud argues, people attempt to overcome the suffering caused by their incompletion and inadequacy.

> The crudest, but also the most effective among these methods of influence is the chemical one—intoxication. I do not think that anyone completely understands its mechanism, but it is a fact that there are foreign substances which, when present in the blood or tissues, directly cause us pleasurable sensations; and they also so alter the conditions governing our sensibility that we become incapable of receiving unpleasurable impulses. (25)

The artist refines the strategies of the pharmacist. From this point of view, art is, in effect, a drug synthesized to relieve the symptoms of loss and deprivation. In art, Freud concludes, "satisfaction is obtained from illusions, which are recognized as such without the discrepancy between them and reality being allowed to interfere with enjoyment" (27). Psychoanalytic theory claims to show how thin the line can be separating the hallucinations of the addict and the fantasies of the artists from the delusions of the madman. To avoid falling into the prison house of solitary madness, individuals tend to join together to create shared fantasies. The result, according to Freud, is religion.

> A special importance attaches to the case in which this attempt to procure a certainty of happiness and a protection against suffering through a delusional remolding of reality is made by a considerable number of people in common. The religions of mankind must be classed among the mass-delusions of this kind. No one, needless to say, who shares a delusion ever recognizes it as such. (28)

A shared delusion is nonetheless still a delusion. While effecting inward transformation, chemical, artistic, and religious fixes cannot bring about outward changes necessary for pleasure. This transformation of reality and its principles is what technology promises. To explain the modern, Freud once again returns to the "primitive."

> Technology is not, of course, new. To trace its origin one must return to prehistoric times. In the beginning was light . . . fire . . . heat. If we go back far enough, we find that the first acts of civilization were the use of tools, the gaining of control over fire and the construction of dwellings. Among these the control over fire stands out as a quite extraordinary and unexampled achievement, while the others opened paths that man has followed ever since, and the stimulus to which is easily guessed. With every tool man is perfecting his own organs, whether motor or sensory, or is removing the limits of their functioning. (37)

Tools forged in the heat of fire function as "extensions of their [creators'] organs." But which organ is at stake in technology? Freud appends to his myth of the origin of technology a footnote in which he explains: "The legends that we possess leave no doubt about the originally phallic view taken of tongues of flame as they shoot upwards" (37). If fire is the trope for technology, the organ of technology appears to be the phallus, whose appearance returns us once again to the maternal matrix.

In the sentence following the one whose footnote discusses the phallic significance of fire, Freud lists the technological developments that have helped man correct his defects and overcome his inadequacies: motor power, ships and aircraft, spectacles, the telescope and microscope, the photographic camera, and the gramophone disk. He concludes this catalogue with the instrument he believes most effectively represents the function of technology: the telephone. "With the help of the telephone he can hear at distances that would be respected as unattainable even in a fairy tale. Writing was in its origin the voice of an absent person; and the dwelling-house was a substitute for the mother's womb, the first lodging, for which in all likelihood man still longs, and in which he was safe and felt at ease" (38).

The string of associations released in this brief passage is dazzling. The lines Freud connects suggest that the telephone, which is a synecdoche for technology, binds us back to our original "dwelling-house." Within this psychic economy, the telephone is "a substitute for the mother's womb." Our deepest desire, our most profound longing, Freud insists, is to return to the womb-tomb of Mother Earth, where eros and thanatos are one. "These things that, by his science and technology," Freud admits, "man has brought about on this earth . . . not only sound like a fairy tale, they are an actual fulfillment of every—or almost every—fairy tale wish."

> Long ago [man] formed an ideal conception of omnipotence and omniscience which he embodied in his gods. To these gods he attributed everything that seemed unattainable to his wishes, or that was forbidden to him. One may say, therefore, that these gods were cultural ideals. Today he has come very close to the attainment of this ideal, he has almost become

a god himself. . . . Man has, as it were, become a kind of prosthetic God. When he puts on all his auxiliary organs he is truly magnificent; but those organs have not grown on to him and they still give him much trouble at times. Nevertheless, he is entitled to console himself with the thought that this development will not come to an end precisely with the year 1930 A.D. Future ages will bring with them new and probably unimaginably great advances in this field of civilization and will increase man's likeness to God still more. (38–39)

Freud's prediction was more accurate than he ever could have imagined. He could not have anticipated the globalized telecommunications matrix that now encompasses us all. Nor could he have known that "The Dream" would become real in virtual realities that form, in the words of the cyberpunk writer William Gibson, a "consensual hallucination." His analysis of the close relationship of religion, art, and technology remains one of the best guides to unraveling the web in which we are caught.

## SCIENCE FICTION

Richard Powers's writing career, like my introduction to his work, began with an uncanny experience with a photograph. After spending much of his youth in Indonesia, Powers returned to Illinois to attend high school and university. Like "Richard Powers," he intended to study science at the University of Illinois but changed direction when he took a freshman literature course. After completing his undergraduate degree, Powers began a graduate program in English during the heyday of critical theory but quickly became disillusioned with what he described as the "shrill solipsism" of literary theory. He completed a master's degree, dropped out of graduate school, and got a job writing code for a company in Boston. For Powers, like a character in one of his novels, "a good, polished program was everything . . . poetry was supposed to be."[4] While strapped to the computer turning out code by day and reading Walter Benjamin at night, Powers's imagination was busy creating an alternative reality that increasingly became his home. One day, chance intervened and changed his life.

In the early eighties, I was living in the Fens in Boston right behind the Museum of Fine Arts. If you go there before noon on Saturdays, you could get into the museum for nothing. One weekend, they were having this exhibition of a German photographer I'd never heard of, who was August Sander. It was the first American retrospective of his work. I have a visceral memory of coming in the doorway, banking to the left, turning up, and seeing the first picture there. It was called *Young Westerwald Farmers on Their Way to the Dance*, 1914. I had this palpable sense of recognition, this feeling that I was walking into their gaze, and they'd been waiting seventy years for someone to return the gaze. I went up to the photograph and read the caption and had this instant realization that not only were they *not* on the way to the dance, but that somehow I had been reading about this moment for the last year and a half. Everything I read seemed to converge onto this act of looking, this birth of the twentieth century— the age of total war, the age of the apotheosis of the machine, the age of mechanical reproduction. This was a Saturday. On Monday, I went in to my job and gave two weeks notice and started working on *Three Farmers*.[5]

*Three Farmers on Their Way to the Dance* (1985) has all the characteristics that have become Powers's signature. He weaves together three narrative strands: first, the story of the three young European men depicted in Sander's photograph as they suffer through World War I; second, the story of Peter Mays, who edits a technology journal and is preoccupied with photography; and third, the narrator's critical reflections on photographic technology and Henry Ford.

If William Gaddis is the most theologically sophisticated novelist America has produced, Richard Powers is the most scientifically literate novelist in the history of American literature. He is a philosopher's novelist— his works are bursting with big ideas and difficult questions. Powers, like Freud, is intrigued by the complex interplay of art, religion, and technology.

Though he never directly invokes Freud, his novels explore the experience of abandonment and the longing to return to an origin that forever eludes us. Reviewing his 2000 novel *Plowing the Dark*, the late John Leonard writes:

> On the road, on the raft, on the lam—ours is a culture of Shane-like vanishing acts, an agitated itchiness from Huck Finn to the Weather Underground, with intermediate stops at the Last of the Mohicans, the Lost Generation, Dean Moriarty, Billy Pilgrim, Rabbit Angstrom, and Henderson the Rain King. It's no big surprise to find lonesome rangers on every page of Powers—teachers who leave hospitals to wander in the atomic desert; scientists who desert their labs for night shift scut work, secretly composing music; librarians who quit their decimal systems to look for the human genome; doctors running away from war crimes and nightmare third-world childhoods; novelists hiding out in a neuroscience research project; single-mother real estate agents marooned in metastatic randomness; Adie who has lost her art.
>
> What does startle is the urgent longing of these pilgrims to go home again, if they can figure out where home is. In one of his novels, *Galatea 2.2*, Powers describes another, *The Gold Bug Variations*, as "a songbook of homesickness." But so are they all. And history keeps getting in the way. In each novel, he seems to hope that by striking out in two directions at once, then rigging a convergence, he can circle back to the sanctuary.[6]

Powers transforms the genre of science fiction from futuristic tales to imaginative explorations of the implications of present-day contemporary scientific theories and technologies. All his novels are organized around a particular scientific idea or technological innovation: *Three Farmers on Their Way to a Dance* (1985), photography and the assembly line; *Prisoner's Dilemma* (1988), game theory; *The Gold Bug Variations* (1991), genetic code; *Operation Wandering Soul* (1993), psychological and surgical technology; *Galatea 2.2* (1995), artificial intelligence; *Gain* (1998), market mechanisms and industrial pollution; *Plowing the Dark* (2000), virtual reality; *The Time of Our Singing* (2003), the relation of physics to medieval, baroque, classical, romantic, and modern music, including jazz and blues; *The Echo Maker*, (2006) cognitive science; and *Generosity: An Enhancement* (2009), neuroscience and psychopharmacology.

Each work is a composite of plots and subplots that join characters from multiple worlds and ideas that initially seem unrelated. The novels taken together appear to be a mosaic whose pixilated parts somehow form a coherent whole. Reading a Powers novel is like looking at a Chuck Close painting—examined close up, each piece of the mosaic seems a self-contained part sealed off from all the others. But as one slowly assumes a broader perspective, the separate parts gradually self-organize until they suddenly click together to form a coherent whole. In *The Gold Bug Variations*, which has been described as "the most daunting American novel since *Moby-Dick*," a Midwestern molecular biologist, Stuart Ressler, is on the verge of cracking the genetic code when he falls in love with a lab assistant and disappears.[7] Twenty-five years later, a librarian and her art historian lover team up to find out what happened to Ressler. Their quest takes them through a dizzying series of connections: self-replicating molecules, differential engines, Klein bottles, polypeptides, Pythagoras, Pascal, Rilke, singing, ATMs, Brueghel, Vermeer, protein chains, Poe, Bach, and "tetragrammatonic golem recipes." Though seemingly disconnected, Powers detects a common thread joining these disparate phenomena. "In Bach's polyphony, as in the double helix, as in kabbala, variations on just four notes, four nucleotides and four letters in the name of God spell out everything we need to know about 'that string of base-pairs coding for all inheritance, desire, ambition, the naming of need itself—first love, forgiveness, frailty.'"[8]

Such baffling connections not only permeate each book but also expand to create an intricate web that encompasses all his works. When asked about the disciplinary diversity of his novels, Powers's response is as revealing of our time as of his work:

The economics of higher education now prevent the kind of interdisciplinary vision that I'm describing. I think that a literary critic's work would only be enhanced by a more sophisticated sense of, say, evolutionary paleontology, or molecular biology, or cognitive science, or cosmology. We want to be able to ask answerable questions, but we also want to be able to situate those answers in a broader geography, an engagement with larger human questions. And that's how my books work; they work by saying you cannot understand a person minimally, you cannot understand a person simply through his supposedly causal psychological profile. You can't understand a person completely in any sense, unless that sense takes into consideration all the contexts that that person inhabits. And a person at the end of the second millennium inhabits more contexts than any specialized discipline can easily name. We are shaped by runaway technology, by the apotheosis of business and markets, by sciences that occasionally seem on the verge of completing themselves or collapsing under its own runaway success. This is the world we live in. If you think of the novel as a supreme connection machine—the most complex artifact of networking that we've ever developed—then you have to ask how a novelist would dare to leave out 95% of the picture.[9]

It is hard to imagine a better description of the structure of Powers's novels than "a supreme connection machine—the most complex artifact of networking that we've ever developed." When so understood, the fabric of his oeuvre reflects the world in which he writes and we live. It is fractal—the same patterns operate at every level within and among his works. Rather than gradually unfolding linear narratives within narratives, he fashions stories in which each work emerges from and folds back into the other to form recursive loops that draw readers into the creative process. To see how Powers's works work, I will concentrate on the interplay of art, religion, and technology in his seminal novel *Plowing the Dark*. As I have suggested, Powers does not shy away from difficult ideas and big questions. In an age of jaded cynicism and recycled ideas, he dares to ask: Why do people believe in religion? What is the purpose of art? Does technology transform reality? What is the nature of life?

# CAVES

*Plato*

Philosophy, religion, and art began in a cave. In his well-known allegory of the cave in book 7 of *The Republic*, Plato describes a group of people huddled around a fire who mistake the shadows projected on the wall for reality. The philosopher, who is freed from this prison house, has a clear vision of the pure forms that are the substance of reality. Christianity and Islam both trace their origins to the underworld—early Christians gathered in caves once used by the followers of Mithra and as Roman catacombs. And for the Prophet Muhammed, the cave is the site of illumination rather than ignorance and bondage. Succumbing to a life crisis at the rather typical age of forty, Muhammed retreated to a cave named Jeba Hira in the mountains around Mecca. There, during the month of Ramadan, he received his first revelation from God and three years later started preaching a message that has transformed the world.

The relation of art to caves is more obscure but no less important. In his suggestive book *Lascaux; or, The Birth of Art*, Georges Bataille maintains that "Lascaux provides our earliest *tangible* trace, our first sign of art and also of man." He proceeds to argue that there have been two pivotal events in human history—the making of tools and the creation of art. "Tool-making was the invention of *Homo faber*—of him who, while no longer an animal, was not yet fully a man. That sufficiently well describes Neanderthal Man. Art began with full-grown man, *Homo sapiens*, who first entered the stage in the early Upper Paleolithic times: in the Aurignacian period." For Bataille, art is constitutive of human being as such. But the tale he tells is not free from ambiguity because there is something disturbing about the heritage that makes us human. "At Lascaux," he insists,

> more troubling even than the deep descent into the earth, what preys upon and transfixes us is the vision, present before our very eyes, of all that is most remote. This message, moreover, is intensified by an inhuman strangeness. Following along the rock walls, we see a kind of cavalcade of animals. But this animality is nonetheless *for us* the first sign, the blind unthinking sign and yet the living intimate sign, of *our* presence in the real world.[10]

It is difficult to read "this message . . . intensified by an inhuman strangeness" without recalling Freud's account of the uncanny. From a psychoanalytic perspective, caves that are openings in Mother Earth are figures of the beginning that is our end. Powers is aware of the multiple connotations of caves and traces direct lines connecting primitive caverns and today's most sophisticated information, communications, and media networks as well as telepresence and virtual reality technologies. For one of the central characters in *Plowing the Dark*, the Koran is a lifeline that allows him to imagine an alternative reality that makes the pain of daily life endurable. "You listen to the archangel Gabriel, dictating to the Prophet in his subterranean cave. This story extends itself only in the hinted wisps, as if all readers already know the plot. But the more gloriously cryptic, the better" (323). Alluding to Plato's cave, another character insists that what appears to be real is but the faint shadow of forms that now can be coded. "The lamp, the food, the brass keys, all led him deeper into the labyrinth, from one state-of-the-art implementation to the next. Each line of his code inched toward that higher library of manipulable Forms" (112–113). For latter-day demiurges, these codes create a virtual reality chamber that is the contemporary version of Lascaux.

> You have to read this. The author claims that the Upper Paleolithic caves were the first VR.
>
> *Sure.* Spiegel twisted his palm in the air. *What else can you call them?*
>
> *No. Literally. Theater-sized, total-immersion staging chambers where they'd drag initiates by torchlight. The shock of the supernatural surround-and-light show supposedly altered the viewer's consciousness.* Lim stopped, amazed by the idea. *Can you imagine? Catching your first ever glimpse of images, flickering out of pitch-darkness. Like nothing you've ever seen. Your deepest mental illusions made real.*
>
> Adie held up her hand to stop the stream, until she could improvise a bridge across it. *You're saying that cave art begets all this?* She waved to include the whole RL. *That Lascaux starts a chain reaction that leads to . . . ?*
>
> *I'm saying that art explodes at exactly the same moment as tool-based culture. That cave pictures prepared the leap, after a million and a half years of*

*static existence. That pictures were the tool that enabled human liftoff, the Ur-tech that planted the idea of a separate symbolic existence in the mind of—* . . .

I read somewhere that Lascaux has become a simulation of itself? Tourism was killing the paintings. So the authorities built these complete underground replicas so that—

Lim's impatience cut him dead. *You still don't get it. They were simulations to begin with. Consciousness holding itself up to its own light, for a look. An initiation ceremony for the new universe of symbolic thought* . . . *The mind is the first virtual reality.*                                        (129–130)

From the ancient to the modern. During the 1990s, there was no better place to explore the Internet and virtual reality technologies than the school where Powers was an undergraduate—the University of Illinois, Champaign-Urbana, which is the home of the National Center for Super-computing Applications (NCSA). Two of the most important developments of the Internet era came from the University of Illinois. The first graphical Web browser—Mosaic—was released by the NCSA in 1993. A team led by Marc Andreessen, who was still an undergraduate at the time, created this wildly popular browser that led to the Internet boom of the 1990s. Andreessen and his colleagues later revised Mosaic to create Netscape. In his book *Architects of the Web: One Thousand Days That Built the Future of Business*, Robert Reid notes that Andreessen and his fellow geeks sought

> to rectify many of the shortcomings of the very primitive prototypes then floating around the Internet. Most significantly, their work transformed the appeal of the Web from niche uses in the technical area to mass-market appeal. In particular, these University of Illinois students made two key changes to the web browser, which hyper-boosted its appeal: they added graphics to what was otherwise boring text-based software, and, most important, they ported the software from so-called Unix computers that were popular only in technical and academic circles, to the Microsoft Windows operating system, which is used on more than 80 percent of the computers in the world, especially personal and commercial computers.[11]

Mosaic not only changed the face of the Internet but literally transformed the world.

It is tempting to read connotations into "Mosaic" suggestive of the three religions of the book: the Byzantine art that is characteristic of Hagia Sophia, the great church and mosque where Christianity and Islam meet, as well as the person who led the Jewish people out of bondage and into exile. The name of the first Web browser Mosaic echoes in Powers's description of one of the principal characters in *Plowing the Dark*, "a mini-Moses, still shepherding around the dream of starting an artist's colony where he could gather all those who needed a hideout from the real world" (8). But, alas, Andreessen denies all such connotations. In a personal e-mail he recalls:

> *Hi Mark—great to hear from you! Unfortunately Mosaic is purely prosaic :-). At the time, all of the good projects in the industry were being given acronyms. (All of the bad projects got random strings of characters and numbers, e.g. every Sony product in existence.) I thought if I gave it a name, it might stick in people's heads. The name Mosaic just seemed evocative.*
>
> *Later I found out the religious connotations. Which are appropriate . . . unfortunately my childhood religious education was limited to whatever burned-out hippies the local Methodist church could attract as pastors :-).*
>
> *Best,*
> *Marc*

Meaning, however, does not have to be intentional to be significant.

The second innovation that plays a leading role in *Plowing the Dark* was developed in the Electronic Visualization Laboratory at the University of Illinois, Chicago. The CAVE—Cave Automatic Virtual Environment—was first introduced at the 1992 SIGGRAPH convention. Explicitly referring to Plato's cave, the CAVE is an immersive virtual reality environment in which art comes to life and life appears to be a work of art. The actual environment is a 10 × 10 × 9 foot structure located in a 35 × 25 × 13 foot room, which is completely dark. The walls of the cave are rear-projection screens where high-resolution projectors display images through reflecting mirrors. Inside the chamber, users wear 3D stereoscopic LCD shutter glasses whose lenses are synchronized with computers to create different 3D images for each eye. There is also a 3D audio system that transmits sound from multiple speakers carefully positioned at precise angles throughout the room. The projection technology of the CAVE fashions a more realistic environment by creating perspective based on the viewer's position rather than a predetermined angle of vision. The walls of the room, in other words, must constantly know where the viewer is located. This is accomplished by feedback loops between a sensor mounted on the goggles and computers that constantly interpolate moving positions from data transmitted in real time.

At the time Powers was writing his novel, this technology was being used to simulate architectural spaces, project walk-through hyperbolic geometries for exploring strange attractors, and create a manipulatable model displaying the brain's anatomy and metabolism and an anatomical atlas of a near-term fetus. Powers is completely conversant with these scientific theories and technological innovations. Indeed, it is possible to learn more from his novels than from many textbooks and technical journals. Like an experienced teacher, he has the ability to explain difficult concepts clearly and concisely to the uninitiated. In the final analysis, however, his interests are not primarily scientific but philosophical, artistic, and even religious.

## KILLING TIME

When I first met Powers after my lecture at Hofstra, I did not know that he had cloistered himself in a small apartment nearby and was writing *Plowing the Dark*. In a 2003 interview, he explained that this book was inspired by a lecture he heard Terry Waite give. In the 1980s, Waite, serving as the envoy of the Archbishop of Canterbury, traveled to Lebanon to try to win the release of four hostages. During the negotiations, he himself was taken hostage and was held captive from 1987 to 1991. Reflecting on Waite's talk, Powers recalled:

*interview*  *secular*

After the lecture, he took questions from the audience and someone bluntly asked, What was the main thing you learned in being locked up for five years? In the moment after my stomach lurched at the question, I ran through all the possible answers: love life while you can; never take people for granted again. But his answer was shocking. He said, "Contemporary humanity has lost the ability to engage in productive solitude."

What most struck Powers about Waite's comment was how well it expressed his understanding of his own craft. The acts of writing and reading, Powers believes, are, in effect, religious activities designed to lift one outside travails of time by creating an alternative reality less fraught than quotidian existence.

> The currency he [Waite] was speaking of is very much the care and tending of individual salvation. To me, his comment legitimized the process of reading and writing. The thing that makes reading and writing suspect in the eyes of the market economy is that it's not corrupted. It's a threat to the GDP, to the gene engineer. It's an invisible, sedate, almost inert process. Reading is the last act of secular prayer.

Like a medieval monk, Powers retreated to a tiny apartment above a garage in Setauket, Long Island. "I wanted to see what the world looked like," he explains, "when I was thrown back entirely upon my imagination, cut off from all material sources."[12]

The novel Powers composes in his simulated cave is structured around three cells located in Seattle; Beirut, Lebanon; and Lebanon, Ohio. *Plowing the Dark* weaves together two stories of events taking place on opposite sides of the world. The book begins in two empty white rooms that mirror each other. The first is a computer lab reminiscent of Microsoft where a team of researchers is developing a virtual reality environment named the Cavern. The second is in Beirut, where an English teacher fleeing the confines of a failed marriage is mistaken for a CIA agent, kidnapped, and held captive from the late 1980s until the early 1990s, which is, of course, the precise period during which Waite was imprisoned. Powers explains the importance of his own isolation for writing the novel:

It mirrors the central experiences of the novel's two main characters—imprisonment in a Beirut prison; and the isolation produced by technology, the isolation of people immersed in virtual reality. These two kinds of removal from society required me to have a first hand visceral solitude. And knowing that I was going to write about such excruciating solitude gave me an excuse for creating my own immobile condition—although at times I think that's just an excuse, because I really do believe that most writers start out learning how to cope with isolation and end up desiring it.[13]

In order to fast track their virtual reality research, the company funding the virtual reality research, TeraSys, sets up the Realization Laboratory. Here as elsewhere, names matter for Powers. In common usage, Virtual Reality (VR) is contrasted with Real Life (RL); by naming the research facility the Realization Lab—RL—Powers scrambles this neat opposition and obscures the line separating the real and the virtual. In addition to the typical geek squad of bitjockeys from different Asian countries, the main characters in the RL narrative are erstwhile college roommates from the 1960s and former artists—Adie Klarpol (*Klar*, clear, transparent, pure; *Pol*, pole), Steven Spiegel (*Spiegel*, mirror, reflecting surface), and Ted Zimmerman (*Zimmer*, room, apartment, chamber). This threesome attended the University of Wisconsin in the early 1970s, shortly after students protesting the Viet Nam war bombed Sterling Hall, killing a university physics researcher and injuring four others. Adie was a budding painter, sometimes poet, and the girlfriend of the campus stud, Ted, who was already an accomplished composer. Stevie, like Powers, came to the university to study science but was converted to literature when he heard Adie recite lines from the final stanza of Yeats's "Sailing to Byzantium."

> Once out of nature I shall never take
> My bodily form from any natural thing . . .

These lines return repeatedly and form the leitmotif of the novel. Powers suggests that we are always sailing toward Byzantium—the dream of art,

religion, and technology is to step out of nature by leaving bodily existence behind.

To step out of nature would be to kill time. In this work, Powers is preoccupied with time and the struggle to master or escape it. The opposition
between time and timelessness (or eternity) mirrors the tension between
body and mind and, by extension, real life and virtual reality. In the first
lines of the novel, Powers frames the question of time in terms of the space
where his narratives unfold.

> *This room is never anything o'clock.*
>
> *Minutes slip through it like a thief in gloves. Hours fail even to raise the
> dust. Outside, deadlines expire. Buzzers erupt. Deals build to their frenzied
> conclusions. But in this chamber, now and forever combine.*
>
> *This room lingers on the perpetual pitch of here. Its low local twilight
> outlasts the day's politics. It hangs fixed, between discovery and invention. It
> floats in pure potential, a strongbox in the inviolate vault.*
>
> *Time does not keep these parts, nor do these parts keep time . . .*
>
> *Out in the template world, flowers still spill from the bud. Fruit runs from
> ripe to rot. Faces still recognize each other in surprise over a fire sale. Mar-
> riages go on reconciling and cracking up. Addicts swear never again. Children
> succumb in their beds after a long fever. But on this island, in this room: the
> faint rumble, the standing hum of a place that passes all understanding.* (3)

To program a place that passes all understanding would be to create a heaven
of sorts.

While the chamber seems timeless, the world is not. The late 1980s and
early 1990s was an unusually tumultuous period in world history—the end
of the Soviet Union, the collapse of the Berlin Wall, Tiananmen Square, the
early days of the dot-com boom, the emergence of financial capitalism, the
spread of Islamic fundamentalism, and the outbreak of the Gulf War. While
seemingly random, these events suggest an emergent pattern that Powers
had already identified in his study of neural networks and artificial intelligence. These outside events inevitably intrude on the Realization Lab.

Growing unrest in Eastern Europe and the impending fall of the Soviet Union lead to a revealing discussion among the virtual reality researchers.

> *This is not about forms of government or appropriations of power or anything of the sort. This is about the globalization of markets, the apotheosis of consumerism. Your . . . human chain*—Kaladjian spat both words out—*is nothing more than a glorified product-promotional placement.*
>
> *Well I'm not going to stand around discussing the fall of Eastern Europe with this crypto-fascist.*
>
> *Absolutely astonishing*, Dale Bergen said, to no one. *It seems to be self-assembling.*
>
> Michael Vulgamott snorted. *You mean the human chain, or the global socialist meltdown?*
>
> *I'm just a biologist*, Bergen answered. *I couldn't tell you about the thing's politics. But from this distance, it looks an awful lot like a long polypeptide growing itself out of side chains.*
>
> Adie broke in on the speculating circle. *This isn't happening*, she said. *Again? Didn't this dream die two months ago? I can't take any more developments. I'm overloading.*
>
> *You think you're overloading?* Jackdaw gestured toward a screen where news of the latest upheaval coursed through the system. *You ought to see what's happening to the network access points. Every time there's a new development, the whole Net grinds into gridlock.* (189–190)

This is a very important exchange. Powers suggests that emergent self-organizing systems are similarly structured and function the same way in all media. In other words, molecular processes, neural networks in the brain, weather systems, financial markets, and media networks are isomorphic and display the same operational logic. Furthermore, these systems are, like Powers's novels, fractal—they have the same structure at every level. One of the primary goals of the research conducted at the Realization Lab is to understand how these complex systems work so that predictive models can be developed.

When the novel opens, Stevie is working for TeraSys, and Adie is a magazine illustrator in New York City. In 1979, Adie launched a promising career in art with her show *Halations*. Attracted to her as well as to her art, Stevie asks Adie about the title of her show.

> *A well-received show, as these things go. Some kind of awful literary*
> *name . . .*
> "Halations." *What's so awful about that?*
> *What does it mean, anyway? It sounds like bad breath caused by asthma.*
> *It's a technical term. Describing what I did.*
> *Pastel penumbra halo stains. Lots of high-frequency colors. Not uninter-*
> *esting. Inkblot tests on mirror hallucinogens. Seemingly abstract, until you*
> *looked closely enough to make out the ghosted high realism. There was one*
> *called* Infinite Coastline, *if I remember right. Kind of a hand-drawn Man-*
> *delbrot, a couple of years before everybody in the industrialized nations was*
> *dosed out on Mandelbrots.* (92–93)

This apparently inconsequential remark establishes a series of surprising associations. "Infinite Coastline" is a direct reference to Mark Tansey's "Coastline Measure" (1987), which is an illustration of Mandelbrot's fractals.[14] Fractals, which became very popular in high and low art during the 1980s, are based on self-iterating mathematical equations that form feedback loops whose recursions generate stunningly lifelike figures. What few people realize is that Mandelbrot discovered fractals while studying financial markets. In his seminal book *Fractals and Scaling in Finance: Discontinuity, Concentration, Risk*, he establishes principles that form the foundation of all statistical approaches to economics and finance. Fractals, therefore, mark a fascinating intersection of art and mathematics that lies at the heart of the research going on at the Realization Lab.

While code runs the machines that generate virtual reality, art fashions the surface that creates all the buzz. Since the geeks in RL cannot paint and are artistically illiterate, Stevie calls Adie to try to persuade her to come to Seattle and join the team. With her artistic career in shambles but her dream of creating a better world still alive, Adie resists, saying that she already sold out once and is not going to do so again. Digital technologies of reproduction, she insists, destroy originality and creativity, which are essential to art. Stevie pushes back, reminding her of William Gaddis's lesson in *Agape Agape*—art actually created the information age because the original punchcard computer is the direct descendent of the player piano. "*Art made all this happen, you know. The whole digital age. Music did it. Hollerith got his idea from the punched data card from the player piano. From the Jacquard tapestry loom*" (216).[15] Not fully persuaded but nonetheless intrigued, Adie agrees to visit Seattle and check out RL.

One look and she is hooked. Echoing Freud's take on technology, she exclaims, "*that's like drugs*" (169). Stevie agrees and might well have replied, "Yup. Just like what we were doing in the sixties. Same trip, different junk." The machine that blows Adie's mind is a prototype total immersion environment named the Cavern, which is directly modeled on the CAVE. Donning goggles and data gloves and tethered by cables linking her to data processors, Adie loops and soars through virtual space until vertigo overcomes her. The experience is exhilarating, but Adie still resists, saying she is an artist and that this is not art. Stevie does not disagree but draws a different conclusion. "*It's not paint.*" "*No paint involved at all. No original expression required, Ade. It's all drawing by numbers out here. Don't think of it as art. Think of it as a massive data structure. What SoHo doesn't know won't hurt it*" (17).

The more time she spends in this alternate reality, the more appealing it becomes. Eventually, Adie relents and agrees to work with Stevie and his team. The virtual world the geeks have created more closely resembles a cartoon than the real world. For the Cavern to be commercially viable, it has to be an environment that is as realistic as possible. While agreeing to work on the project, Adie does not give up her commitment to art. Indeed, the more deeply she becomes immersed in the virtual, the more closely it seems to resemble art; conversely, her growing appreciation of the Cavern reveals virtual dimensions of art she never before had recognized. As her work progresses, Adie gradually comes to suspect that art and technology are not so different after all but are actually playing the same game.

---

Having come of age as an artist during the go-go 1980s, when copying and counterfeiting were all the rage, Adie knows how to play the appropriation game. Drawing on the resources of a vast data bank with programs mimicking the styles of countless great artists, she creates a copy of a copy of an original that is forever lost. The two paintings she decides to replicate in the Cavern's Jungle Room are Henri Rousseau's "The Dream" (1910) and Vincent van Gogh's "Bedroom in Arles" (1888). With seemingly endless processing power at her disposal, Adie not only reproduces "The Dream" but actually brings it to life. Rousseau's popular painting depicts an Edenic jungle before the fall as a paradise in which the natural world and human beings exist in undisturbed harmony. The realization of this dream would be the fulfillment of humankind's deepest and most enduring wishes. Powers describes Adie's uncanny creation with words that carry religious, psychological, and cosmological connotations. As Freud leads us to suspect, this enveloping forest feels strangely familiar.

> Your eye recognizes the place all at once, it has never been there. Or say your eye *has* been there, long ago. Back before childhood's childhood. Before your eye was even an eye. And say that you've toted this spurge around inside ever since, a keepsake of long-abandoned cover.
>
> Origins converge in the Jungle Room. Choose your myth or preference: the garden banishment, the wayward chromosome. Either way, this green is a return engagement. Nostalgia sprawls from the overgrown nooks. Life leverages every cranny. Moonlit creepers spread a welcome mat. The pennant of mangrove branches announces Old Home Week. . . .
>
> Something yearns to return to first vegetation, only this time at a cool remove. The body wants back in its abandoned nest, but now free to come and go, like a shameless tourist, without the fatal danger of travel, free to name the lush sprawl of this place from the safe vantage of a divan.     (67)

To return to the Garden from which we originally came would be to close the circle that marks the end of time.

But Adie's artistic concerns and even spiritual longings are not shared by all the members of the research team. While she is busy creating knockoffs of works by Rousseau and van Gogh, others are using the Cavern's VR technology to create simulations to manage events in the so-called real world. This research has two primary aims: first, to develop models that can predict the activity and measure the risk of complex weather, biological, financial, and economic systems; and second, to engineer simulators that can be used for everything from entertainment and theme parks to sophisticated weapons systems for the military. In addition to the Jungle Room, the Cavern has a Weather Room, Large Molecule Docking Room, Therapy Room, Economics Room, and Futures Room.

Powers realizes that this research, which has grown considerably since his novel was published, raises the most basic questions about life itself. Is life—human as well as nonhuman—computational? If so, is it digital or analog? Is there a code of codes that programs the cosmic order? In *Plowing the Dark*, the strongest believer in the possibility of calculating all aspects of human life is an Irish economist named Ronan O'Reilly, who created the Economics Room and the Futures Room to program statistical models of human behavior. Late one night, the usual banter turns to the unexpected subject of religion. Two of O'Reilly's colleagues from Sri Lanka are watching a television show on Mormonism and are baffled. Assuming O'Reilly is Christian, they ask him to explain Mormon belief and express incredulity at what they hear. O'Reilly turns their questions back on them by asking about their fundamental beliefs, and, when they deflect his questions, he grows impatient with their evasive answers.

> *You both believe—as all good lab rats do—that reality is basically computational, whether or not we'll ever lay our hands on a good, clean copy of the computation. At the core of your deepest convictions about the universe lies a Monte Carlo simulation.*[16]
>
> *Sounds about right*, Vulgamott said.
>
> *Even miracle-preaching evangelists, God love them, make their point statistically. Every modern mind is out there with a yardstick, a stopwatch, and a chi-square.*

*Hang on. You're not saying there's a hidden order behind all this?* Vulga-mott cast his eyes abroad. *Something bigger than statistics?*

O'Reilly smiled. *What do you mean, hidden order? That the universe is formalizable, but not from where we're standing? That it's unformalizable? Now there's a one-word contradiction in terms.*

*Ronan, baba. Some of us believe in contradictions in terms.*

O'Reilly faced down Rajasundaran. *Even mysticism is a non-Euclidean geometry. No, gentlemen. The world is a numbers racket all the way down.*

(82–83)

What O'Reilly does not realize is that his argument proves the point he is trying to dismiss. If it's numbers all the way down, the ancient philosophers and theologians were right all along—codes and algorithms are nothing more than the latest version of Plato's Forms and the early Christian apologists' Logos. Philosophers, theologians, and VR researchers might be chasing the same holy grail.

Powers recognizes the importance of this issue and returns to it later in the novel. A few days after O'Reilly's conversation, Kaladjian, a programmer from Armenia, demonstrates the virtual environment he has created for Adie. As she flies through space freed from the burden of flesh, she is captivated by the experience.

> She looked out across a sweeping interstellar pinwheel, its slow spokes lapping around her midriff. Each wash of stars unfolded another billion years of cosmic evolution. She swelled to the size of God's recording angel, attending at the day of Creation.
>
> *It's . . . magnificent. I had no idea.* She felt her eyes spilling over, and did not care. There was no foolishness, no vanity, no shame in anything a body felt on this. (265)

When Kaladjian is sure she is hooked, he literally pulls the plug. "'*Yes. Now here is the math behind it.*' He pushed a button and the expanding universe fell away into a few polynomials, breathtaking in their slightness" (265). At this moment it is as if Adie were staring into the mind of God.

But questions remain, and lingering uncertainties generate more questions. Is code the final word? Is the world real or virtual? Are there rules to the Game of Life? Are nature and history programmed, i.e., scripted in advance? Is the world running on a cosmic computer? Is what we take for reality a faint shadow of a metacode or algorithm of algorithms that has not yet been deciphered? Are programmers latter-day demiurges who bring together form and matter to fashion the engine of creation? Does high-speed computer technology make it possible to decode all of life's mysteries? Powers does not answer these questions directly but, taking the long view of human development, suggests that the Cavern is the culmination of an ancient religious and philosophical quest.

> Millennia pass in the war against matter. Every invention bootstraps off the next. The tale advances; thought extends its grasp over things until it arrives at the final interface. The ultimate display, the one that closes the gap between sign and thing.
>
> In this continuous room, images go real. . . . The room of the cave is something more than allegory. But the room of the cave is something less than real. Its wall shadows ripple with an undercurrent of substance, more than representation, but not yet stuff. Notion springs to life from the same, deep source in which the outdoors is scripted—what the run-on Greek once called the Forms. (400)

The final interface . . . the ultimate display that closes the gap between sign and thing. . . . Notion springs to life . . . what the Greeks once called the Forms. Perhaps the human race is finally on the brink of emerging from Plato's cave. When images become real, we return to the questions of home and homelessness that haunt uncanny chambers from Lascaux to the Cavern.

But what might "the final interface" be? Paradoxically, it is an interface that is not an interface. The dream inspiring VR technology is to render the virtual real and the real virtual by erasing the interface separating mind and matter. As "human intelligence migrate[s] wholesale into its artifacts," technology has the capacity "to break the bonds of matter and make the mind real" (395, 396). At this point, art comes to life and life becomes a work of art; programmers and engineers create what artists promise but never deliver—a *Gesamtkunstwerk* grander than Wagner ever imagined. Stevie explains to Adie,

> *The computer changes the tasks. Other inventions alter the conditions of human existence. The computer alters the human form. It's our complement, our partner, our vindication. The goal of all the previous stopgap inventions. It builds us an entirely new home . . . You know what we're working on, don't you? Time travel, Ade. The matter transporter. Embodied art; a life-sized poem that we can live inside. It's the grail we've been after since the first campfire recital. The defeat of time and space. The final victory of the imagination . . . Invented worlds that respond to what we're doing, where the interface disappears. Places we can meet in, across any distance. Places where we can change all the rules, one at a time, to see what happens. Fleshed-out mental labs to explore and extend. VR reinvents the terms of existence. It redefines what it means to be human. All those old dead-end ontological undergrad conundrums? They've now become questions of engineering.*
>
> (159–160)

"The final victory of the imagination" is code rather than poetry or, more precisely, code as poetry. "*Software,*" Stevie explains to Adie, "*is the final victory of description over thing*" (307). In the enchanted realm of VR, saying is doing and doing is making—"In the beginning is the Word." The vision inspiring the Cavern is the latest chapter of the ancient dream of killing time by escaping the body. If the world is computational, the future is calculable, and time is but an illusory shadow of a program that has already been coded. The body lends life weight and the sense of gravity that VR is designed to overcome. Adie struggles to grasp Stevie's understanding of the stakes of their research:

> The technology meant nothing. The technology would disappear, go transparent. In a generation or two, no one would even see it. Someone

would discover how to implant billions of transistors directly into the temporal lobes, on two little squares of metal foil . . . The clumsy mass of distracting machine would vanish into software, into the impulse that had invented it. Into pure conception . . . It was not even a tool, really. More of a medium, the universal one. However much the Cavern had been built from nouns, it dreamed the dream of the unmediated, active verb. It lived where ideas stepped off the blackboard into real being. It represented humanity's final victory over the tyranny of matter.                    (267)

Like ancient Gnostic initiates gathering in subterranean caverns to undergo rituals that will beam them up to the distant heavens, cybernauts rev up their processors until their speed reaches escape velocity. Kaladjian draws the final conclusion: "*We're approaching the point of full symbolic liberation*" (336). But it is left for the tattooed and pierced code junkie, Jacksaw, to give the date for "The Great Escape." "*You know, 2030 is right around the time that we'll finally be out of here*" (339).

Science fiction or fictionalized scientific facts? It's hard to know. With proliferating prostheses, implants, transplants, the engineering of molecules, and the reengineering of the genetic code, it is difficult to be sure if there is any longer a line between form and matter, body and mind, original and copy, or virtual and real. Powers's science fiction anticipates the argument of the respected computer scientist, inventor, entrepreneur, and futurist Ray Kurtzweil, who writes in his controversial 2005 book, *The Singularity Is Near: When Humans Transcend Biology*:

The Singularity will allow us to transcend these limitations of our biological bodies and brains. We will gain power over our fates. Our mortality will be in our own hands. We will be able to live as long as we want (a subtly different statement from saying we will live forever). We will fully understand human thinking and will vastly extend and expand its reach. By the end of this century, the nonbiological portion of our intelligence will be trillions of times more powerful than unaided human intelligence . . .

The Singularity will represent the culmination of the merger of our biological thinking and existence with our technology, resulting in a world that is still human but that transcends our biological roots. There will be no distinction post-Singularity, between human and machine or between physical and virtual reality.[17]

For people interested in exploring this new frontier, Kurtzweil has established a virtual university: http://singularityu.org. According to the website, "Singularity University is an interdisciplinary university whose mission is to assemble, educate and inspire leaders who strive to understand and facilitate the development of exponentially advancing technologies in order to address humanity's grand challenges." Undergraduate, graduate, and executive programs include the following areas: Futures Studies and Forecasting, Networks and Computing Systems, Biotechnology and Bioinformatics, Nanotechnology, AI and Robotics, and Space and Physical Sciences. Predictably, Singularity University is all the rage in Silicon Valley. In a promotional video, Google's co-founder Serge Brin declares, "If I was [n.b.] a student, this is where I would want to be." (It appears that Serge should have taken a few more English courses at Stanford.)

Again, it's hard to know if this is science fiction or fictionalized science. As I write these words, an article appears on the front page of the *New York Times*: "Scientists Worry Machines May Outsmart Man." That might have been from a review of Michael Crichton's novel *Prey*. John Markoff reports, "Impressed and alarmed by advances in artificial intelligence, a group of computer scientists is debating whether there should be limits on research that might lead to loss of human control over computer-based systems that carry a growing share of society's workload, from waging war to chatting with customers on the phone." Eric Horvitz, a researcher for Microsoft and president of the Association for the Advancement of Artificial Intelligence, convened a conference to respond to what he regards as the realistic prospect of

superintelligent machines and artificial intelligence systems run amok. . . .
The idea of an "intelligence explosion" in which smart machines would

design even more intelligent machines was proposed by the mathematician I. J. Good in 1965. Later, in lectures and science fiction novels, the computer scientist Vernor Vinge popularized the notion of a moment when humans will create smarter-than-human machines, causing such rapid change that "the human era will be ended." He called this shift *the Singularity*.

## MARKING TIME

But, alas, Plato's grotto, Lascaux, and the Cavern are not the only caves in *Plowing the Dark*. Jebel Hira, the cave in the mountains near Mecca where the archangel Gabriel dictated God's words to the Prophet Muhammad, is another piece in Powers's intricate mosaic. While artists, programmers, and engineers at the Realization Lab are sealed in a bubble plotting designs for their migration to the next dimension, a very different story is unfolding on the other side of the globe.

Trapped in an unhappy marriage and a dead-end job in Chicago, Taimur Martin flees to Beirut, where he secures a position teaching English. Though his mother is Muslim, he knows little about the Middle East and almost nothing about Islamic culture. In one of his first classes, he tries to engage the students by making what he intended as an ironic comment about the CIA. A fundamentalist student who is literalistic and has never heard of irony misunderstands the remark and reports to one of the terrorist cells that Taimur is a government agent. Several days later, Shi'ite guerrillas, who know nothing of the suspicions surrounding him, randomly kidnap Taimur and hold him captive for five years. Tai's story is a fictive version of Terry Waite's experience, which, as I have noted, initially inspired the novel.

Though Powers draws an explicit parallel between Tai's prison cell and the Cavern, the worlds could not be more different. The Cavern is a white room that is ten feet wide and twelve feet long; the root cellar where Tai is held is ten feet by six feet but is dark, damp, and filthy. The style of the two narratives is as different as the stories they tell. While Powers uses first-person dialogue for his account of the Realization Lab, he tells Taimur's story in the second person:

> The crib where they've dumped you is too dark to see. Inch by inch, your fingertips cover its surface. Good for passing a couple of hours, if nothing else. You are on a dirt floor, in a more or less rectangular room maybe ten feet by six. The floor is little more than the flight of five steps they shove you down. It stinks of soot and vegetables. Three of the walls are wooden; one is stone. The crumbling ceiling is too low to stand up under. Your heart begins to race, despite your forced calm. You will perish here. Suffocate. You will never see the light of day.                    (69)

Every detail of Taimur's world is calculated to contrast with RL.

Real/Virtual
Material/Immaterial
Body/Mind
Dirty/Clean
Random/Computational
Uncontrollable/Controlled
Hell/Heaven

Powers goes into graphic detail about the filthy conditions in which Tai is held. He is fed fetid gruel that throws his stomach and intestines into convulsions, but he is only allowed out of his cell to go to the toilet once a day. He has no choice but to shit and piss in his cell and then must endure the stench. He hears bugs and creatures he cannot see and sometimes is awoken by a cockroach crawling across his face. Though he eventually disciplines himself to eat in order to survive, he grows steadily weaker as the days, weeks, months, and years wear on.

At first Tai assumes his kidnapping is a mistake and tries to explain that he is only a teacher who has recently come to Beirut to teach English to the Lebanese. But his captors either do not understand or do not believe him.

As the story unfolds, it becomes clear that nothing is farther from the Seattle lab than this Beirut prison. Yet as the two stories unfold, they become intertwined in a way that suggests that these seemingly opposite worlds share more than it appears. Details accumulate that make it necessary to reread the opening lines of the novel as a description of Taimur's cell, as well as RL.

> *The room is never anything o'clock.*
>
> *Minutes slip through it like a thief in gloves. Hours fail even to raise the dust. Outside, deadlines expire. Buzzers erupt. Deals build to their frenzied conclusions. But in this chamber, now and forever combine.* (3)

The now that is forever in Beirut is not the same as the now that is forever in Seattle. Far from the moment of release when time is left behind, the now becomes the endless expanse of time that is inescapable.

The question of time is the cement that holds the two aspects of Powers's mosaic together. While programmers at RL plot the future in order to control time, Taimur is relentlessly subjected to the contingencies that mark the openness of the future. His kidnapping was a mistake—a random error that never could have been calculated in advance. The play of chance is the sting of time—if contingency can be figured and risk modeled, the future is closed and time is an illusion.

> Taken by surprise. Taken by accident. An insignificant foreign language teacher who never took sides in his life. Half Islamic, for God's sake. You mean nothing to your government. Nothing you can be swapped for. You're of no value to your captors whatsoever. . . . You wake up still horrified, unwilling to go near yourself. But by noon, you creep back again. You replay the mistake, consider the spy. It passes the time, at least. And time is more of an enemy than any other terrorist. (47)

No one would seem to need a technological fix to reach escape velocity more than Taimur. Though more frightful than any terrorist, Tai's relation to time is more complex and interesting than that of his counterparts on the other side of the globe. Imagine—just try to imagine—what it would be like to be trapped in a dark, stinking cell for five years! With no interruption other than a morning toilet break and an occasional outburst from the guards that has no more rhyme or reason than your kidnapping, days blur into one another until time becomes an unfathomable abyss.

In time, whole days start to vanish. For a long while the orderly egg carton of the calendar has regulated your mind, kept it, if not productive, at least aligned. But now the carton starts to crumple, the eggs begin to break against one another in an angry omelet.

You carry on numbering the days, desperate for form, although the tally no longer correlates with anything. The week arrives when you can't make it from one Friday call to prayer to the next without disorientation. It pulls you up out of a night's sleep and runs you under the freezing fire hose—this drift into terror, into utter timelessness. (321)

What the dreamers in RL do not know is that timelessness not only promises the eternal ecstasy of escape but also harbors the terror of endless imprisonment. The only thing worse than dying too young is living too long.

As days pass, Tai is forced to admit that escape is impossible and release most unlikely. Trapped in a time warp, he knows nothing of the world-historical events raging outside—the collapse of communism, heralded in apocalyptic terms as "the end of history"; demise of the Soviet Union; turmoil in the global financial markets, the Gulf War. What makes time so terrifying is its undifferentiated flow, in which everything passes but nothing changes. Tai realizes that the only way to cope with his situation is to manage time by punctuating its flux. "But which day? You can't say, and it crazes you. You've lost count, by as much as two full days. Lost your link to the world that they've stolen you away from. Market day, school day, wash day, holiday, birthday: you fall into limbo. You can't live, without a date to live in" (98). While the researchers seek release *from* time, Tai seeks release *through* time.

Tai's strategy is to turn to two ancient methods of marking time—ritual and story. "Desperate for form," he establishes a series of rituals intended to impose structure on his formless days. As he settles into a routine, terror is transformed into fear, which is more manageable. But rituals are repetitious and quickly become meaningless if they are not placed in a broader context. From the time *Paleanthropus* gathered around fires in ancient caves, human beings have told themselves stories to get through the night. Whether fiction or nonfiction, narrative creates meaning by translating serial events into coherent stories with a clear beginning, middle, and end. Though rarely noted, there is an unresolvable paradox in all storytelling—narrative simultaneously marks time by articulating temporal sequence and relieves the press of time by lending comprehensive form to contingency and chronicity.

In the absence of books, Tai recalls stories his Persian mother used to read to him in Farsi. These narratives wrap him in a blanket as warm and reassuring as the cave is cold and distressing. But memory is weak, and time is strong. When he has exhausted the library of his mind, Taimur begs his captors to give him a real book. They resist but do not say no, so he asks them to bring him a copy of one of his favorite childhood books—*Great Expectations*. Several days later, much to his surprise, an unexpected "presence settles in his cell." Hesitant at first, he finally picks up the book.

> Your sight scans up the book's length, seeking out the title that will sentence or deliver you. Terror is no less than desire with the chrome stripped away. In your atrophied eyes, the letters read like a line of alien hieroglyphs. Bizarre analphabetic randomness. English has no such series. Then your pulse shoots into your ears. *Great*. Your word. Your title. . . . For a long time, your eyes refuse the title's second word. Instead, they insist on the word that the word should be. But the surety of print survives your stare. You look again, and the title skids off into senselessness. You remove your blindfold and look dead on. *Expectations* somehow mutates into *Escapes*. (254)

Not *Great Expectations* but *Great Escapes*—not a great work of literature but a cheap collection of stories Tai never would have read in his previous life. But these throwaway tales become a lifeline that allows him to mark time. "*Great Escapes* must be your daily introit and gradual. A single paragraph to serve as a matins service, another two sentences every other hour. The need to make astonishment last far exceeds your immediate urge to swallow it whole. The point is not to finish but to find yourself somewhere, forever starting" (256). But, of course, Tai does finish *Great Escapes*, and with its completion what Bataille aptly describes as "the deleterious absurdity of time" returns with a vengeance.[18] When he pleas for another book, his captors give him a copy of the Qur'an. Once again, Tai is less interested in the substance of the story than the structure of the narrative. As if to impose a digital code on an analog tale, he parcels the Qur'an into ten-verse sections, which he reads one day at a time. "Each ten-verse maze holds you longer than the Sunday *Times* crossword ever did" (323). As he reads day after day, Tai's cell is transformed into the Prophet's cave: "You lie in the Prophet's slime-laden cave, taking the complete dictation all over again" (324). Ritual is a repetition compulsion that marks time by imposing form on formlessness. Myth and history are not opposite; to the contrary, history originates with the eternal return of the same. As Tai repeats the verses day after day after day, his cave not only morphs into the Prophet's cave, but both cells become virtually indistinguishable from the Cavern. While Adie floats through the Garden that is forever lost, Tai slips into a dream that seems to be real. "You and lucidity have been parting company without your knowing. Mind has been resorting to the quietist drift, a protective hallucination finally gentler than the alternative" (323).

In another Lebanon half a world away, somewhere between Beirut and Seattle, the "protective hallucination" is beginning to show cracks. With virtual reality technology reaching liftoff velocity, Stevie and Adie are brought back down to earth by the third member of their collegiate triangle. Ted, the handsome stud whom girls found irresistible, had come down with multiple sclerosis several years earlier. His career as a composer having failed, he is teaching extension courses in a prison located in Lebanon, Ohio, for a third-rate college. The prison is built on what was the original site of a utopian Shaker community. With a looming deadline for the design of a new prototype for the Cavern to be used in marketing VR technology, Steve and

Adie receive word that Ted's condition has taken a turn for the worse and decide they must visit him. By the time they reconnect with their friend, Ted is confined to a wheelchair and has to be strapped into his bed in a bare cinderblock room. As cells proliferate, prisons become darker. Zimmerman has become a true *Zimmer* man, confined to his cell-like room and never going out. To relieve the boredom and sense of entrapment, Stevie and Adie push Ted's wheelchair from the nursing home down the main street of town, stopping at shops he used to frequent. His pleasure with the outing deepens the despair of the return to his room.

"Where the body is chained," Powers avers, "the brain travels." Travel, however, takes people in different directions. What painting is for Adie, virtual reality is for Stevie, and literature and religion are for Taimur, music is for Ted. Technology becomes the supplement that enables Ted to pursue music even as his body betrays him. When Stevie uses a synthesizer to play the chamber symphony Ted has been composing for years, he and Adie are startled by what they hear. Body reprograms mind even as mind permeates body. Gone are the edge, irony, and flamboyance of Ted's youthful atonal compositions, and in their place there is beautiful tonal music, intended to soothe and reassure, that "proved nothing but its own raw need for redemption" (319). "*If I could just finish all four movements,*" Ted despairs. "*It's music . . . that people might love. That people might think about . . . and feel. Not like that alien stuff we used to make*" (319). As if recalling Wyatt's infinite deferral of ending, Stevie and Adie know he will never finish what he has started, because he does not have enough time. We never do. Before leaving for the last time, they lift Ted's naked body onto the bedpan and help him prepare for a night that has no end.

Depressed beyond words, Stevie and Adie return to the motel, where they engage in frenzied sex for hours. When mind finally returns to body, the two lie side by side, and Stevie asks Adie to repeat the words that changed his life.

> By the tips of her fingers, Stevie felt that his temples were wet. *Remind me,* he said.
>
> She rustled up close to his ear. *Remind you what?*

*Once out of nature. To look for something better than this body.*

She stroked his temples, counterclockwise [n.b.]. Each trace round the circle undid one spent year. Then she placed his words—the past, the poem that he was quoting. Her fingers clenched. *Go on*, she commanded. Desperate. *Say it. Say the rest.*

He could not refuse her anything. He'd given her worse, more irreversible, already this night. His own voice rang strange to him, speaking into the black:

*Once out of nature I shall never take*
*My bodily form from any natural thing,*
*But such a form as Grecian goldsmiths make*
*Of hammered gold and gold enamelling . . .*

*That's it*, she whispered into the gaping motel room. *That's the room we're supposed to build.* And set upon the golden bough to sing. *The place we're after. Byzantium.* (321)

But where is Byzantium?

## AFTER BYZANTIUM

Byzantium is the place where opposites meet but do not quite come together. In an interview, Powers explains the significance of Yeats's poem in *Plowing the Dark.*

*interview*

> One of the motifs that I use in the book is Yeats's "Sailing to Byzantium." The last project that the heroine in Seattle takes on is the construction of the Hagia Sophia, which is the crowning achievement of Byzantium. Yeats's Byzantium is the magic place where the inimical war between spirit and body is finally resolved. As it's resolved in this atemporal setting. "Once out of nature I shall never take / My bodily form from any

natural thing." It's exactly that. The idea that the soul doesn't want to be fastened to a dying animal. That's what drives the desire for art, the desire for a materially transcendent technology.[19]

Byzantium, of course, is also where West meets East and Christianity encounters Islam. The greatest expression of Byzantine art and architecture, Hagia Sophia, was *"for close to a thousand years, the greatest church in Christendom. And for another five hundred years after that, the greatest mosque in Islam"* (341). This is where great iconoclastic controversies have raged for centuries and, indeed, continue today.

Ancient theological disputes in the three religions of the Book probe questions that the most recent technology raises: can the Real be represented? The hidden mosaics that adorn the walls of Hagia Sophia reveal the passions that images stir. In his influential essay "The Precession of the Simulacrum," Jean Baudrillard underscores the theological stakes of contemporary media and VR technology:

But what becomes of the divinity [i.e., the Real] when it reveals itself in icons, when it is multiplied in simulacra? Does it remain the supreme authority, simply incarnated in images as a visible theology? Or is it volatized into simulacra that alone deploy their pomp and power of fascination—the visible machinery of icons being substituted for the pure and intelligible Idea of God? This is precisely what was feared by the Iconoclasts, whose millennial quarrel is still with us today. Their rage to destroy images rose precisely because they sensed this omnipotence of simulacra, this facility they have of effacing God from the consciousness of men, and the overwhelming, destructive truth that they suggest: that ultimately there has never been any God, that only the simulacrum exists, indeed that God himself has only ever been his own simulacrum. Had they been able to believe that images only occulted or masked the Platonic Idea of God, there would have been no reason to destroy them. One can live with the idea of a distorted truth. But their metaphysical despair came from the idea that the images concealed nothing at all, that in fact they were not images, such as the original model would have made them, but actually perfect simulacra forever radiant with their own fascination. But this death of the divine referential has to be exorcised at all cost.[20]

Iconoclasts understand the power of images better than the people who worship them.

Though she is unaware of the theological genealogy of virtual reality, Adie cannot give up the dream of "perfect simulacra forever radiant with their own fascination." She decides that she will recreate Hagia Sophia for the Cavern's final demonstration. Far from erasing the original, her simulation merely updates an earlier virtual environment using the latest technological fix. "Mosaic saints man the walls at strategic points. Deep-color tile squares of hammered gold leaf dusted over a layer of glass tesserae and finished with a layer of glass paste become the world's first bitmaps. Up close, their resolutions pixilated into discrete rectangles. But from down below, at the eye's prescribed distance, the folds of a gown hang full," and geometrically fashioned "faces escape the waste of history into some stilled, further conviction" (343). The Fall is always a fall into time and history that disrupts the eternal harmony of our original home. Far from *la recherche du temps perdu*, life becomes the search for a timelessness that is always already past. Hagia Sophia is the simulacrum of the prelapsarian garden that Adie artfully recreates as "The Dream" in the Jungle Room. In this work, it becomes clear that art, religion, and technology are all chasing the same dream. It takes fellow Irishman O'Reilly, whose calculations and machinations are designed to master time, to explain the point of Yeats's poem to Adie and Stevie.

> *The man never found a place where he could put down and live in good conscience. A place where heart and head could sit at the same table. That was his Byzantium fantasy. The zero point, the fulcrum for the whole insane machine of civilization. Sages standing in God's holy fire. The mechanical bird—tiny, gold-enameled gears and sprockets, singing perfectly, forever, of all things.*
>
> *Beats the hell out of anything that Silicon Valley has come up with yet,* Stevie said. *Or even the Japanese, for that matter.*

*But you see, it's all the same project. That's what's so demoralizing. The thing that's best in people, the thing that wants to be pure and whole and permanent, the thing that won't rest until it builds its eternal bird . . .* (335)

The end is near, the volume almost finished, only a few pages remain. To Taimur or, perhaps, the reader locked in a room reading *Plowing the Dark*, Powers writes:

> You learn to steer your fragile machine. You skim above the surface of a dark sea. You dive beneath these scattered reefs and float in your birthright air. The flight feels like reading, like skimming a thousand exhilarated pages, but without the brakes and ballast of an ending. . . . You fly too freely, or the land's geometry is wrong. Some titan fails to hold up his corner of the air's tent. Or you simply reach the edge of a story that, even at this final stage, remains eternally under construction. . . . The scene crashes before you do. The room of the cave slams to a breakpoint and empties itself into error's buffer. There on the wall where the oceans and olives and temples were, where the marble crags ran from their spine down into their unbroken chasm, the machine seizes up, the faulty allegory crumbles, the debugger spits out a continuous scroll of words.
>
> Only through this crack can you see where things lead. You step through the broken symbols and into something brighter. (401)

And into something darker. Byzantium always remains virtual because the zero point that is the navel of the universe as well as the dream forever withdraws to leave us to follow in its wake. Since Byzantium is never present, we are destined forever to sail toward a horizon we cannot reach.

When all the images are stripped away and only code and algorithms remain, the Cavern appears to be a "House of Leaves" that is bigger on the inside than it is on the outside. "In the mystery of sealed volumes, the space is larger than its container" (408). The volume might be a book, cathedral, mosque, cave, prison cell, or even the body itself. There is always noise that cannot be filtered, data that cannot be processed, and "desire that outlives its burn."

> *We're approaching the point of full symbolic liberation.* Loque almost sang it, gospel-style.
> *What's the point?* Ebsen asked. *Wasn't there enough imagery out there already?*
> But reality had never been large enough, because the body had never been large enough for the thing it hosted. Where else but in the imagination could such a kludge live? (336–337)

Efforts to the contrary notwithstanding, in the very effort to cover the abyss, the imagination reveals a concealment that can never be decoded. This opening keeps everything in play by constantly generating the "*hum of a place that passes all understanding*" (3).

While Adie and Stevie are putting the finishing touches on their rendering of Hagia Sophia, Taimur is released as abruptly and inexplicably as he had been seized. Overwhelmed by how much the world has changed during his five years of captivity, Tai, dazed and confused, rediscovers the lesson Terry Waite had learned about "the lost ability to engage in productive solitude." Powers writes, "There is a truth only solitude reveals. An insight that action destroys, one scattered by the slightest worldly affair: the fact of our abandonment here, in a far corner of sketched space. This is the truth that enterprise would deny. How many years have you fought to hold at bay this hideous aloneness, only now discovering that it shelters the one fact of any value?" (414) And then, in an unexpected twist, Powers concludes his mosaic on an explicitly theological note:

> You turn in the entranceway of illusion, gaping down the airplane aisle, and you make it out. For God's sake, call it God. That's what we've called it forever, and it's so cheap, so self-promoting, to invent new vocabulary for every goddamned thing, at this late a date. The place where you've been

> unfolds inside you. A space so large it will surely kill you, by never giving
> you the chance to earn it. (414)

"The place where you've been unfolds inside you," yet you cannot contain it. Everyone is bigger on the inside than on the outside because the imagination can never be contained by the figures it forms. It is as if Adie's virtual Parasite Room is in reality an uncanny internal cavern that can never be fathomed. Is this room the "place past place" where ghosts holy and unholy dwell? And what might be the name of this nameless place? Powers gives an answer that is not an answer: "For God's sake, call it God." Literature, Technology, Religion . . . Mind/Body, Spirit/Matter, Eternity/Time, VR/RL—"*it's all the same project.*"

# 3

# FIGURING NOTHING

Mark Danielewski, *House of Leaves*

*Make no mistake, those who write long books have nothing to say.*
*Of course those who write short books have even less to say.*

—Mark Z. Danielewski

**THE TEXT** is about nothing—always *about* nothing. Nothing is what keeps the text in play by rendering it irreducibly open and in/finitely complex. The nothingness haunting the text marks its border by exceeding it. This excess is the siteless site where difference endlessly emerges. The void that empties everything of itself is the incomprehensible gift that never stops giving. Art figures the unfigurable by giving what cannot be taken.

o o o

## WIRED

Today's students *live* online and in the cloud. Far from a mere tool they occasionally utilize, the Web is a space they inhabit and that inhabits them. This house in which they dwell does not, however, always feel like a home because familiarity with technology does not erase the strangeness of the domain into which we are migrating. As Myspace becomes Ourspace, it's a safe bet that in the twenty-first century, the virtual will increasingly displace, which is not to say replace, places and things that once seemed real. As virtual relations are becoming as important or even more important than real relations, real relations inevitably become entangled in virtual connections that both complicate and enrich them. Neither *Leibe* nor *Arbeit* remains the same in a wired world. The webs in which we are evermore entangled are not merely computer networks but are also global financial, media, and information networks. These changes are far from superficial; as we become inseparably joined to these prostheses by feedback loops, our very being is transformed. Young people, who are already living this future, are wired differently from previous generations. If one is patient enough to listen, though most adults are not, it quickly becomes clear that they do not see or think like their parents. The point is not that they think different ideas but that they actually *think differently*. The common complaint about students not reading enough is misguided; they read—perhaps not always as much as their parents and professors think they should—but they do not read the way their parents and teachers read. Their texts, which are not only verbal but more often are visual, auditory, and multimedia, have, like the contemporary world, lost their coherence and, thus, display little narrative continuity. As word gives way to image, old protocols no longer work, yet new logics have not been adequately formulated. Critics who insist it has ever been thus are wrong— something fundamental or, more precisely, nonfundamental is shifting, and this shift poses serious intellectual and pedagogical challenges.

How can the apparent gap between students who are wired differently and teachers who want to introduce them to the influential works in art, literature, philosophy, and religion be bridged? Do Hegel, Kierkegaard, Nietzsche, Melville, Poe, Stevens, Heidegger, and Derrida have anything to say to multitasking kids plugged into iPods, iPads, Facebook, Twitter, YouTube, and World of Warcraft? Conversely, do the children of network culture have anything to teach older generations about the ghosts who continue to haunt them—or at least some of them?

For the past twenty years, I have been attempting to bring together theory and practice by deploying a range of new technologies in my teaching. The consistent aim of these efforts has been to practice theory and theorize practice. These experiments require redrawing the traditional line separating teacher and students. The students and I have entered into a contract in which I pledge to teach them how my world can illuminate theirs and they promise to teach me how their world can reveal new aspects of mine. Every iteration of my courses has been different: Imagologies, Electronic Frontier, Cyberscapes, Networking, Real Fakes . . . In the early 1990s, I began experimenting by using teleconferencing technology to create a global classroom, with sites as distant as Helsinki and Melbourne. This led to efforts to webcast classes first locally and then globally through the Global Education Network (www.GEN.com).[1] While this strategy effectively blew away classroom walls that once seemed impermeable, it did not fundamentally change what went on in the classroom. The seminar table had been expanded, but the texts discussed around it too often remained the same. To create the possibility of thinking, reading, and writing differently, I decided to develop courses in which students would be required to take a lab where they developed the skills necessary for working with multimedia. Since I do not know these technologies as well as the students, I have asked them to design and teach the labs. Instead of writing term papers, members of the class are required to produce an analytic and critical treatment of the issues we consider in the course in the form of a multimedia format. With the increasing sophistication of software and expanding bandwidth, it is now possible to distribute this material on the Web.

A recent version of this ongoing experiment was called Real Fakes. The following is the catalog description of the course:

Cloning, genetic engineering, transplants, implants, cosmetic surgery, artificial life, artificial intelligence, nanotechnology, *faux* fashion, sampling, art about art, photographs of photographs, films about films, identity theft, derivatives, facial transplants, Enron, virtual reality, reality TV: the line long separating fake/real, artificial/natural, illusory/true, and inauthentic/authentic has disappeared. Fascination with the fake is as old as the imagination itself. But the shift from mechanical to digital and electronic means of production and reproduction has taken simulation to another level. What are the aesthetic, philosophical, social, ethical, and political implications of the multifaceted disappearance of the real? In addition to readings and discussions, there will be visits by a detective, a journalist, and experts on art forgery and counterfeiting.

Students were required to read theoretical texts such as Kierkegaard's "Shadowgraphs: A Psychological Pastime," Benjamin's *Arcades Project*, Baudrillard's "Simulacra and Simulations," Eco's *Travels in Hyperreality*, Foucault's *This Is Not a Pipe*, and Derrida's " 'Counterfeit Money' " and explore the work of artists such as P. T. Barnum, Tom Stoppard, Marcel Duchamp, Andy Warhol, J. S. G. Boggs, David Wilson, and Jeff Koons. In addition to participating in class discussions, students had to contribute to the construction of a website (www.realfakes.org), which was a knockoff of the *National Enquirer*'s home page. Course and site combined to create an extended text that was open and constantly changing in unexpected ways. This course expressed my abiding conviction that teaching and research are not only complementary but essential to each other: research without teaching is empty; teaching without research is blind. The multiple dimensions of different versions of this course formed part of an ongoing research project that continues to transform my thinking and writing.

## BLINDNESS AND INSIGHT

There are books I teach because I understand them and believe students should know what they have to offer, and there are books I teach because I do not understand them and know I can come to terms with them only with the help of students. After considerable deliberation, I decided to conclude Real Fakes with Mark Danielewski's remarkable *House of Leaves*, a 709-page book that eludes every established genre. Though a work of fiction, it is not quite a novel. Who, after all, has ever heard of a novel that includes its own commentary and analysis, as well as appendices, illustrations, footnotes, and even a thirty-two-page index that is unlike any index you have ever seen? From the cover design to the last page, *House of Leaves* is a labyrinthine work of enormous complexity. One of the reasons I selected this unusual book was that it is as sophisticated an examination of the problem of the real and the fake or the original and the counterfeit in the age of electronic reproduction as any theoretical work I know. *House of Leaves* is something like *The Recognitions* for the digital age. This theme is actually identified in the first paragraph of the first chapter of the book:

> While enthusiasts and detractors will continue to empty entire diction-
> aries attempting to describe or deride it, "authenticity" still remains the
> word most likely to stir a debate. In fact, this leading obsession—to vali-
> date or invalidate the reels and tapes—invariably brings up a collateral
> and more general concern: whether or not, with the advent of digital tech-
> nology, image has forsaken its once unimpeachable hold on the truth.[2]

*How* Danielewski writes is as intriguing as *what* he writes. Freely mixing high and low culture, he weaves together literary theory, architectural theory, film theory, philosophy, theology, psychoanalysis, modern and post-modern art and literature, detective fiction, and punk rock to create a book that baffles as much as it dazzles. The complexity of the work is compounded by a graphic design that *enacts* or *performs* the ideas the multiple authors and characters explore. *House of Leaves* is as hypertextual as a printed book can possibly be: its multiple layers fold into one another to form a work that places unusual demands on readers.

The length and complexity of *House of Leaves* made me hesitant to assign it to undergraduates and lifetime learners. But I was intrigued by the work and wanted to experiment with it. As I prepared for the first class, I had no idea what to expect, so I decided to begin the discussion by asking them what they thought of the book. Predictably, the adults in the class threw up their hands and declared they were unable to make any sense of it, but the reaction of the students was completely unexpected. Far from being daunted, they were completely absorbed by the text. In almost four decades of teaching, I have never been so surprised by the response to a book I had assigned. It was as if the students had been waiting to read this book their whole lives. *House of Leaves* might not have been their home, but it is where the youth of network culture live at some level, and the students in Real Fakes knew it.[3]

At the most superficial level, *House of Leaves* is about a documentary film entitled *The Navidson Record*, which might or might not have been made. With their marriage in shambles, the Pulitzer Prize–winning photojournalist Will Navidson, his partner Karen Green, and their two children Chad and Daisy retreat from the city to a seemingly cozy house on Ash Tree Lane in a quiet Virginia suburb to repair their disintegrating family. But everything goes awry when the house turns out to be haunted. Returning from a wedding in Seattle, they sense "something in the house had changed. Though they had only been away for four days, the change was enormous. It was not, however, obvious—like for instance a fire, a robbery, or an act of vandalism. Quite the contrary, the horror was atypical. No one could deny there had been an intrusion, but it was so odd that no one knew how to respond" (24). After carefully examining every nook and cranny, Navidson discovers that the house is, impossibly, one-quarter inch larger on the inside than it is on the outside. As the house continues to expand while appearing to remain unchanged, Navidson calls on his dope-smoking twin Tom and other friends and associates to help him explore the cavernous abyss opening in their midst. Rather than a prison to be escaped, this cave draws people in with the promise to reveal a secret that can never be revealed. Having committed his life to the truth of the image, the prize-winning photographer records all the explorations of his haunted house with a video camera and eventually produces *The Navidson Record* from this footage.

There are many autobiographical references to the contentious relation of Danielewski and his sister to their filmmaker father and influential mother throughout *House of Leaves*. The narrative quickly becomes impossibly convoluted until, in good modernist fashion, it folds back on itself and becomes a book about the book. The ever-shifting labyrinth the characters explore is, among many other things, the book Danielewski is writing. In good postmodernist fashion, the modernist fold is interrupted, and the self-referentiality of the work of art does not come full circle but reveals a gap that can be neither closed nor concealed even though it is never really revealed. In this house, nothing is certain—*nothing* is certain; indeed, questions begin before the first page of the work "proper." What seems to be the first edition is listed as the second edition because the purportedly documentary film around which the book is constructed appears to be based on an earlier work. "*The Navidson Record* did not first appear as it does today. Nearly seven years ago what surfaced was 'The Five and a Half Minute Hallway'— a five and a half minute optical illusion barely exceeding the abilities of any NYU film school graduate. The problem, of course, was the accompanying statement that claimed all of it was true" (4). Fact based on illusion yields fiction, and claims about the film raise questions about the book. In a manner reminiscent of *The Recognitions*, we discover counterfeits of counterfeits being passed off as the real thing.

But the puzzles are even more profound because it is not clear who has written *House of Leaves*. Though Danielewski's name appears on the cover and the copyright page, the title page indicates that Zampanò is the author and Johnny Truant has contributed an introduction and extensive notes. To compound confusion, in real life (or is it RL?) Danielewski signs all his personal e-mails Ƶ. Zampanò turns out to have been a blind recluse who wrote an extensive commentary on *The Navidson Record*. When Johnny Truant, whose name suggests that he is a Johnny-come-lately, and his friend Lude, whose real name is Harry, discover Zampanò's body in his cryptlike apartment, Johnny inherits a monstrous trunk that contains pages and pages of the old man's reflections on the film. The twenty-something-year-old kid, who intermittently works in a tattoo parlor and is in love with a hooker named Thumper, assumes the onerous responsibility of organizing Zampanò's ramblings into something resembling a coherent narrative. Johnny appends notes explaining his editorial procedures and adding his own observations and reflections, which are so extensive that they eventually overwhelm

Zampanò's text. As his prose becomes more convoluted, it becomes clear that his recent breakup with his girlfriend Clara English has had a significant impact on his writing. The texts are initially distinguished by contrasting typefaces, but as the work unfolds and refolds the difference between them becomes increasingly obscure. In his confusing introduction to the work, Johnny goes so far as to cast doubt on Zampanò's identity.

> He called himself Zampanò. It was the name he put down on his apartment lease and on several other fragments I found. I never came across any sort of ID, whether a passport, license or other official document insinuating that yes, he was An-Actual-&-Accounted-For person.
>
> Who knows where his name really came from. Maybe it's authentic, maybe made up, maybe borrowed, a *nom de plume* or—my personal favorite—*nom de guerre*. (xii)

As if this were not enough, Johnny, if he can be trusted, confirms suspicions about Navidson and his film.

> After all as I fast discovered, Zampanò's entire project is about a film which doesn't even exist. You can look, I have, but no matter how long you search you will never find *The Navidson Record* in theaters or video stores. Furthermore, most of what's said by famous people has been made up. I tried contacting all of them. Those that took the time to respond told me they had never heard of Will Navidson let alone Zampanò. (xix–xx)

A book about a nonexistent film that claims to be true is, in a certain sense, a book about nothing.

But if Zampanò did not write the text, who did? Perhaps Johnny. The more deeply immersed in his work he becomes, the more like Zampanò Johnny appears to be. However, since Zampanò dies before the tale begins, we only see him through Johnny's eyes. Though casting doubt on Zampanò and Navidson, Johnny never claims to be the author of the work. Some commentators have suggested that the book was actually written by Johnny's mother, who, after slipping into madness, is confined to the Three Attic Whalestoe Institute. Whether the mad woman is confined to the attic or is trapped in the belly of the whale, the figure of the absent mother haunts *House of Leaves*. We learn about the mother through her letters to Johnny, which are appended to the text. The letter from the director of the institute informing Johnny of the death of his mother indicates that her name was Pelafina Heather Lièvre. In the first sentence of the concluding paragraph of his letter, the director "misspells" her name. "Again we wish to extend our sympathies over the death of Ms. Livre [*sic*]" (643). While *livre* means book, Li(e)vre is a visual pun that betrays the lie at the heart of the book. In *House of Leaves*, no name is proper.

Nor are dates insignificant. The book "begins" and "ends" on Halloween. Johnny dates his introduction October 31, 1998, and when we last see Navidson, he is in Dorset, Vermont, filming "his costume clad children" in the local Halloween parade.

> In those final shots, Navidson gives a wink to the genre his work will always resist but inevitably join. Halloween. Jack O'lanterns. Vampires, witches, and politicians. A whole slew of eight year old ghouls haunting the streets of Dorset, plundering its homes for apples and blackness forever closing in above them. . . .
>
> Navidson does not close with the caramel covered face of a Casper the friendly ghost. He ends instead on what he knows is true and always will be true. Letting the parade pass from sight, he focuses on the empty road beyond, a pale curve vanishing into the woods where nothing moves and a street lamp flickers on and off until at last it flickers out and darkness sweeps in like a hand.
>
> December 25, 1996                                                    (527–528)

. . . the empty road beyond . . . where nothing moves . . . and darkness sweeps in like a hand. The nothing figured in darkness is what *The Navidson Record*, which, of course, does not exist, is all about. Zampanò, who, Johnny informs us, is "blind as a bat," "sees" the darkness Navidson struggles to film.

Zampanò writes constantly about seeing. What we see, how we see and what in turn we can't see. Over and over again, in one form or another, he returns to the subject of light, space, shape, line, color, focus, tone, contrast, movement, rhythm, perspective, and composition. None of which is surprising considering Zampanò's piece centers on a documentary called *The Navidson Record* made by a Pulitzer Prize–winning photojournalist who must somehow capture the most difficult subject of all: the sight of darkness itself. (xxi)

To film darkness would be to convey the insight blindness brings.

This book about the book layers text upon text. In addition to Navidson's film, Zampanò's commentary, and Johnny's commentary on the commentary, *House of Leaves* includes an elaborate textual apparatus citing scholarly comments, articles, and books either about the text or relevant to it. Some are real and some are fake, and it remains unclear who has assembled these academic studies. It seems unlikely that the strung-out Johnny would be familiar with such works, but no obvious alternative is suggested. A prefatory note from the nameless editor warns the reader:

> This novel is a work of fiction. Any references to real people, events, establishments, organizations or locales are intended only to give the fiction a sense of reality and authenticity. Other names, characters and incidents are either the product of the author's imagination or are used fictitiously, as are those fictionalized events and incidents which involve real persons and did not occur or are set in the future.

But this only complicates the puzzle because the author whose imagination has conjured other authors goes unnamed. Moreover, though many of the authors cited are real and the articles and books noted have actually been published, many of the passages quoted are made up, and pages referenced are either incorrect or do not exist. These textual plays have a theoretical purpose. Having studied at Yale during the halcyon days of deconstruction, Danielewski knows his literary theory inside out. Tucked away at the bottom of the blank page that follows the page where Navidson's film runs out, the name of "the processing lab" is listed: "*Yale" (490).

Many of the readings of *House of Leaves* included in the notes are brilliant; indeed, they are worthy of publication in the best literary journals or with leading university presses. Every time the reader imagines a new way to interpret the text, he turns the page only to discover a footnote or a footnote to a footnote in which some "author" has anticipated his analysis. It is as if a precocious graduate student in literary theory had written a demanding work of fiction that includes every possible interpretation of it that might be proffered by the professors sitting on his doctoral committee. In a 2003 interview, Danielewski remarks: "I don't mind admitting that I was extremely self-conscious about everything that went into *House of Leaves*. In fact—and I know this will sound like a very bold remark, but I will say it anyway since it remains the truth—I have yet to hear an interpretation of *House of Leaves* that I had not anticipated. I have yet to be surprised, but I'm hoping."[4] While the claim is hyperbolic, Danielewski's ironic take on literary criticism is trenchant. In this book, the writer outsmarts critics who claim to be writers. And to make it all even sweeter, Danielewski knows it.

A commentary on an original that never existed, a commentary on that commentary, footnotes to books and articles analyzing the "novel," exhibits, letters, poems, appendices, real and fake quotations, collages, index . . . Johnny characterizes Danielewski's book when he describes Zampanò's manuscript:

> Endless snarls of words, sometimes twisting into meaning, sometimes into nothing at all, frequently breaking apart, always branching off into other pieces I'd come across later—on old napkins, the tattered edges of an envelope, once even on the back of a postage stamp; everything is anything but empty; each fragment completely covered with the creep of years and years of ink pronouncements; layered, crossed out, amended; handwritten, typed; legible, illegible; impenetrable, lucid; torn, stained, scotch taped; some bits crisp and clean, others faded, burnt or folded and refolded so many times the creases have obliterated whole passages

of god knows what—sense? truth? deceit? a legacy of prophecy or lunacy or nothing of the kind?, and in the end achieving, designating, describing, recreating—find your own words; I have no more; or plenty more but why? and all to tell—what? (xvii)

Nothing perhaps. Original or copy? Authentic or inauthentic? Primary or secondary? Genuine or counterfeit? Real or fake?

## ENTRANCES WITHOUT EXITS

*House of Leaves* has multiple entrances but no exits. To enter this house is to wander through the underworld—Plato's cave, Dante's hell, Freud's unconscious, Poe's tomb, Melville's whale, God's house . . . tattoo parlors, bars, clubs, rave parties, rock-and-roll punk concerts, underground film theaters, strip joints, brothels, acid trips, crack houses, the Internet . . . In the absence of the original, beginning is difficult, and starts often seem false. Epigram upon epigram upon epigram: 1. "This is not for you"—which of course makes the book irresistible; 2. "*Muss es sein?*" which is the title of a work by Beethoven, though it sounds like a line lifted from Heidegger or perhaps even Lacan; 3. "*I saw a film today, oh boy . . .* ", which is supposed to be a line from an unnamed song by the Beatles. Can we take this book seriously? If so, how is it to be read, and how is it to be taught?

*House of Leaves* is a book about how to read in a world where the real, however it is figured, is always slipping away. Any effort to summarize the book, any attempt to say what the book is *about*, is bound to fail. The most that can be said is that the book is about the impossibility of saying what the book is about. How, then, can such a book be taught? After considerable reflection, I decided that the only way I could teach the book was by trying to show the students *how* to read it, by tracking a few of its tangled lines. Among the many threads we might have followed, I selected a particular series of connections, chain of associations, perhaps lines of *filiation* that held interest for me:

As I have noted, when Navidson and his family returned from Seattle, there had been an intrusion in the house so slight—a mere quarter inch—as to be virtually imperceptible. Nothing yet everything had changed. After describing Chad and Daisy running through the house "playing, giggling, completely oblivious to the deeper implications" of the intrusion, Zampanò shifts the narrative in a direction that initially seems incongruous. "What took place amounts to a strange spatial violation which has already been described in a number of ways—namely surprising, unsettling, disturbing but most of all uncanny. In German the word for 'uncanny' is 'unheimlich' which Heidegger in his book *Sein und Zeit* thought worthy of some consideration" (24). This observation is followed by a quotation in German from the section of *Being and Time* entitled "The Basic State-of-Mind of Anxiety as a Distinctive Way in which Dasein is Disclosed." In a footnote, Johnny provides the English translation, which, he stresses, was "a real bitch to find." He concludes that this text by "a former Nazi tweaking on who knows what . . . only goes to prove the existence of crack back in the early twentieth century. Certainly this geezer must have gotten hung up on a pretty wicked rock habit to start spouting such nonsense" (25).[5] Initially this seems to be merely parody, but the more one reads the clearer it becomes that these musings must be taken seriously. By citing the passage in which Heidegger associates the *unheimlich* with the psychological experience of anxiety, Zampanò underscores the relationship between the house and the mind or, more precisely, the unconscious. Freud, of course, anticipated Heidegger's account of the uncanny. He begins his famous essay "*Das Unheimliche*" by tracing the etymological implications of "uncanny" in several languages. As we have seen in the analysis of *Plowing the Dark*, the English term, Freud explains, suggests a haunted house: "English . . . Uncomfortable, uneasy, gloomy, dismal, uncanny, ghastly; (of a house) haunted; (of a man) a repulsive fellow." After his long linguistic excursus, he concludes that the most satisfactory definition of *unheimlich* has been provided by Schelling: " '*Unheimlich*' is the name for everything that ought to have remained . . . secret and hidden but *has come to light."* For Freud, this interplay of concealing and revealing suggests the female genitals, whose veiling and unveiling, he believes, lie at the heart of the experience of the uncanny. What most intrigues Freud about the notion of the uncanny, however, is its irreducible ambiguity. Commenting on the multiple nuances of the word, he writes:

> What interests us most in this long extract is to find that among its different shades of meaning the word "*heimlich*" exhibits one which is identical with its opposite, "*unheimlich.*" What is *heimlich* thus comes to be *unheimlich.* . . . In general we are reminded that the word "*heimlich*" is not unambiguous, but belongs to two sets of ideas, which, without being contradictory, are yet very different: on the one hand, it means what is familiar and agreeable, and on the other, what is concealed and kept out of sight.[6]

What is *heimlich*, thus, turns out to be *unheimlich*. And this is precisely what happens to the Navidson house.

In the passage from *Being and Time* that Zampanò cites, Heidegger interprets the uncanny as the experience of "not-being-at-home." In contrast to "tranquilized self-assurance—'Being-at-home,'" the uncanny unsettles in a way that leaves everything insecure. What makes the uncanny so disturbing is that it is provoked by *nothing*. "In anxiety," Heidegger writes, "one feels *uncanny*. Here the peculiar indefiniteness of that which Dasein finds itself alongside in anxiety, comes proximally to expression: the 'nothing and nowhere'" (25). As Kierkegaard first pointed out in *The Concept of Anxiety* (1844), anxiety, in contrast to fear, which always has a specific object, is a response to nothing, i.e., to no definite thing. The indefiniteness of this no-thing is precisely what makes anxiety so difficult to manage, control, and master. After all, how is it possible to cope with what is never present yet is not absent? For those who suffer anxiety, the experience is so unsettling that it is never again possible to be at home in the world. When understood in this way, anxiety is one of the names for "the unnamable horror" that haunts the house on Ash Tree Lane as well as *House of Leaves*.

It is Johnny Truant rather than Heidegger who brings the experience of anxiety to life. One afternoon, while working as an apprentice at the tattoo shop, Johnny suddenly has the strange feeling that "something's really off. I'm off." What makes this experience all the more unsettling is that "nothing has happened, absolutely nothing" (26). As he begins to have trouble breathing, Johnny is seized by the conviction that he has "caught sight of some tremendous beast crouched off in the shadows . . . beyond the point of reason." But, he reports,

> when I finally do turn, jerking around like the scared-shitless shit-for-brains I am, I discover only a deserted corridor, or what is merely a *recently* deserted corridor; this thing, whatever it had been, obviously beyond the grasp of my imagination or for that matter my emotions, having departed into alcoves of darkness, seeping into corners & floors, cracks & outlets, gone even to the walls. Lights now normal. The smell history. Though my fingers still tremble and I've yet to stop choking on large irregular gulps of air, as I keep spinning around like a stupid top spinning around on top of nothing, looking everywhere, even though there's absolutely nothing, nothing anywhere. (27)

The thing—the dreadful thing haunting Johnny is "absolutely nothing, nothing anywhere"—and everywhere. Neither present nor absent, this nothing is, in the words of a fictitious work of a critic Johnny cites later, "unpresent"[7] but not precisely absent. How is this *unpresent* to be understood?

On June 6, 1950, Heidegger delivered a prescient lecture to the Bayerische Akademie der Schönen Kunst, which later was published under the title "The Thing." Reflecting on "the abolition of distance" brought about by rapidly developing information technologies, he writes,

> all distances in time and space are shrinking. Man now reaches overnight, by plane, places that formerly took weeks and months of travel. He now receives instant information, by radio, of events that he formerly learned about only years later, if at all. . . . The peak of this abolition of every

possibility of remoteness is reached by television, which will soon pervade and dominate the whole machinery of communication.[8]

In the years since Heidegger wrote these words, the collapse of distance has accelerated, but nearness remains elusive, and people fall victim to the feeling of "helpless anxiety." Trying to diagnose what occasions this anxiety, Heidegger reflects: "The terrifying is unsettling; it places everything outside its own nature. What is it that unsettles and thus terrifies? It shows itself and hides itself in the *way* in which everything presences, namely, in the fact that despite all overcoming of distances the nearness of things remains absent." This absence continues to haunt a world drawn ever closer together by information and telecommunications technologies. But what *is* it?

To answer this question, Heidegger takes the unlikely example of a clay jug. The jug, he explains, is first and foremost a *thing*. But "what is a thing?" As always, the most basic questions turn out to be the most difficult. Instead of identifying the thing as an object (*Gegen-stand* or ob-ject) that stands over against or opposite a subject, Heidegger describes the thing as what "stands forth" or emerges. Then in a claim that is critical for understanding *House of Leaves* as well as all the texts it gathers together, he argues: "no representation of what is present, in the sense of what stands over against us as an object, ever reaches to the thing *qua* thing." The thing, in other words, is *unrepresentable* and as such is never present, though it is not absent. As Johnny insists, "this thing" is "obviously beyond the grasp of [the] imagination." To clarify his admittedly obscure analysis, Heidegger explains what it means for the jug to stand forth. After defining the jug by its function as a holding vessel, he proceeds to explain,

> When we fill the jug with wine, do we pour the wine into the sides and bottom? At most, we pour the wine between the sides and over the bottom. Sides and bottom are, to be sure, what is impermeable in the vessel. But what is impermeable is not yet what does the holding. When we fill the jug, the pouring that fills it flows into the empty jug. The emptiness, the void is what does the vessel's holding. The empty space, this nothing

of the jug, is what the jug is as the holding vessel. . . . But if the holding is done by the jug's void, then the potter who forms sides and bottom on his wheel does not, strictly speaking, make the jug. He only shapes the clay. No—he shapes the void. For it, in it, and out of it, he forms the clay into the form. From start to finish the potter takes hold of the impalpable void and brings it forth as the container in the shape of a containing vessel. The jug's void determines all the handling in the process of making the vessel. The vessel's thingness does not lie at all in the material of which it consists, but in the void that holds.

As we will see in more detail in the final chapter, the thing is nothing— the no-thing that allows the jug to stand forth or appear as the object we think we know. So understood, nothing is not the opposite of the thing; to the contrary, thing and nothing are inseparably interrelated—there can be no thing without nothing. For this reason, nothing haunts everything and, thus, is everywhere yet nowhere. What makes no-thing so strange is that it is a beyond that is not elsewhere but is the proximate betwixt 'n' between that is always in a midst that is not our own.

The writerly equivalent of the relation between the void and the clay of the jug is the interplay between the white space of the blank page and the black ink of formed letters of the text. As speech emerges from silence, so writing emerges from a void that is never completely erased. Yet precisely this emptiness is what much—perhaps most—writing is designed to avoid. As Johnny explains, narratives are developed to make the world comprehensible, hospitable, habitable: "We create stories to protect ourselves" (20). But to protect ourselves from what? Above all else, stories are supposed to protect us from the emptiness, meaninglessness, absence, and the nothingness they nonetheless harbor. All such efforts, however, prove futile because nothing cannot be a-voided; there can be no story without the haunting emptiness it is written to fill. No matter how many stories there are, every house is haunted and every story is a ghost story.

As fits of anxiety deepen and panic approaches, Johnny frets: "I don't know what I need but for no apparent reason, I'm going terribly south.

Nothing has happened, absolutely nothing" (26). It is precisely because *nothing* has happened that Johnny is heading south. The farther south he journeys, the closer opposites become, until they collapse to create a *concidentia oppositorum* that is simultaneously destructive and creative. No one understood the unexpected terror of southern parts better than Edgar Allan Poe. Far from a verdant world of pleasure and leisure, the southern hemisphere is, for Poe, the region where warmth turns cold and life meets death. The two most memorable works in which Poe takes the reader to the bottomless bottom of the world are *The Narrative of Arthur Gordon Pym* and "MS. Found in a Bottle." Poe, like many in his day, believed the South Pole was a vortex toward which all the waters of the world inevitably rush. As one approaches the pole, snow and ice create a blinding whiteout that turns everything dark. In "MS. Found in a Bottle," an anonymous narrator sets out on a voyage to the archipelago of the Sunda Islands only to find himself, along with a nameless Swede, the victim of an horrific shipwreck. Impossibly, the narrator records the experience in a journal that survives the disaster: "Just before sinking within the turgid sea, its central fires suddenly went out, as if hurriedly extinguished by some unaccountable power. It was a dim, silver-like rim, alone, as it rushed down the unfathomable ocean."[9] When they surface, he reports, "we were enshrouded in pitch darkness, so that we could not have seen an object at twenty paces from the ship. Eternal night continued to envelop us." Clinging to the wreckage, the two survivors drift in darkness until the Swede can no longer hang on and slips into "the abyss." Left alone, the narrator sees or thinks he sees "a gigantic ship" bearing down on him. He miraculously escapes, boards the vessel, and records what he discovers: "I have made many observations upon the structure of the vessel. Although well armed, she is not, I think, a ship of war. Her rigging, build, and general equipment, all negative a supposition of this kind. What she *is not*, I can easily perceive; what she *is*, I fear it is impossible to say." Like the distant *deus absconditus*, it is only possible to say what the ship is saying it *is not*. As the story unfolds, the narrator discovers that the ship is haunted. Members of the crew, speaking "a foreign tongue . . . glide to and fro like the ghosts of buried centuries." With "the blackness of eternal night, and a chaos of foamless water" swirling, the ship is caught in a strong current and rushes "howling and shrieking by the white ice, thunders on to the southward with a velocity like the headlong dashing of a cataract." The tale concludes,

> To conceive the horror of my sensations is, I presume, utterly impossible; yet a curiosity to penetrate the mysteries of these awful regions, predominates even over my despair, and will reconcile me to the most hideous aspect of death. It is evident that we are hurrying onwards to some exciting knowledge—some never-to-be-imparted secret, whose attainment is destruction. Perhaps this current leads us to the southern pole itself. It must be confessed that a supposition apparently so wild has every probability in its favor.

More fantastic than the tale itself is the "fact" that the narrator somehow manages to stuff his manuscript into a bottle and toss it into the sea at the very last moment.

After the disaster, the text surfaces from the abyss. This abyss is not merely the sea but is the unrepresentable void that makes the creation of the work of art possible. Like *House of Leaves*, "MS. Found in a Bottle" explores the unfathomable depths of the imagination and the intractable enigma of writing. Far from avoiding the void, writing, when it is not trivial, struggles to communicate the incommunicable by imparting "some never-to-be-imparted secret, whose attainment is destruction." Writing *sensu strictissimo* is always what Maurice Blanchot calls "the writing of the disaster."[10]

Danielewski or Johnny—it is never possible to be sure who the author is—rewrites "MS. Found in a Bottle" as the tale of the disaster of a ship named the *Atrocity*. The Swede becomes a Norwegian, and the South becomes the North Pole, but the story remains the same. When only eighteen, Johnny meets "an eccentric gay millionaire from Norway" who goes by the name Tex Geisa and delights in telling "weird sea stories" that always rush to the same inevitable ending. (Geisha-Tex is a community of artists fascinated by surface rather than depth or, perhaps, by the depths of surfaces. They are devoted to digital art, tattooing, skin art, body modification, wallpaper, and photography.). For Johnny, Tex is as weird as the tales he spins,

> delivering one after another in his equally strange monotone, strangely reminiscent of something else, whirlpools, polar bears, storms and sinking ships, one sinking ship after another, in fact that was the conclusion to every single story he told so that we, his strange audience, learned not to wonder about the end but paid more attention to the inevitable rush of icy water, whirlpools and polar bears. (297)

Tex's tales remind Johnny of yet another story:

> though not the same, a completely different story after all, built upon story after story, so many, how many? stories high, but building what? and why?—like for instance, why—the approaching "it" providing momentarily vague—did it have to leave Longyearbyen, Norway and head North in the dead of summer? Up there summer means day, a constant ebb of days flowing into more days, nothing but constant light washing over all that ice and water, creating strange ice blinks on the horizon, flashing out a code, a distress signal?—maybe; or some other prehistoric meaning?— maybe; or nothing at all?—also maybe; nothing's all . . . (297–298)

"Nothing's all." This is not the first time that Johnny has suspected that nothing's all. But now the implications of his suspicion appear more far-reaching. Perhaps the nothing that is all is the never-to-be-imparted secret whose attainment is our destruction. If the secret is nothing, the distress signal would turn out to be a code that cannot be cracked. And if the code cannot be cracked, the message becomes unreadable, and unreadability becomes the message in the bottle.

With "wind whistling through the corridors like the voice of god," the *Atrocity*, in spite of its size and experienced crew, sinks in the violent northern seas. Rushing to their watery graves, the sailors hear a monstrous growl loose *inside*! their ship, tearing, slashing, hurling anyone aside who dares hesitate before it, bow before it, pray before it . . . breaking some, ripping apart others, burying all of them, and it's still only water, gutting the inside, destroying the pumps, impotent things impossibly set against transporting outside that which has always waited outside but now on gaining entrance, on finding itself inside, has started to make an outside of the whole—there is no more inside . . .

When the outside is inside, *nothing* remains the same.

As horrible as this disaster is, there is, as Poe knew all too well, a worse fate: to be buried alive. Unbeknownst to most of the *Atrocity's* crew members, the ship had two holds, "one secret, the other extremely flammable." When the ship erupted in flames, one unnamed crewman sealed himself in the secret hold. But like the lines of a story, the walls of the compartment provide only temporary shelter: "in that second hold where one man hid, having sealed the doors, creating a momentary bit of inside, a place to live in, to breathe in, a man who survived the blast and the water and instead lived to feel another kind of death, a closing in of such impenetrable darkness, far blacker than any Haitian night or recounted murder" (299). The reprieve proves temporary because the sailor's fate is sealed as tightly as his crypt. Like the manuscript in the bottle rising from the abyss, the sinking ship leaves traces to be deciphered on the surface of the sea:

slicing down into the blackness, vanishing in under twelve minutes from the midnight sun, so much sun and glistening light, sparking signals to the horizon, reminiscent of a message written once upon a time, a long, long time ago, though now no more, lost, or am I wrong again? never written at all, let alone before . . . unlawful hopes? . . . retroactive crimes? . . . unknowable rapes? an attempt to conceal the Hand at all, though I still know the message, I think, in all those blinks of light upon the ice, inferring something from what is not there or ever was to begin with, otherwise who's left to catch the signs? crack the codes? (299)

What hand has written these signs? Can they be caught? Can the code be cracked?

As the last moments of the entombed Norwegian's life are recounted, the narrative indirectly confirms what we have suspected all along—the story of the *Atrocity* is Johnny's as well as our own. Johnny cannot stay afloat because the outside is no longer outside but now is *inside*.

> I'm losing any sense of who he was, no name, no history, only the awful panic he felt, universal to us all, as he sunk inside that *thing* [emphasis added], down into the unyielding waters, until peace finally did follow panic, a sad and mournful peace but somewhat pleasant after all, even though he lay there alone, chest heaving, yes, understanding home, understanding hope, and losing all of it, all long long gone a long long time ago . . .  (300)

This unnamable thing is the "terrifying and unsettling" nothing Heidegger names the uncanny. Sunk inside the thing that is sunk within oneself, every space that once seemed habitable now becomes *unheimlich*. If the something inferred turns out to be nothing, signs and codes remain opaque, and when signs are indecipherable and codes cannot be cracked, texts become labyrinths from which there is no exit.

A few pages—most of which are blank—after the end of the *Atrocity* narrative, a new chapter begins:

## XIII

### The Minotaur[123]

> Alarga en la pradera una pausada
> Sombra, pero ya el hecho de nombrarlo
> Y de conjeturar su circunstancia
> Lo hace ficción del arte y no criatura
> Viviente de las que andan por la tierra.

—Jorge Luis Borges[255]

In note 255, the anonymous editor provides a translation of the Borges text: " . . . a slow shadow spreads across the prairie, / but still, the act of naming it, of guessing / what is its nature and its circumstances / creates a fiction, not a living creature, / not one of those who wander on earth." Just as Poe's effort to name the unnamable produces his tales, so, Borges suggests, the act of naming the shadow creates a fiction. Note 123 appears 203 pages earlier in a passage that, like the title, is *sous rature*.[11] Footnotes to footnotes transform the text about the labyrinth into a labyrinth. In one note, Johnny explains that the crossed-out sections had been deleted by Zampanò. The passages Johnny restores summarize the story of the labyrinth Daedalus constructed as well as several interpretations of the myth. Some of the notes within notes refer to published books, others refer to fictitious authors and articles. The last line on the page on which this textual labyrinth is inscribed cites the influential essay "Structure, Sign, and Play in the Discourse of the Human Sciences," in which Derrida summarizes some of the most important aspects of his theory of textuality. Stressing the significance of "the question of structure and centrality," Johnny, or whoever is providing these notes, quotes two passages in both French and English. Once again, the issue is the unthinkable outside that is inside systems and structures that are supposed to provide stability, purpose, and meaning.

> The function of [a] center was not only to orient, balance, and organize the structure—one cannot in fact conceive of an unorganized structure— but above all to make sure that the organizing principle of the structure would limit what we might call the *play* of the structure. By orienting and organizing the coherence of the system, the center of a structure permits the play of its elements inside the total form. And even today the notion of a structure lacking any center represents the unthinkable itself. . . . This is why the classical thought concerning structure could say that the center is, paradoxically, *within* the structure and *outside* it. The center is at the center of the totality, and yet, since the center does not belong to the totality (is not part of the totality), the totality *has its center elsewhere*. The center is not the center. (112)

Systems and structures include as a condition of their own possibility an excess that they cannot incorporate. The displacement of the center renders the text irreducibly open and thereby erases every bottom line.

Though it is not readily apparent, this footnote is not the first time a Derridean trace appears in *House of Leaves*. The obscure black cover of the book bears the outline of a labyrinth whose center represents a variation of either Borges's spiral staircase or the outline of a drawing in a footnote of Derrida's essay "Tympan." As the preface to Derrida's collection of essays titled *Margins of Philosophy*, "Tympan" is, in effect, the margin of *Margins*. "Tympan" is important not only for the argument it presents but also for the design of the essay. Breaking with traditional monographic typography, Derrida divides the text into a wide column, devoted to a critical reassessment of Hegel's philosophy, and a narrow marginal column that consists of a lengthy quotation from Michel Leiris's *Biffures*. *Biffure*, it is important to note, means crossing out, canceling, erasure. The drawing Derrida reproduces is Lafaye's *Tympanum* (1717).

"Tympanum" has multiple meanings—it is the membrane that forms the eardrum as well as the diaphragm of a telephone. In architecture, the tympanum is the recessed, ornamental panel enclosed by the cornices of a triangular pediment. A closely related word, *tympan*, refers in printing to a padding of paper or cloth placed over the plate of a printing press to provide support for the sheet being printed. A tympan is also the tightly stretched sheet or membrane that forms the head of a drum. Finally, in old French, *tympaniser* means to criticize or ridicule publicly.

Derrida begins his critique of Hegel by playing with all of these meanings of *tympan* and more.

> To tympanize—philosophy.
>
> *Being at the limit*: these words do not yet form a proposition, and even less a discourse. But there is enough in them, provided that one plays upon it, to engender almost all the sentences in this book.
>
> Does philosophy answer this need? How is it to be understood? Philosophy? The need?[12]

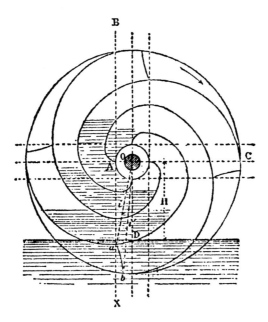

3.1  Jacques Derrida, "Tympan."

*Source:* Jacques Derrida, *Margins of Philosophy*, trans. Alan Bass (Chicago: University of Chicago Press, 1982), xxi.

As in most of Derrida's work, the proper name Hegel stands for Western philosophy as such. While the details of the argument need not concern us here, the conclusion is important. Philosophy, Derrida argues, presupposes yet cannot comprehend the limit or margin that constitutes it. In attempting to turn on itself to complete a circle of transparent self-reflexivity or self-referentiality, philosophy inevitably exposes the gap that can be neither bridged nor closed. By pushing philosophy to its *logical* conclusion, in the quest for Absolute Knowledge, Hegel unwittingly exposes philosophy to the limit it can never grasp. Instead of avoiding this margin or limit that philosophy cannot think, Derrida relentlessly probes it in all his writing.

The only explicit reference to "Tympan" in *House of Leaves* appears on page 401, where Zampanò cites this essay in an effort to "clarify" his association of Borges's spiral staircase first with the shell (i.e., house) of a snail and then with quotations drawn from Bachelard's *The Poetics of Space*, which probes the psyche by exploring every nook and cranny of a house. Once again, footnotes proliferate; a note that provides Bachelard's "original text" includes the reference to Derrida's essay. After quoting Derrida's text in French, Johnny adds:

> In his own note buried within the already existing footnote, in this case *not* 5 but enlarged now to 9, Alan Bass (—Trans for *Margins of Philosophy* (Chicago: University of Chicago Press, 1981)) further illuminates the above by making the following comments here below:
>
> "There is an elaborate play on the words *limaçon* and *conquer* here. *Limaçon* (aside from meaning snail) means spiral staircase and the spiral canal that is part of the inner ear. *Conque* means both conch and concha, the largest cavity of the external ear."
>
> [386]"Tympanum, Dionysianism, labyrinth, Ariadne's thread. We are now traveling through (upright, walking, dancing), included and enveloped within it, never to emerge, the form of an ear constructed around a barrier, going round its inner walls, a city, therefore (labyrinth, semicircular canals—warning: the spiral walkways do not hold) circling around like a stairway winding around a lock, a dike (dam) stretched out toward the sea; closed in on itself and open to the sea's path. Full and empty of its water, the anamnesis of the concha resonates alone on the beach." As translated by Alan Bass.—Ed.

As Derrida folds into Danielewski who folds into Derrida, the reader becomes implicated in the text that now appears to be implicated in him. Inasmuch as the ear is a labyrinth, the labyrinth into which *House of Leaves* leads us is not merely outside but is inside as an outside we incorporate but cannot assimilate.

The typographical gestures of "Tympan" are neither incidental nor accidental but are integral to the argument of the essay. The tympan that Derrida traces in *Margins* cannot be directly represented in words or images but can be performed or enacted through strategies of textual design. The interplay of the columns as well as the blank or white space joining and separating them implies the elusive margin of difference that the text presupposes but cannot articulate. Originally published in 1972, "Tympan" is, in effect, the preliminary draft for a more extensive and demanding work that appears two years later. *Glas* is one of the most remarkable and challenging works in the history of philosophy (if that is what it is).[13] Written before the era of word processing, it is a hypertext *avant la lettre* and, as such, is the prototype for *House of Leaves*.

While the connections are subtle, the lines joining *House of Leaves* and *Glas* unexpectedly pass through Paul Auster's *New York Trilogy*.[14] In the moments immediately after Navidson's film runs out, Karen turns around "to discover the real emptiness waiting behind her." Zampanò fabricates several critical interpretations of Karen's experience, the most interesting of which refers to Paul Auster.

> Karen's action inspired Paul Auster to conjure up a short internal mono-
> logue tracing the directions of her thoughts.[422]
>
> [422] Paul Auster's "Ribbons," *Glas Ohms*, v. xiii, n. 83, August 11, 1993, p. 2.
>
> (522)[15]

Danielewski plays on a suggestive slippage between *Glas* and glass in the passage. In French, *glas* means knell, passing-bell, tolling. The *glas funèbre*, which is very important for Derrida, is the death knell that sounds as the funeral procession passes the church. Danielewski includes two strategic references to *Glas* in an appended section entitled, significantly, "Bits." A bit, of course, is, among other things, "a unit of information equivalent to the choice of either of two equally likely states of an information-carrying system" as well as a small piece or fragment. The fragments of *Glas* elude the binary logic of bits.

> Incomplete. Syllables to describe a life. Any life.
> I cannot even discuss Günter Nitschke or Norberg-Schulz. I merely wanted Glas (Paris: Editions Galilée, 1974). That is all. But the bastards reply it is unavailable. Swine. All of them. Swine. Swine. Swine.

---

Mr. Leavy, Jr. and of course Mr. Rand will have to do.[16]
April 22, 1991

Let us space.
Jacques Derrida
*Glas*

(654)

The association of *Glas* with the *New York Trilogy* is, in characteristic Austerian fashion, a matter of chance. The English translation of Derrida's *Truth in Painting* mistranslates *Glas* as "glass," thereby establishing an association with Auster's *New York Trilogy*. Auster's philosophical detective story consists of three volumes whose titles underscore their relevance for Danielewski's work: *City of Glass*, *Ghosts*, and *The Locked Room*. The ghost of Poe haunts both Auster and Danielewski. *City of Glass*, which takes place on the Upper West Side of Manhattan in the neighborhood where Poe once lived is, among other things, a rewriting of "MS. in a Bottle" and *The Narrative of Arthur Gordon Pym*. Danielewski, in turn, rewrites Auster's rewriting of Poe in the *Atrocity* episode. The second hold of Danielewski's sinking ship becomes "the locked room" in which the tolling of *Glas* echoes.

A final, seemingly insignificant detail. Who is Norberg-Schulz, and why does his name appear in the supplementary bit devoted to *Glas*? The dean of the Institute of Architecture at the University of Oslo, Christian Norberg-Schultz has developed a phenomenological approach to architecture that is deeply influenced by Heidegger's philosophy. In his most important work, *The Concept of Dwelling: On the Way to Figurative Architecture*, Norberg-Schultz takes Heidegger's essay "The Thing" as his point of departure for his analysis of dwelling.

> What, then, *are* these things, which reveal their meaning through their configuration? Heidegger offers an answer in his famous essay, where he defines the thing as a "gathering of world." He recalls that the original meaning of the word "thing" is "gathering," and illustrates this significant

fact with a phenomenological analysis of a jug. Then he goes on defining the world which is gathered by the thing as a "fourfold" of earth, sky, mortals and divinities, which belong together in a "mirror-play," where "each of the four mirrors in its own way the essence of the others." In other words, the things are what they are relative to the basic structure of the world. The things make the world appear and therefore condition man.[17]

What Norberg-Schulz overlooks is as important as what he considers. In his preoccupation with things, he fails to examine the thing and therefore does not explain why every dwelling is *unheimlich*. As I have stressed, Heidegger's thing is the no-thing that obsesses Danielewski and haunts *House of Leaves*.

"Endless snarls of words, sometimes twisting into meaning, sometimes into nothing at all, frequently breaking apart, always branching into other

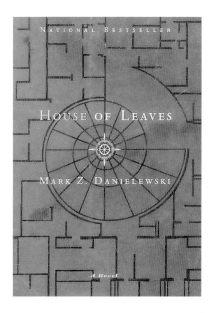

3.2  Mark Danielewski, cover, *House of Leaves*.

*Source:* Mark Danielewski, *House of Leaves* (New York: Random House, 2000).

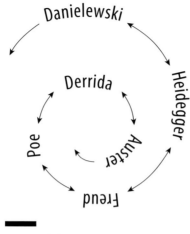

3.3 Untitled.

pieces I'd come across later . . . " The connections, associations, filiations are endless, which is not to say infinite. Trace the connections of any name, date, episode, or reference, and you will become entangled in shifty connections that ceaselessly transform meaning as they multiply. In this way, the text becomes a labyrinth whose very openness leaves no exit. As we have discovered, however, this is no ordinary labyrinth because it has no center. A labyrinth without a center is a network, and, as Derrida insists, "even today the notion of a structure lacking any center represents the unthinkable itself." The network, then, (impossibly) represents the unthinkable itself.

## LIFE ONLINE

The students patiently followed my philosophical and theoretical ramblings and absorbed as much as they could tolerate. But it was clear that they were anxious to get on to other issues. They understood intuitively what I came to see only gradually: *House of Leaves* is not merely a book but is actually a node in the World Wide Web, where more and more people live today. The book, in other words, is a web, and the Web is a house of leaves. The Web, after all, is exactly like a house that is bigger on the inside than it is on the outside. Screens are not terminals but are windows opening onto spaces that keep expanding faster and faster. Though he never explicitly associates the text with the Web, Danielewski leaves clues, which, once recognized, seem obvious. Most important, every time the word *house* appears in the text, it is printed in blue. Click "house," and the tangled world of the Web opens. The more one explores *House of Leaves*, the clearer it becomes that the work exceeds the limits of the book—any book. The book turns out to be a printed interlude in a work that began and continues to emerge online. Instead of the usual publisher's hype, the text on the jacket flap describes the actual history of the work.

> Years ago, when *House of Leaves* was first being passed around, it was nothing more than a badly bundled heap of paper, parts of which would occasionally surface on the Internet. No one could have anticipated the small but devoted following this terrifying story would soon command. Starting with an odd assortment of marginalized youth . . . the book eventually made its way into the hands of older generations, who not only found themselves in those strangely arranged pages but also discovered a way back into the lives of their estranged children.

In *House of Leaves*, parents and teachers discover that the house they had thought was their own has been taken over by their kids and students.

Johnny weaves the history of the work into reflections recorded in a journal he keeps while he tries to regain a semblance of equilibrium by riding the rails with other homeless migrants across the country. Passing through Flagstaff, only a few miles from James Turrell's Roden Crater, he jumps off the freight car and, while hanging out in a park, is drawn into a nearby bar by alluring music. While drinking cheap beer and talking with the locals, Johnny is startled to hear the band playing a song named "I Live at the End of a Five-and-a-Half-Minute Hallway," which is the title of one of the most unsettling parts of *The Navidson Record*. Unable to believe his ears, he approaches the band and asks whether anybody has heard of a film with the same title. The response only deepens the mystery:

> the drummer shook his head and explained that the lyrics were inspired by a book he'd found on the Internet quite some time ago. The guitar player walked over to the duffel bag lying behind one of their Vox amps. After digging around for a second he found what he was looking for.
>
> "Take a look for yourself," he said, handing me a big brick of tattered paper. "But be careful," he added in a conspiratorial whisper. "It'll change your life."
>
> Here's what the title page said:
> House of Leaves
> by Zampanò
> with introduction and
> notes by Johnny Truant
> Circle Round a Stone Publication
> First Edition (513)

As the conversation continues to unfold, it becomes clear that the band has not only read but is deeply involved with the book. Johnny reports that "they had discussed the footnotes, the names and even the encoded appearance of Thamyris on page 387, something I'd transcribed without ever detecting" (541). Unlike Danielewski, Johnny admits that he has neither completely understood what he has written nor has anticipated every response to "his" work. Seeming to mistake fiction for fact, the musicians say they often wonder what ever happened to Johnny. Though tempted to disclose his identity, Johnny finally decides to return the book with a simple thank you as he leaves the bar to continue his journey.

When one has "lost sense of what's real and what's not," the line separating fact and fiction becomes obscure. Not only are facts often fictions, but fictions sometimes turn out to be fact. In fact, "5 and ½ Minute Hallway" was inspired by *House of Leaves*. Danielewski's sister is a rock singer who performs under the stage name Poe. Her second CD, *Haunted*, includes the song "5 and ½ Minute Hallway," which is an extended dialogue with *House of Leaves*. Lines of the book appear in songs on the CD, or lines of the song are reinscribed in the book—it is impossible to know which way these lines run. For all their differences, *House of Leaves* and *Haunted* are the "same" work. Brother writes and sister sings: "No-one should brave the underworld alone." Poe's voice echoes through Mark's house, and Mark's words echo in Poe's songs.

By the time I introduced Poe into our class discussion, the students were already far ahead of me. They not only had discovered the complicated relationship between *House of Leaves* and *Haunted* but had immediately grasped its significance. Poe joined the roster of authors that already included Mark, Zampanò, Johnny, Navidson, and the countless writers and critics quoted and cited in notes. Like the members of the band in the Flagstaff bar, the students had become absorbed in the text. They were not reading the book as much as the book was reading them. When I realized what the book was doing to them, I asked them to post their responses to *House of Leaves* on one of the course websites. Several students reported that they had started listening to Poe's music while reading the book.

> When I first started reading this book, I was honestly bored. I was even reading it out in the sun.[18] I don't know when I was sucked in—but 6 hours later I finally put it down. Even after I put it down, I found myself thinking analytically about the text. (How often does that happen with an ordinary book?) I tried to figure out the names as anagrams in the margins of my textbooks. I got the Poe CD and listened to it . . . a lot. Especially when reading the book. (I think it's even scarier than the book—for example, she puts a cut of her deceased father in.) I couldn't fall asleep at night, wondering what the hell that labyrinth in the house meant (was it the world experienced by a blind person? Or the closet for everyone's skeletons/repressed memories? When Navy compared the house to God, the homonym prey/pray popped into my mind). Crazy things like that.[19]

For student after student, reading the book actually became the haunting experience the "novel" describes.

> I loved the way you get sucked into the book like the house sucks up everything that goes into it. Normally when I read a book, I read sections then take breaks to get a sense of my world back . . . yet Truant's footnotes took over my sense of breaks as I experienced his life outside of Zampanò's book. It was like an alternative reality that I kept relating to when I would carry on my life and reflect in my thoughts.[20]

As I pondered their posts and listened to what they said in class, I began to realize that they were actually living in *House of Leaves*, or, perhaps more accurately, they discovered that it was living in them.

> Reading *House of Leaves* was more than just reading a book for class; it was an actual experience. At first, I was completely spooked out by hallways and Daisy's "always," but the more I read, the more I wanted to figure things out. I became Johnny Truant II. True to name, I actually skipped one of my classes because I was so engrossed by the story. Like Johnny, I tried to piece the clues together to make sense of it all. Even though I was not as obsessed, I still felt the need to pry and google everything that looked suspect. Of course, there were many frustrating dead ends, but that was part of the experience.[21]

The more they Googled, the more they felt the need to Google. The labyrinth of the book led to the labyrinth of the Web, which led back to the book until the two became seamless. Students discovered countless websites with thousands of posts investigating every clue, checking every reference, and tracking every association. As they searched and researched, the Web invaded the classroom until we were forced to admit that we were all in a room that was bigger on the inside than it was on the outside. Returning to *House of Leaves* from the Web, students had a deeper appreciation for the book's graphic design. Though Danielewski stresses the influence of film on the design of the book, the work is actually more hypertextual than filmic. The twists and turns of the words on the page enact the convolutions of the text. One of the most insightful students in the class offered a telling account of his reading experience:

> I do know, however, that my experience of reading the book mimics the experience of the characters as they are represented to me—Tom, Navy, Karen, Chad, Daisy, Reston, etc., but also Zampanò, Johnny, and even the "Editors," so that my experience resonates on every differ- ent level, through and with all mediators, of the novel. That's genius: Danielewski has constructed, in effect, a "choose your own adven- ture" that places readers at the center of the action without them con- sciously realizing it. By making me hunt for the location of footnotes or scour the web for clues to references or codes, or even by forcing me to physically turn the text upside down at times or to learn Morse code just to get the plot, Danielewski has brought the outside inside: my reading—not only my interpretation, but the actual physical process of my reading—is central to the story even though it cannot be con- tained by the book's covers.[22]

As the book edged beyond its covers, we began to realize that both the class and the website we were building for Real Fakes were part of *House of Leaves*. In Danielewski's world, which is, of course, our own, it is impossible to draw the line between original and copy, authentic and inauthentic, legitimate and illegitimate, real and fake.

As students continued to click and search, sign led to sign and reference to reference until exhilaration ended in frustration and we heard echoes of a detective singing: "all clues no solutions." But matters were even more confusing because the students were no longer sure which clues were reli- able and which were not. The discussion reached a turning point when one student took the class to the website for the *Idiot's Guide to* House of Leaves (http://www.houseofleaves.4t.com/guide.html), where he had discovered the following post:

> Depending on the version of *House of Leaves* you hold in front of you as you look at this page, several things could appear different to you. If you have a US hardcover edition of the novel, you'll notice strange four character patterns covering the endpapers. Are those characters just there to make cool designs?
>
> No, actually the characters are Hexidecimal [*sic*] code, when compiled in a hex editor and made into an AIFF file, the code actually plays as Mark Z. Danielewski's sister Poe singing "Johnny, Angry, Johnny" in a 2 second clip from her track "Angry Johnny" from the album release "Hello."[23]

Codes within codes within codes until *nothing* is decipherable and, thus, *nothing* remains certain—undeniably certain. Passages, of course, exist in books as well as houses. Are these passages credible or incredible? Where do they begin and where do they end? Without the key, how can any room be unlocked? How can the meaning of any work be decided? Are the codes by which we read and live discovered or invented? Real or fake? Can Melville's *Confidence-Man* provide a "counterfeit detector" for this book? Where is the line between credibility and credulity? Suspicions aroused, students turned to a passage I had resisted pointing out: "Unfortunately, the anfractuosity of some labyrinths may actually prohibit a permanent solution. More confounding still, its complexity may exceed the imagination of even the designer. Therefore anyone lost within must recognize that no one, not even a god or an Other, comprehends the entire maze and therefore there can never be a definitive answer" (115).

Perhaps, then, *House of Leaves*—like life itself—is an elaborate confidence game. We cannot be certain. This is the point to which Danielewski leads the reader, and this is the point to which I had been steadily leading the class. Only when they realized that every house is always haunted by uncertainty were they ready to face the most unexpected and unsettling question of all: *God.*

# FATHER'S HOUSE

Poe is haunted by her father. Her CD begins with her mother's voice on an answering machine and Poe's uncanny singsong words announcing the death of the father.

> Mother's answering machine: Hello, nobody's home. Leave a message
>     after the beep and somebody will get back to you.
> Daughter: I thought you should know
> Daddy died today
> He closed his eyes and left here
> At 12:03
> He sends his love
> He wanted you to know
> He isn't holding a grudge
> And if you are you should let go
> Pick up, pick up please, mom? hello?

Failing to connect, the daughter hangs up, and Poe begins to sing.

> Ba da pa pa ba da pa pa . . .
> Come here
> Pretty please
> Can you tell me where I am
> You won't you say something
> I need to get my bearings
> I'm lost
> And the shadows keep on changing
> And I'm haunted . . .

Throughout the CD, Poe's songs are interrupted by the father's voice echoing from beyond the grave. The liner notes, which include pictures of her father and mother as well as a photograph of her father's obituary, begin with a dedication and explanation:

*This album is dedicated to my father Tad Z. Danielewski* (1921–1993)

A few years after my father died my brother and I came across a box of cassettes—recordings of my father's voice. One was a letter to my brother that he had spoken into a tape recorder long ago: another was the recording of a speech he had given during his years as a teacher: a few more contained random recordings of forgotten family noise. Hearing his voice again shook me to my foundation. At first I couldn't bear to listen to him, then I couldn't stop. Finally I began sampling him. It was an eerie process. Had I resurrected a ghost? In some ways I had. Ultimately I entered into a dialogue with the ghost. Pieces of that dialogue compose the story contained in this album.

Tad Ƶ, once again Ƶ, Danielewski had been a filmmaker who spent years working on a documentary film entitled *Spain: Open Door*, which the Spanish government eventually confiscated because it included material the authorities deemed unacceptable. Though rumors about it being stored in hidden vaults persisted, the complete film was never recovered. The relation of *House of Leaves* and *Haunted* to *Spain: Open Door* is the mirror image of the relation of Zampanò's screenplay and Johnny's commentary/diary to *The Navidson Record*. The hallways of the house are the webs of the mind where the ghost of papa roams.

And I'm haunted
By the lives that I have loved
And actions I have hated
I'm haunted
By the promises I've made
And others I have broken
I'm haunted

By the lives that wove the web
Inside my haunted head
Hallways . . . always
I'll always want you
I'll always need you
I'll always love you
And I will always miss you
Ba da pa pa ba da pa pa . . .

But papa never returns, and because of his nonarrival, Poe *must* sing, and Mark—which Mark?—*must* write.

Between "Terrified Heart" and "5 and ½ Minute Hallway," Poe's singing is interrupted by the recorded voice of the dead father: "Communication is not just words; communication is architecture. Because of course it is quite obvious that a house which would be built without the sense . . . without that desire for communication, would not look the way your house looks today!" Nor would a house look the way ordinary houses look if the architect wanted to communicate the incommunicable. Rather, the house would look something like *House of Leaves*.

A few pages after the excursus on the myth of the labyrinth, which includes Derrida's claim that "today the notion of a structure lacking any center represents the unthinkable itself," Exploration #4 is interrupted by a long reflection on the architecture of the house. Citing a fictitious work by Sebastiano Pérouse de Montclos (*Palladian Grammar and Metaphysical Appropriations: Navidson's Villa Malcontenta* [Englewood Cliffs: Prentice-Hall, 1996]), Zampanò (or whoever is the author of this section) stresses that while there is general agreement that the labyrinth is a house, there is no consensus about who the occupant of the house might be. At this point, the narrative takes an unexpected turn.

Therefore the question soon arises whether or not it is someone's house. Though if so whose? Whose was it or even whose *is* it? Thus giving voice to another suspicion: could the owner still be there? Questions which echo the snippet of gospel Navidson alludes to in his letter to Karen— St. John, chapter 14—where Jesus says:

> In my Father's house are many rooms: if it *were* not *so*, I would have told you. I go to prepare a place for you . . .
>
> Something to be taken literally as well as ironically. (121)

To name *House of Leaves* the Father's house makes it no less uncanny. Two pages before this biblical reference, an extended footnote to the following passage begins in a window framed in blue. "This desire for exteriority is no doubt further amplified by the utter blankness found within. Nothing there provides a reason to linger. In part because not one object, let alone fixture or other manner of finish [*sic*] work has ever been discovered there.¹⁴⁴" *Nothing* provides a reason to linger, and the longer we linger the stranger nothing becomes.

The windows in which footnote 144 appears are framed in blue and run for twenty-five pages. In a manner reminiscent of negative theology, the house is defined by what it is not: "Not only are there no hot-air registers, return vents, or radiators, cast iron, or other, or cooling systems . . . " Far from transparent, these Windows are filled with words, and the list in every window is repeated in reverse on the following page.

The opacity of the windows reveals nothing by trying to list everything. As windows open within Windows, the architecture of the text becomes ever more hypertextual. A long note that forms the margin of eight left-hand pages lists every conceivable twentieth-century house that the Navidson house (i.e., *House of Leaves*) is *not*. The corresponding inverted margin of eight right-hand pages lists countless modern and postmodern architects. While many names are recognizable, it is impossible to be sure how many are real and how many are fake. Notes within notes create textual gyrations that are almost impossible to follow: Coleridge, "The Rime of the Ancient Mariner"; Poe, "The Fall of the House of Usher"; Walker Percy, *The Moviegoer*; Jean Genet, *Notre Dame des Fleurs*; Pynchon's gator patrol in *V*, J. L. Borges, "The Garden of Forking Paths; Conrad, *Heart of Darkness*; Lawrence

"As photojournalists, we have the responsibility to document society and to preserve its images as a matter of historical record. It is clear that the emerging electronic technologies provide new challenges to the integrity of photographic images. The technology enables the manipulation of the content of an image in such a way that the change is virtually undetectable. In light of this, we, the National Press Photographers Association, reaffirm the basis of our ethics: Accurate representation is the benchmark of our profession."[185]

Then in 1992, MIT professor William J. Mitchell offered this powerful summation:

"Protagonists of the institutions of journalism, with their interest in being trusted, of the legal system, with their need for provably reliable evidence, and of science, with their foundational faith in the recording instrument, may well fight hard to maintain the hegemony of the standard photographic image—but others will see the emergence of digital imaging as a welcome opportunity to expose the aporias in photography's construction of the visual world, to deconstruct the very ideas of photographic objectivity and closure, and to resist what has become an increasingly sclerotic pictorial tradition."

[185] See chapter 20 in Howard Chapnick's *Truth Needs No Ally: Inside Photojournalism* (University of Missouri Press, 1994).
William J. Mitchell's *The Reconfigured Eye: Visual Truth In The Post-Photographic Era* (Cambridge, Massachusetts: The MIT Press, 1994), p. 8.

143

### 3.4 Mark Danielewski, *House of Leaves*.

Source: Mark Danielewski, *House of Leaves* (New York: Random House, 2000).

Ironically, the very technology that instructs us to mistrust the image also creates the means by which to accredit it.

As author Murphy Gruner once remarked:

"Just as is true with Chandler's Marlowe, the viewer is won over simply because the shirts are rumpled, the soles are worn, and there's that ever present hat. These days nothing deserves our faith less than the slick and expensive. Which is how video and film technology comes to us: rumpled or slick.

"Rumpled Technology—capital M for Marlowe—hails from Good Guys, Radio Shack or Fry's Electronics. It is cheap, available and very dangerous. One needs only to consider *The George Holliday Rodney King Video* to recognize the power of such low-end technology. Furthermore, as the recording time for tapes and digital disks increases, as battery life is extended, and as camera size is reduced, the larger the window will grow for capturing events as they occur.

"Slick Technology—capital S for Slick—is the opposite: expensive, cumbersome, and time consuming. But it too is also very powerful. Digital manipulation allows for the creation of almost anything the imagination can come up with, all in the safe confines of an editing suite, equipped with 24 hour catering and an on site masseuse."[186]

[186] Murphy Gruner's *Document Detectives* (New York: Pantheon, 1995), p. 37.
[187] One can imagine a group of ~~Documentary Detectives~~ whose ~~sole purpose is to uphold~~ ~~Truth & Truth~~ by guaranteeing ~~the authenticity~~ of all works. Such seal ~~of approval would~~ create a sense of ~~public faith which~~ could only be maintained ~~if said~~ ~~Documentary Detec-~~ ~~tives were as fierce~~ as pit bulls and as ~~scrupulous as saints.~~ Of course, this is ~~more the kind of~~ thing a novelist or ~~playwright would~~ deal with, and as I am pointedly not a novelist or a playwright I will leave that tale to someone else—

Or TMT. Truth And Truth therefore becoming another name for the nitrating of toluene or $C_7H_5N_3O_6$—not to be confused with $C_{18}H_{10}M_2O_3$—in other words one word: trinitrotoluene, TNT[188] telegraphing a weird coalition of sense. On one hand transcendent and lasting and on the other violent and extremely flammable.

144

Weschler, *Mr. Wilson's Cabinet of Wonders*; Sartre, *Huis Clos*; Maurice Merleau-Ponty, *The Phenomenology of Perception*; and on and on and on. Taken together, these pages are both a parody of the *via negativa* and an ingenious literary reformulation of it.

The last two windows are the most interesting. Framed in blue, one is white and the obverse is black (143–144). It is as if paintings by Kasimir Malevich and Ad Rheinardt were placed back to back to reveal nothing; pure light becomes utter darkness, and total darkness turns into blinding light. White and black are simultaneously separated and joined by the slim margin of the page, which, of course, is the space of writing. Associations proliferate in this play of black and white: Poe is Poe is Mark is Mark. In *House of Leaves*, writing is the interplay of black and white that figures what can never be figured. On the page following the darkness of the black window, there is a large white square that contains nothing. The text about this nothing summarizes the argument of the erstwhile dean of MIT's School of Architecture, William J. Mitchell's *The Reconfigured Eye: Visual Truth in the Post-Photographic Era*, in which he analyzes the unreliability of images in the age of digital reproduction. What remains unsaid or is said by not saying it is that when attempting to represent the unrepresentable, it is not only digital images that are unreliable.

In a manner reminiscent of Heidegger's jug, *House of Leaves* is *about* nothing. When all is said and done—and all must be said and done—Navidson discovers *nothing*. In an entry, which, like the introduction (but separated from it by 516 pages), is dated Halloween 1998, Johnny confesses:

> I start to run, trying to find a way to something new, something safe, darting from the sight of others, the clamor of living.
>
> There is something stronger here. Beyond my imagination. It terrifies me. But what is it? And why has it retained me? Wasn't darkness nothingness? Wasn't that Navidson's discovery? Wasn't it Zampanò's? Or have I misconstrued it all? Missed the obvious, something still undiscovered waiting there deep within me, outside of me, powerful and extremely patient, unafraid to remain, even though it is and always has been free.   (516)

How *can* one imagine what lies within the imagination as an inexhaustible beyond that is not its own? The film is the book is the film . . . These strange loops encircle the nothingness without which they would not be. Nothing is the condition of the possibility of the book and the condition of the impossibility of its completion. By ceaselessly figuring what is always slipping away, Danielewski and all of his coauthors allow the void from which the work of art emerges to appear by withdrawing. The disclosure of this nondisclosure is what keeps the work in play. Though no-thing provokes dread, it is also the void without which there is no creativity.

With the recognition that all emerges from and returns to nothing, the contours of the house shift yet again. In a long discussion of John Hollander's analysis of the importance of echoes in Wordsworth's poetry, Zampanò associates "the hollow" with "the hallowed":

> It is not by accident that choirs singing Psalms are most always recorded with ample reverb. Divinity seems to be defined by echo. Whether the Vienna Boys Choir or monks chanting away on some chart climbing CD, the hallowed always seems to abide in the province of the hollow. The reason for this is not too complex. An echo, while implying an enormity of a space, at the same time also defines it, limits it, and even temporarily inhabits it. (46)

Since the ghosts haunting this house turn out to be holy, the Father's house and the Father become indistinguishable.

At a pivotal point when Navidson seems to be slipping into madness, Zampanò interrupts his narrative with footnotes that cannot be unraveled.

*Non ein videbit me homo et vivet.*[365]

Note 365 reads simply: "Sorry." This is followed by two notes numbered 366, neither of which appears in the body of the text:

> No clue.[366]
> Maurice Blanchot translates this as "whoever sees God dies."—Ed.
> (388)

On the following page, Navidson begins a letter to Karen in which he expresses doubts about his photography. In the crucial paragraph, he unexpectedly raises the question of God.

> Do you believe in God? I don't think I ever asked you that one. Well I do now. But my God isn't your Catholic varietal or your Judaic or Mormon or Baptist or Seventh Day Adventist or whatever/whoever. No burning bush, no angels, no cross. God's a house. Which is not to say that our house is God's house or even a house of God. What I mean to say is that our house *is* God
> XXXXXXXXXXXXXXXXXXXXXXXXXXXXXXXXXXXXXXXXXXXXX
> XXXXXXXXXXXXXXXXXXXXXXXXXXXXXXXXXXXXXXXXXXXXX
> XXXXXXXXXXXXXXXXXXXXX.                                    (390)

God is a house—not just any house but a house that is haunted by something it cannot contain and that is, therefore, bigger on the inside than it is on the outside. As such, the house is infinite. This infinite is not simply transcendent but is outside as an inside that cannot be incorporated. The infinite, in other words, is in/finite. Neither here nor elsewhere, the in/finite approaches by withdrawing through infinite displacements: . . . Book . . . Film . . . House . . . Nothing . . . God . . . Real . . . The inaccessibility of the real refigures the relationship between the real and the fake to create what can only be described as a realfake. While the real and the fake are opposites, the notion of the realfake is a paradox or even a contradiction. But what if the real and the fake are not precisely opposite but are codependent, i.e., each simultaneously emerges and withdraws in and through the other? Since the real is never accessible as such, it can only "show" itself by hiding. In this play of hide-and-seek, hiding turns out to be a strange revelation—revealing, in other words, is reveiling. When semblance is dissemblance, the fake is real because the real can only appear fake. In the world of realfakes, everything that once seemed certain and secure begins to tremble, even if ever so slightly.

Out of the blue, beyond any cause you can trace, you'll suddenly realize things are not how you perceived them to be at all. For some reason, you will no longer be the person you believed you once were. You'll detect slow and subtle shifts going on all around you, more importantly shifts in you. Worse, you'll realize it's always been shifting, like a shimmer of sorts, a vast shimmer, only dark like a room. But you won't understand why or how. You'll have forgotten what granted you this awareness in the first place.

Old shelters—television, magazines, movies—won't protect you anymore. You might try scribbling in a journal, on a napkin, maybe even in the margins of this book. That's when you'll discover you no longer trust the very walls you always took for granted. Even the hallways you've walked a hundred times will feel longer, much longer, and the shadows, any shadow at all, will suddenly seem deeper, much, much deeper.

(xxii–xxiii)

o o o

After the text, after the index, after the credits, the "final" page that proves not to be final after all:

●

Y g g
d

r

a

s

i

1

What miracle is this? This giant tree.
It stands ten thousand feet high
But doesn't reach the ground. Still it stands.
Its roots must hold the sky.

O

Black and white . . . full and empty . . . It all ends with O. What's the point?

Perhaps the tree holds a clue. Rising to the sky and with branches spreading over the world, Yggdrasil, which usually is identified as an ash, is the cosmic tree that plays an important role in the German creation myth *Prose Edda*. Every day, the gods hold a council at the foot of this tree. Here as in many other myths, the cosmic tree is the *axis mundi*, which is supposed to provide a center to a world that otherwise remains labyrinthian. Danielewski shatters the *axis mundi* by uprooting the cosmic tree, which "doesn't reach the ground." This destruction is, however, creative: the withering leaves of Yggdrasil become the ashes from which *House of Leaves* is born.

O

When to stop? Where to stop? How to stop?

> July 27, 1991
> Make no mistake, those who write long books have nothing to say.
> Of course those who write short books have even less to say.          (545)

*House of Leaves* is a long book—a *very* long book. Indeed, this book is so long that it is *virtually* endless.

A clue—perhaps, but we can never be certain. At one point, Zampanò includes a section entitled "A Partial Transcript Of What Some Have Thought," which supposedly was compiled by Karen. Between fictitious entries attributed to Harold Bloom and Douglas Hoftstadter, a suggestive passage appears.[24]

> **A Poe t. 21 years old. No tattoos. No piercings.**
> Setting: In front of a giant transformer.
> Poe t: No capitals. [she takes out a paper napkin and reads from it] i was online. i had no recollection of how i got there. of how i got sucked in there. it was pitch black. i suspected the power had failed. i started moving. i had no idea which direction i was headed. i kept moving. i had the

feeling i was being watched. i asked "who's there?" the echoes created a
passage and disappeared. i followed them (360)

The first line attributed to Hoftstadter reads:

Similar to Zeno's arrow, consider the following equation: $1/a = \lambda$ where $1/\infty = 0$. Zeno. . . . Zero.

$$\infty = 0$$

$$0 = \infty$$

Is it significant that these clues appear on page 360?[25] It is impossible to
know. What we do know by now is that *House of Leaves* turns everything
completely around—360 degrees, as it were—by turning everything inside
out and outside in. What makes the work so uncanny is that it sucks us into a
web that is virtually in-finite. Every point in the text is connected with other
points within and beyond the book proper. Like Poe(t), we have been online
all along, even when we thought we were unplugged. . . . no recollection of
how we got here . . . of how we got sucked in . . . no idea of which direction
we are headed . . . echoes create passages . . . When connections multiply and
lines become tangled, meaning shifts—endlessly, in-finitely. As meaning
slips away, meanings proliferate. In the labyrinth of decentered webs, walls
and floors turn to nothing and the vertigo of the abyss becomes the giddi-
ness of creativity—*ad infinitum.* Though it will never be our home, the Web
might be the haunted house that is the "embodiment" of God today.

O
O
O

See: www.realfakes.org

O
O
O

# 4

## "HOLY SHIT!"

Don DeLillo, *Underworld*

> *To become an artist means nothing but consecrating oneself to the gods of the underworld.*
>
> —Friedrich Schlegel

> *Garbage has to be the poem of our time because Garbage is spiritual . . .*
>
> —A. R. Ammons

> *What we excrete comes back to consume us.*
>
> —Don DeLillo

## PROLOGUE

### The Pit and the Pyramid

with a high whine the garbage trucks slowly
circling the pyramid rising intone the morning

and atop the mound's plateau birds circling
hear and roil alive in winklings of wings

denser than windy forest shelves: and meanwhile
a truck already arrived spills its goods from

the black hatch and the birds as in a single computer-
formed net plunge in celebration, hallelujahs

of rejoicing: the driver gets out of his truck
and wanders over to the cliff on the spill and

looks off from the high point into the rose-fine
rising of day, the air pure, the wings of the

bird white and clean as angel-food cake: holy, holy,
holy, the driver cries and flicks his cigarette

in a spiritual swoop that floats and floats before
it touches the ground: here, the driver knows,

where the consummations gather, where the disposal flows out of form,
where the last translations

cast away their immutable bits and scraps,
flits of steel, shivers of bottle and tumbler,

here is the gateway to the beginning, here the portal
of renewing change, the birdshit, even, melding

enrichingly with debris, a loam for the roots
of placenta: oh, nature, the man on the edge

of the cardboard-laced cliff exclaims, that there
could be a straightaway from the toxic past into

the fusion-lit reaches of a coming time! Our
sins are so many, here heaped, shapes given to

false matter, hamburger meat left out[1]


"Yeah, yeah, I know, Mom, I should have called.[2] But there aren't any phones in the middle of the damn desert somewhere south of nowhere. Besides, you sent me to that godforsaken place to get me away from Dennis. What the hell did you think my father could do? He's too screwed up himself to help anybody else. Sitting in that cabin day after day, staring into empty space, reading poetry—Rilke, Pound, and Zukofsky—and rattlin' on and on about the self, time, and silence. That's right, *talking* and *talking* about silence. Jeeesus Christ! He says to me, 'You need to know things the others don't know. It's what no one knows about you that allows you to know your-self.' Yeah, well, what if others know more about me than I do? You could fill this whole goddamn desert with what I don't know about myself.

"Half the time I have no idea what he's talking about—mumbles some-thing about time healing my wounds. 'Day turns to night eventually, but it's a matter of light and darkness, it's not passing time, mortal time. There's none of the usual terror. It's different here, time is enormous, that's what I feel here, palpably. Time that precedes us and survives us.' Well, maybe the enormity of time doesn't fill him with terror, but it sure scares the shit out of me. And then there's his sicko sidekick—Jimmy, Jimmy whatshisname—Jimmy Findlay or something like that. Mr. 'DeadBeat' films wantin' to make a movie about counterinsurgency strategy in the Iraq war. No script, no action, just a headshot of Mr. 'Defense Intellectual' talking alone in front of a bare wall with cracks and chipped paint. 'Haiku war,' 'Renditions,' and crazi-est of all, this 'Omega Point' deal.

"Seems he picked up the idea from some guy who was a Jesuit paleon-tologist just like his first wife—well, the paleontologist part. I listened to him for a while but couldn't make much sense about what he was saying. Dad and Jimmy usually talked late into the night. Sometimes I couldn't get to sleep, and I'd listen to them through the thin cabin wall. One night—most nights they'd both had too much scotch, or was it vodka, doesn't matter—I hear Dad say, 'There's some law of mathematics or physics that we haven't quite hit upon, where the mind transcends all direction inward. The Omega Point. Whatever the intended meaning of this term, if it has a meaning, if it's not a case of language that's struggling toward some idea outside of our experience.'

"'Omega Point? What does that mean?' 'Father Teilhard knew this, the Omega Point. A leap out of biology. Ask yourself this question. Do we have to be human forever? Consciousness is exhausted. Back to inorganic mat-ter. This is what we want. We want to be stones in a field.' 'Either a sublime transformation of mind and soul or some worldly convulsion. We want it to happen.' 'You think we want it to happen.' 'We want it to happen. Some paroxysm.' 'Think of it. We pass completely out of being. Stones. Unless stones have being. Unless there's some profoundly mystical shift that places being in a stone.'

"When I heard him say this, I totally freaked out. Entropy's got enough going for it without our help. Omega Point, Point Omega mystical shift—more like mystical shit—stoned, maybe, stone, no way. I don't know about him, but I'm not yet ready to pass out of being, so I figured it was time for me to split. But I knew he wouldn't let me go, and you'd never agree to allow me to come home. All his blather about everything disappearing—I figured I'd show him what disappearing really means. I decided to fake my own kidnapping. I had overheard Dad and Jimmy talking about a place not far away called the 'Impact Area.' Access was limited because it was littered with unexploded bombs and artillery shells. One afternoon they left me alone to go to town to stock up on supplies.

"I knew this was my chance. I packed some water and food and took a knife from the kitchen. Then I made my way through canyons, washes, and a long mine road to the edge of the forbidden territory, carefully covering my tracks in the sand so they couldn't easily follow me. When I found a NO TRESPASSING sign, I stopped, pulled the knife out of my backpack and carefully cut my arm just enough to leave a trace of blood on the blade and a few drops in the sand. I then buried the knife in the sand, leaving only enough of the blade exposed to catch the sunlight. I ducked under the barbed-wire fence and slowly made my way through the Impact Area, being very careful to avoid anything that looked like it might blow up. This time I didn't cover my tracks as I headed for the thick sagebrush a few hundred yards away. I brought enough food and water for two days.

"I knew I was somewhere in the Sonora Desert and had heard Jimmy say that the Mojave Desert is to the north. I didn't have a compass so checked out the sun and started walking due west. I thought I knew what I was running from but had no idea what I was walking toward. With all the sand, sage, and rabbit bush, it was slow going, but luckily it wasn't summer, so the heat was tolerable. The first day I saw nothing—absolutely nothing—farther I walked more distant the horizon became. By the afternoon of the second day I was beginning to worry. I figured I would have found signs of life by now but still nothing. This wasn't good—I was running out of food and water and didn't have a plan B.

"Then all of a sudden my luck changed—I thought I glimpsed lights on the horizon in the fading desert heat. At first I was afraid my eyes were playing tricks on me, but I walked on and saw the thin line of a road cutting straight through the desert. Route 111. On the other side of the highway, I saw a bunch of RVs parked among abandoned buildings, rusted cars, trucks, and, most bizarre, boats, boats in the middle of the desert! Crazy, totally crazy.

"As I was carefully making my way through debris, a man in his sixties with a big white beard, wearing a USMC cap, opened the door to his RV and called out, 'Welcome to Slab City—the place that's meant to be nowhere.'

"'Nowhere? Well, then, I must have arrived.'

"'My name is One Can; I guess you could call me the mayor of our little corner of heaven on earth. They say this is where success and failure collide and where utopia and apocalypse meet to dance a dirty tango.'

"Some dance, I thought. 'Man, I sure am glad to see you!'

"'How the hell did you get here?'

"'Long story, but short version is that I was staying with my father "somewhere south of nowhere" and got lost while I was out hiking. I almost ran out of food and water and had no idea what I would do next, and then, like a gift from on high or somewhere else, I saw your lights.'

"'Well, out here in the desert, the Lord works in mysterious ways. Don't worry, everything is gonna be OK now. Come on in and have something to eat and drink.'

"His RV was crammed full with all kinds of junk—piles of old newspapers and magazines, colored bottles, broken toys that looked like they had been collected from a dump.

"'Just clear off all that stuff—don't worry, you can't break anything; everything's already broke. I pick up all kinds of shit around here and make little doodads to sell to the tourists who stop by. I know it's crazy, but this dump has become a tourist attraction.'

"One Can gave me some water, opened a can of ravioli, and put it on the stove to heat. 'So what *is* this place?'

"'Slab City? Home for the homeless. A place where the forgotten come to forget those who have forgotten them. Sorta Palm Springs for people who don't want to be bothered and would rather fish than play golf.'

"'People really live here?'

"'Oh, yeah, about 150 of us year round; from October to April the snowbirds head south, and our little town swells to five thousand.'

"'You stay here all summer?'

"'All summer, all winter. 120 degrees in the summer, who knows how cold in the winter?'

"'Why here?'

"'Why not? No rent, no government, no bother. Place used to be a military base—World War II Marine Barracks Camp Dunlap. Story goes that General Patton trained his troops right here. Military pulled out in the sixties and tore down all the buildings, but they left the cement slabs they were built on. That's where the place gets its name. After the war some guys came back and set up camp; word got out, and people been coming ever since.'

"'But what about water, electricity, sewers—all that stuff?'

"'Don't have any—gotta do it all ourselves. But that's OK, government fucks up everything it's supposed to do. Might not look like it at night, but there's a lot going on here. I'll show you around tomorrow.'

"There was no room for me to sleep in the RV, so he gave me an air mattress and pillow and pointed me toward his Dodge Ram. Lying in the truck trying to make sense of it all, I had never seen so many stars. I was exhausted and soon fell into a deep sleep. Smell not sound woke me the next morning. One Can had coffee brewing and was frying bacon and eggs. We ate together on the picnic table beside the RV.

"'After the Marines, I worked odd jobs. Never could find anybody I could work for but myself. Work wasn't important to me, bikes was. I worked to ride. Had a big hog as long as I can remember, and my family was my biking buddies. Some years back a bunch of us was taking a trip down to Mexico and passed this place. Stayed the night and I liked it. Always stuck in my mind. When my ridin' bitch died, I didn't want to stay in San Diego so decided to quit my job, cash in my chips, buy a used RV, and set up camp in Slab City. Never looked in my rearview mirror. Hell, never moved the RV since I parked it on the slab eight years ago.'

"'And nobody bothers you? The government doesn't mind?'

"'Hell, no, they forgot us faster than we forgot them. Let me show you around; we can clean up later.'

"Clean up? I thought, fat chance. Slab City, turns out, *is* a city—well, more of a small town. Something resembling streets run between rows of what once were barracks. Everyone we saw knew One Can and greeted us warmly. When he explained that I was his friend visiting from back east, they all had stories about why they came and why they would rather be here than anywhere else on earth. They proudly told me about their city—Lizard Tree Library, with Internet access; social clubs; Gopher Flats Country Club, an eighteen-hole course open to everybody ('bring your own golf clubs and beer!'); even a pet cemetery.

"They would have talked all day but One Can dragged me away. 'Come on, let her go, gotta show her our beach.'

"'Beach?' I said in amazement. 'A beach out in the middle of the desert?'

"'Yeah, beach. We got a nice beach on the other side of town. It's called the Salton Sea.'

"I smelled the beach before I saw it. When we finally reached water's edge, I'd never seen such pollution. Dead fish, thick algae, and the stench—so bad I had to cover my nose. But the people lounging on the beach seemed to love it.

"A woman sitting on a beach chair said, 'We even go swimming. It's more saltier than the ocean. It heals your skin. And it's warm, so warm. Nicer than the bathtub.'

"'Fishing in the summer's great. The hotter the water, the better the fishing.'

"A guy with a sailor's cap wasn't so sure. 'Yeah, I know they fish, but that's not edible fish. If they eat that fish they'll get botulism poisoning. That sea is filthy.'

"Others chimed in, 'Filthy's right. Dead fish, dead birds, dead everything over there. We have the odor problem, we have the insect problem.'

"'It's a sewer. Why clean up the most useful sewer? It's perfect that way. It's the greatest sewer the world has ever seen. Leave it that way.'[3]

"'But if it's so bad, why do you stay?' I asked.

"'Where else would we go, lady? Got no money, got no family. Only friends in the world are here in Slab City. Lotta people in them big cities would kill to have a community like we got.'

"One Can interrupted, 'Hey, there's one other place I want you to see, but it's a couple of miles away, so we gotta take the truck.' His Dodge Ram looked about as reliable as the junked cars permanently parked along the streets of Slab City.

"'There's this guy, Leonard Knight, lives in a little cabin that sits on the rear of his 1930s Chevy two-ton truck. Been livin' there for years; he's created this thing he calls Salvation Mountain.'

"As we approached, I couldn't believe my eyes. Out there in the middle of nowhere, there was one of the most amazing pop-art installations I've ever seen. Better than the ones you showed me in that gallery. I hadn't told One Can that I'm an Upper East Sider who knows a bit about the art scene. Warhol, Rauschenberg, and Oldenberg have nothing on Knight. Salvation Mountain reminded me of what that guy in LA is doing—Sam Rodin, I think that's his name—called it Watts Towers. Art made from junk—waste made into art. Not bad. Knight's mountain in the desert is more impressive because there are no rich gallery hoppers checking it out. For Knight, it seems it's not really about money but about art and even religion in a weird way. I don't know. At any rate, he makes his message clear, 'God Loves Everyone'; right above the Salvation Mountain sign, he had painted 'God Never Fails.' One Can gave me a picture. This guy's cut steps into the side of the hill, and at the top there is a big cross. Used bales of straw to create nooks and crannies, sorta like the caves where the desert monks used to hang out. I remember in an art history class once the prof showed us slides of these amazing frescoes painted on the walls of tiny little caves carved into the cliffs in the middle of Turkey. Monks used to live in those caves for years and

4.1 Salvation Mountain.

*Source:* Salvation Mountain at Slab City, Ed Darack, Science Faction, Corbis Images.

years and never see anybody. Cappadocia, I think that's what the place is called. But Knight's mountain's not dull sandstone; it's day-glo, maybe night-glo too for all I know. His mountain is covered with bright, gaudy colors—a cross between folk and pop art. Over a hundred thousand gallons of acrylic paint since he started, and people are still invited to bring their own paint and contribute to the ongoing work of art. Right below the cross, 'God Is Love' written in big letters, and below that a huge red heart with the words: 'Jesus, I am a sinner please come upon my body and into my heart.' No East Coast irony here. Straight from the heart.

"I told One Can, 'I've never seen anything like it. It's better than good.'

"After roaming around the work for a while, we got into the truck and headed back to his RV. By this time, it was late afternoon and he asked me if I wanted a beer.

"We settled under his awning drinking and talking. After seeing Salvation Mountain, I had to fess up. 'Look, One Can, I gotta tell you, I'm an uptown girl who likes the downtown art scene. I live on the Upper East Side of Manhattan but hang out a lot in the art galleries down in Chelsea and SoHo. And I want to tell you, what you showed me this afternoon is more interesting than any art I've seen for a long time.'

"'You sound surprised.'

"'Yeeeeah, I *am* surprised. Out here in the middle of the desert, that kind of art?'

"'Hey, lots of those NYC dudes come out here to the desert to make art when the gallery scene gets overheated. I know, I read about them.'

"'But Salvation Mountain? Give me a break, that tops art that brings big bucks. Eat your heart out, Jeff Koons.'

"'You like the stuff. Sounds like you're fixin' to stay. You're welcome to stay here as long as you want, but you really should let your mom and dad know you are OK. Whatever your problems with them, I'm sure they're worried sick.'

"'Yeah, I know. It's just that it's great to be away from all the hassles and bitchin'. That's really nice of you, and I *am* tempted to stay. Never thought I'd say so, but Slab City sorta grows on you.'

"'Like a fungus.'

"'Whatever. I guess I really should get back to New York, but I have no idea how to get there from here.'

"'I might be able to help. Tomorrow I'm heading up to Vegas for a few days. Go twice a year no matter what. Usually lose more than I win, but winning and losing ain't what it's all about. You can ride along and catch a plane from there.'

"'That would be great! Sure you don't mind?'

"'Not at all. But I'm leaving early so we have to get a good night's sleep.'

"The drive from Slab City to Las Vegas was long, hot, and boring. Country music broke the monotony—well, some of it. The more I learned about One Can, the more intrigued I became. The reason he was living in Slab City, he told me, was not only because there was no rent, no taxes, no government. He was disgusted with where the country was heading—politics, the military, business—the whole nine yards. But what drove him craziest was the waste, everywhere waste.

"'The shit just kept piling up,' he said, 'more and more, deeper and deeper—soon it's gonna bury us. Imagine, not the Russians, like they told us in the Marines, but our own shit's gonna bury us. Maybe the commies were right—capitalism can't live without its shit, can't live with it.'

"As an act of quiet protest, One Can had chosen to live amid the ruins of civilization. Something like a desert ascetic working on his personal recycling project. He thought and read. Most surprising of all, he had taught himself quite a bit about art.

"'You were talking about art yesterday. That whole New York scene—I don't know, just seems phony to me. A couple of years ago, I heard a radio program about some guy who left New York and came out west. Built this big thing up there in the Great Salt Lake. *Spiral Jetty* I think he called it. I just couldn't get over it—millions of dollars, trucks, dozers, cranes, crews, years of work. And for what? This thing out in the middle of nowhere that the lake would flood and nobody would see.'

"'And he wasn't the only one.'

"'Yeah, I know. After hearing about that project, I started poking around. You know our little library's got a computer hooked up to the Internet. Found a couple of other guys. They all think they're cowboys. There's this guy up in Arizona somewhere, bought a friggin' volcano and's turning it into some kind of artwork. I read he's been working on it for thirty years and spent millions of dollars on it. Says he needs another fifty million to finish it. Some other guy started this whole thing with a couple of cuts on the edge of a big mesa in the desert about eighty miles from Vegas. Rumor has it that he's been working on some humungous project about 130 miles north of Vegas. But nobody's sure what he's up to cuz he keeps it secret, and his place is tighter than Area 51.'

"'Heizer, Michael Heizer, that's his name. I once met him at the opening of his show in a Chelsea gallery. Ace Gallery. I remember because the owner's name was Doug Christmas. How can you forget that name?'

"After a few hundred miles, One Can got tired and wanted me to drive. City girl that I am, I'd never driven a truck before. Hardly ever driven a car. Luckily it was automatic; I don't have a clue how to drive a stick. One

Can didn't want to stop, and after he'd been so nice, I couldn't say no. We switched off driving and sleeping. Never saw roads so straight. By the time we glimpsed the lights of Vegas, I had to admit I was beginning to like country music. Well, some of it.

" 'So where can I drop you off? I'm gonna stay at the Days Inn at the edge of town. It's cheap. I'll take you wherever you want to go.'

" 'I don't know, I guess the Strip. I have to find an ATM to get some money.' He took me to the center of the Strip and stopped in front of the Venetian. He reached for his wallet and handed me fifty bucks.

" 'No, I can't, not after all you've done.'

" 'Take it, it's nothing; I'll win it back with the first roll of the dice.'

" 'One Can, I . . .'

" 'Forget it; been my pleasure, come back any time.'

"He gave me a hug; I got out and headed into the casino. I got two hundred in cash and headed for the nearest Holiday Inn. It was also cheap. Past few days had been a long ordeal, and I was beat. After checking into the motel, I took a shower, collapsed on the bed, and fell into a dreamless sleep. When I woke up ten hours later, the Strip was just coming to life. But after my detour in the desert, I wanted nothing to do with the bright lights and big city.

"I kept thinking about what One Can had said about Heizer living and working in the middle of the Nevada desert. When I met him in New York, he was like a fish out of water. Jeans, Wrangler shirt, lizard-skin boots, and a belt buckle as big as a rodeo champ's. But it was his face I most remember— steely gray eyes and lines as deep as those he drew in the desert sand. I went downstairs, found a computer, and Googled 'Michael Heizer.' I was shocked by the first item that showed up—a cover story from the February 6, 2005, *New York Times Sunday Magazine* entitled "Art's Last, Lonely Cowboy," written by the *Times* art critic Michael Kimmelman. There staring me in the face was a picture of Heizer standing beside one of the sculptures that formed part of his lifelong project, *City*.

"Article said it's located in the middle of the desert 130 miles north of Vegas somewhere west of nowhere. After decades of refusing to let anybody see his work, he had gone public, big time. I wondered why.

"The article began with Kimmelman's report of his introduction to Heizer; sounds like quite a character. 'You just don't get it, do you?' he said to Kimmelman. 'This is a czarist nation, a fascist state. They control everything. They tap my phone. They'll do anything to stop me. We're the front lines, man, fleas fighting a giant.'

"Welcome to Nevada! I thought. One Can told me a lot about this place. The federal government owns 87 percent of the land in the state—military has more say about what goes on here than the citizens. Few miles north of Las Vegas, right across the highway from the state-of-the-art NASCAR racetrack, all the remaining hydrogen bombs are stored in bunkers that look more like artistic earthworks than dangerous military sites. Less than a hundred miles up the road where the Nuclear Test Site used to be you can still find big holes in the ground and the remains of bombed-out structures. Uncanny skeletons of bleachers still standing, where dignitaries used to watch nuclear blasts. Nellis Air Force Base, where top gun pilots train and stealth bombers take off and land without making a sound, is less than thirty miles from where Heizer lives and works. And, of course, Area 51 is nearby. Magnet for all the world's whacked-out weirdoes. I've heard people who otherwise seem perfectly sane insist that the government's hiding aliens captured years ago in that desolate outpost. The Nevada desert is where the military plays war games 24/7/365. Scattered among the sage and bones that litter the desert are ammo shells and bombs exploded and unexploded. Some kinda desert.

"What pushed Heizer over the edge and forced him to go public, I discovered, was not the military but waste—radioactive waste the government wants to transport across his land. Bush 2 rammed through something called the Yucca Mountain Development Act in 2002. Authorizes the completion of the first national nuclear waste depository. The Office of Civilian Radioactive Waste Management predicted that the Yucca Mountain facility wouldn't be completed and operational until 2020. I had no idea. Why don't people know this is goin' on?[4]

"Heizer's worried, and seems to me he should be. Government's plan calls for the nuclear waste to be shipped to the site by truck or rail in heavy fuel shipping casts. Yucca Mountain is less than a hundred miles from Heizer's place, and a section of the three-hundred-mile Caliente rail corridor passes along the far edge of his property. Kimmelman says the current plan is for the route to cut across Garden Valley, within ear- and eyeshot of Heizer's house and *City*. House would probably be fine. It's a kind of survivalist compound—cinderblock with solar panels, an oasis of cottonwoods and wild plum trees in the middle of a wide, empty plain. But seems his artwork would be damaged. Poor guy moved to the end of the earth to build his immense sculpture and now finds the federal government plotting, as he sees it, to ruin him and everything he's done. Seeing sinister conspiracies everywhere he turns, Heizer told Kimmelman, 'wouldn't be surprised if they sent out a hit squad to kill me!'

"When I finished reading the article, I knew I had to see the *City*, even if Heizer did threaten to shoot anybody who showed up on his land uninvited. It wasn't just Heizer's story that drew me, but the images—I had never seen, never imagined anything like the work he's creating. Seemed the desert wasn't done with me; New York would have to wait another few days. I went back upstairs, slept for another twelve hours, and the next morning rented a car and headed north.

"Driving out of Las Vegas, the road gradually ascends from the low to the high desert, until the highway unexpectedly turns to the right and cuts through a narrow pass. I took off my sunglasses so I could appreciate the richly colored cliffs. As the road bends again to the left, a lake and dense marsh appear like a mirage on the horizon. After twisting and turning through the narrows carved from archaic stone, the road drops into the lush Pahranagat Valley. I stopped at a turnout to read the roadside sign. Here in the middle of the desert there is a string of lakes, marshes, and swamps that are a stopping place and home to countless species of birds. I got back in the car and continued driving.

"A hundred miles later, I came to a small town, no more than a few houses, named Hiko. I saw a sign on one house that said Post Office and decided to go in and ask if anybody knew where the road to Michael Heizer's place is.

"The woman behind the counter directed me to a dirt road a few miles north of town. She warned, 'I wouldn't go there if I was you. Mike don't like visitors.'

"I thanked her and got back in the car. Good thing her directions were precise because I never would have seen the road without them. And I guess she's right about visitors. On a post at the edge of the dirt road, there's a faded sign, 'MIKE'S COUNTRY STAY OUT.'

"I ignored it and drove on. The road was treacherous, some gravel but mostly sand and rocks—small, medium, and large; in places it had been washed out. I later learned that for much of the year, the road is impassable, and even in good weather ruts and dust make driving tough. But it was worth the risk—beyond the narrow entrance to Garden Valley, I discovered a world of amazing beauty. The farther I drove, the more I understood why Heizer had decided to create his monumental earthwork in this distant desert. This desert is a special—perhaps even sacred—place. I saw petroglyphs scattered throughout the area, traces of some of the earliest Native Americans. I couldn't help but wonder if Heizer's art will last as long.

"I heard the last, lonely cowboy before I saw him—a single gunshot broke the desert silence. I had driven thirty-five miles down the sand 'road' when I saw a gate with a 'No Trespassing' sign. I stopped, got out of the car, and as I was about to turn around, a gunshot broke the silence.

"'What the hell are you doing out here? Can't you read the damn signs?'

"I turned and my eyes met his steely eyes and gaunt, lined face. 'Yes, of course, I can read, and I know you don't like visitors, but I came anyhow.'

"'Why? Why won't you leave me alone? Where you from?'

"'Well, that's a long story. New York, I guess.'

"'New York! Jeeeeesus fuckin' Christ! I came out here to get away from goddamn New Yorkers.'

"'But I'm not coming from New York now.'

"'Then where're you coming from?'

"'Slab City.'

"'Slab City? What the hell you doing in Slab City?'

"'Well, I was visiting my dad in the desert and had to get away from him and his crazy sidekick, so I faked my own kidnapping and started walking. Next thing I knew I was in Slab City.'

"'Place's a dump.'

"'Isn't that the point?'

"'Did you see that thing called Salvation Mountain? Not my taste but still pretty damn impressive.'

"'Yeah, I think so too, and sorta like your art.'

"'What do you mean, "like my art?" That guy's work is more like what Claus does. 'Cept he has the balls to use real material rather than all that plastic shit.'

"'Yeah, true. But still, think about it. There he is, living out in the middle of the desert for years and years working on a project he knows he'll never finish. Sound familiar?'

"'I guess. Look, it's too late for you to turn back now. Besides, with those shitty tires, you probably won't make it anyhow. Let's go see what Maureen has to say.'

"He opened the gate and let me drive through.

"'Only one road, pretty hard to get lost. I'll meet you at the house.'

"I drove another mile or so until I saw a stand of cottonwood and a low cinderblock building with a corrugated metal roof. Nearby there was what looked like a work shed with all kinds of equipment scattered around it. Farther on was a fleet of huge machines—dump trucks, bulldozers, a steam shovel, earthmover, and road grader. On the far side of the shed were fences keeping cattle and sheep from straying. I sat in the car and waited for Heizer to catch up. The door to the house opened, and Maureen came out to greet me. She was as hospitable as Mike was hostile.

"'Hi, I'm Maureen Sands, Mike's wife. What are you doing way out here? Mike actually let you through the gate?'

"'Yeah, he did. After I heard the shot, I didn't know what to expect, but he felt sorry for me, I guess.'

"'He always carries that darn pistol. Says it's to shoot rattlesnakes, but it's more than that. Thinks he's some kinda cowboy. Well, welcome. We don't get many visitors out here. What's your name?'

"'Jessie, Jessie Elster.'

"'And where're you from?'

"'New York.'

"'Oh no, does Mike know that?'

"'Sorta. See, I'm from New York but I've been wandering in the desert for the past week or so. Lost track of time.'

"In a few minutes, Mike came in and explained the situation to Maureen.

"'You're welcome to stay the night,' Maureen said. 'We have room and plenty of food.' She showed me to a small bedroom with no windows but a large painting hanging on the wall.

"'Who did that?'

"'I did; I'm a painter.'

"'I like it—it's beautiful, reminds me of the sky out here. Blue, but it's the hints of amber, umber, and red that make the difference.'

"'You have a good eye.'

"'I've spent quite a bit of time looking at art.'

"We had a simple but delicious ranch dinner—beef, potatoes, and beans. I hadn't realized how hungry I was.

"'We raised and produced everything right here in Garden Valley.'

"'But this is the middle of the desert—where do you get the water?'

"'Aquifers. There're huge aquifers under all this basin-range territory. Vegas's been trying to get its hands on that water for years. They'll have to shoot me to get my water.'

"Somehow I knew he wasn't kidding.

"'So why did you come all the way out here?'

"'To see your art.'

"'See my art? Nobody sees my art.'

"'That's not true, I saw your art in the *New York Times*. Doesn't get much more public than that.'

"'That was different. I was trying to stop that goddamn train from coming through here. First the MX missiles and now radioactive waste shit.'

"'You know, we actually met once before.'

"'No way, where?'

" 'A few years ago, at the opening of your show in Ace Gallery in Chelsea.'

" 'Ace Gallery—that damn Doug Christmas. Like all the other gallery guys.'

" 'I was there with a friend and was brash enough to come up and introduce myself. Still have a jacket with a splotch of white paint from brushing up against the wet gallery walls. Guess you cut it pretty close.'

" 'Always do.'

" 'Some of the sculptures you were showing were just like those outside your work shed.'

" 'Where do you think they were made? Trucked all the way to New York.'

" 'I heard you were sick, and when you fell off the radar screen I figured you'd stopped working or died. Then this guy from Slab City that showed me Salvation Mountain started talking about you. He dropped me off in Vegas. I was curious, so I Googled your name and up popped the *Times* article. When I read that, I couldn't return to New York without at least trying to see your work. So here I am.'

" 'If you hadn't come by way of Slab City, I wudda kicked your sweet little ass all the way back to New York.'

" 'Mike, be decent!'

" 'So can I see the *City*?'

" 'Look, I don't let people see the *City* till it's finished.'

" 'But it's never going to be finished.'

" 'Mike, what can it hurt? She's come all this way alone—that has to count for something.'

" 'Well, maybe. But here's the rules—no photographs, and everything we say is off the record. You can never tell anybody I let you see it. Deal?'

" 'Deal. I didn't sleep very well, and I'm not sure Mike ever went to bed. Every time I roused, he was shuffling around the living room. I awoke before dawn and already smelled coffee brewing. Stumbled into the dining room and found Mike sitting at the table reading. 'What are you reading?'

" '*Tibetan Book of the Dead*. Read it a hundred times. Saved my life when I was a kid hanging around Berkeley. Got me off of acid, which was frying my friggin' brain.'

" 'Never read it myself.'

" 'Want some coffee?'

" 'Sure.' It was strong and blacker than black. 'How long you been out here?'

" 'Almost forty years. Used to leave quite a bit, go back to New York. But now almost never leave the place. Nowhere else I'd rather be.'

" 'And you've been working on the *City* all that time.'

" 'More or less. On and off. Depends on money. I finished *Complex One* way back in 1974. But then the money ran out. Had to make art to continue my work. Every dime I make goes into the *City*. But it's still not enough, not near enough.'

" 'How much you spent?'

" 'Not sure, more than twenty-five million, maybe.'

" 'How much more do you need?'

" 'Too much. We'll go take a look when the sun comes up. Morning light is a good time to see it.'

"He disappeared into Maureen's studio, and I was left to browse his bookshelves. Lots of books about Garden Valley written by his father, who was a famous anthropologist.

"Maureen slept in and wasn't awake by the time Mike emerged and said, 'Time to go to the City.'

"We climbed in his truck and drove about half a mile to the work's edge. Mike was silent the whole way. Suddenly he stopped the truck and just sat for a few minutes. From where we were, you would never know anything was there. The desert floor seemed to stretch uninterrupted all the way to the horizon. No matter how hard I looked, I could see nothing.

" 'Go on, go over and take a look.'

"I got out of the truck and walked in the direction he pointed. Within a few steps the entire *City* opened beneath my feet. It's hard to convey the scale of the work. Numbers don't do it justice—one and a quarter miles long and more than a quarter of a mile wide. Nor do comparisons help—as large as the Washington Mall, four, five, ten Yankee Stadiums. Washington, New York—Easterners will never understand; the *City*'s scale and ambition are as big as the West. Lines etched in sand and carved in stone are as clear, clean, and crisp as the desert air. Ideas from my art and philosophy classes at Columbia rushed through my head—ancient and modern, massive and minimal, art and architecture. Differences and oppositions collide but don't appear contradictory. More associations—pyramids, above all pyramids—Egyptian, Mayan, Peruvian, and, yes, Vegas—Mississippian tumuli, Chichen Itza. Every trace of Europe erased, like a slate wiped clean. For some reason, the title of an essay I'd read in a philosophy class came to mind, 'The Pit and the Pyramid.' Poe deciphering signs but not solving all the mysteries. In the *City* massive pits and pyramids pose puzzles people will struggle to interpret for generations to come—unless no one ever sees it.

"What's the point? I wondered. What can possibly be the point of a city built in the desert that nobody ever sees? Sorta like writing a huge book in a world where people no longer read. Imagine aliens, arriving after the apocalypse, stumbling on Heizer's creation. How will they understand it? What will the *City* tell them about our civilization?

" 'Go ahead, you can go down into the work. Just be careful where you step.'

"I slowly made my way down the precisely graded side of the *City*, with Heizer following close behind. Standing in the middle of the pit, the horizon disappeared. I felt like I was in the presence of a modern alchemist who could make pure gold out of sand. The article I read said Heizer adds by subtracting, creates by removing. Emptiness, void, but ever so full. Negative sculpture—his *Double Negative* doubled and then doubled again. Not language but art 'struggling toward some idea outside our experience.' I was beginning to get it. Right before leaving to see my dad, I'd read a book I didn't understand. 'True life is not reducible to words spoken or written, not by anyone, ever. True life takes place when we're alone, thinking, feeling, lost in memory, dreamingly self-aware, the submicroscopic moments.' In the middle of the massive *City*, I thought to myself, what if we have to venture into the supermacroscopic to discover the submicroscopic?

"While I was struggling to absorb all of this, Mike offered a rare comment on his work. 'Look, I'm not gonna tell you what I'm up to but I'll say this, what I'm interested in is making this thing internalized. It is connected to the environment but not to the landscape. Landscape to me is a planar thing, just a view. Environment is everything down to the ecosystem. Big difference.'[5]

"The desert is where landscape disappears and something else opens up. I began to suspect that this might be the geologic time my father left the E Ring of the Pentagon to search for. But Heizer's not Smithson, and the *City's* not about entropy. You don't come here to 'dream of extinction,' to 'endlessly count down,' to 'become dead matter,' to 'pass completely out of being' and become a stone. Different vibes. No, no, something else is going on here, something that's not simply about extinction and death but about creation and life. You come to this desert to feel part of something infinitely bigger than yourself.

"Can't deny it—Heizer's art's a 'spectacle of excess'—it *is* wasteful, perhaps even pointless. What art isn't? Isn't that what art's supposed to be?

" 'But Mike, how can I internalize such an immense work?'

" 'You've entered it, now let it enter you.'

" 'My father always said I hear words from the inside.'

" 'Yeah, well, you can get inside some things only when you get outside yourself and listen to the silence of words. Listen harder.'

"Lifting my eyes to the far rim of the pit, I saw a massive pyramid—*Complex One. Complex One*, another contradiction. How can one be complex? How can the complex be one? Aren't those opposites? *Complex One* is not just any pyramid—it's like the pyramid in that essay—it has its 'tip knocked off.'[6] A pointless pyramid. From a certain angle, *Complex One* looks like a Mayan sacrificial altar. Some of the other sculptural forms in the *City* were more imposing, but none was as disturbing as *Complex One*. What sacrifices—ancient and modern—echo in this uncanny form? And what does it mean to sacrifice—to sacrifice today, here and now?

" 'Lots of material here, but it's not really about the material; it's all about the light. Everything changes with the light. Why don't you stay another night? Spend the whole day in the *City*. I packed water and some lunch for you. I'll leave it up top. You know the way back to the house. I'll see you after dark.'

"What happened to the tough, lonely cowboy? I wondered. Mike was right, the *City* changes with the light. The longer I lingered, the less certain I was whether the light made the sculpture appear or the sculpture made the light appear. There were moments when I could see myself seeing light, and in that instant it was as if I were present at the creation of the world. I was suddenly transported hundreds of miles away to another desert where I had once been present at the moment of creation in the eye of a volcano. Art becoming religion, religion becoming art. That's what those ancient desert monks sitting in their tiny caves looking out at the wilderness and in at surreal frescoes were searching for. The Omega Point, Point Omega. Then, just when the stones were about to speak, my reverie was broken by the passing shadow of a B-1 bomber flying silently less than three hundred feet above my head.

"Dusk was falling, and I had to get back to the house before dark. When I opened the door, Mike was dozing in his chair, and Maureen was in the kitchen making dinner.

"He roused and said, 'Don't want to talk about it. Takes time to process, lots of time.'

"'Yes, I know. Time is the point, isn't it—or one of the points?'

"'I guess. I don't know, I don't know. All the years out here hundreds of miles west of nowhere. Hard to know if it's been worth it.'

"'What do you mean, if it's been worth it? Are you crazy? You've done what no one else has ever done.'

"'And what's that? Begging rich dudes and trophy wives for millions of dollars so I can push tons and tons dirt around in the middle of the desert? They might as well burn their shit.'

"'But this will last and their shit won't.'

"'Maybe. Look, it's not just that those government bastards are invading my space. And it's not just the radiation that eats your guts out. They're gonna destroy my life's work. I've talked to seismologists and geologists, we've run the calculations. The vibrations from that goddamn train will destroy the *City*. And for what? A fucking dump! I won't let the government ruin what I created—I'd rather destroy it myself. If we can't stop the friggin' train from coming, I'll blow up the *City*. I swear, I'll blow it up.'

"'But . . .'

"'Nothing more to say. You gotta get up early to head back to what they call civilization back East.'

"Dawn arrived earlier than usual. By the time I roused, Mike and Maureen were both up and had made coffee and a big ranch breakfast. We made small talk while we ate, and after finishing, I gathered my things and stuffed them in my backpack.

"'Mike, Maureen, I don't know what to say.'

"'Don't say anything. Whatever we say, it's never right. And remember, everything's off the record, no photographs.'

"'Yeah, yeah, I know.'

"'Drop me a note sometime, let me know what you think.'

"Mike walked me to my rental car and kicked the tires. 'They're crap,' he said. 'They'll blow out if you hit a big rock, and then you'll be stuck.'

"He reminded me to call when I reached the paved road, so that he'd know I got there.[7]

"As I looked into the rearview mirror, Mike was standing alone. That's it—nothing more to tell."

"What an adventure! But you shouldn't have done it, you shouldn't have run away from your father. We were worried sick."

"Yeah, I know, but I had to, Mom. I just had to." "But you might have died."

"That's the point. *We're all gonna die.* I'm going back to the desert."


## WASTE

. . . Is it peace,
Is it a philosopher's honeymoon, one finds
On the dump? Is it to sit among mattresses of the dead,
Bottles, pots, shoes, and grass and murmur *aptest eve*:
Is it to hear the blatter of grackles and say
*Invisible priest*; is it to eject, to pull
The day to pieces and cry *stanza my stone*?
Where was it one first heard the truth? The the.[8]

*Underworld*, published in 1997, is one of the richest explorations of the complexities and contradictions of life during the latter half of the twentieth century that has been written in fiction or nonfiction. Don DeLillo connects without integrating the abstract and concrete, global and local, public and private, material and immaterial, planned and random, conspiracy and coincidence. The complexity of *Underworld* begins with the title, which counterfeits a counterfeit. *Underworld*, like *House of Leaves*, seems to take as its point of departure a film that does not exist. DeLillo claims he borrowed the title from a long-lost film, *Unterwelt*, by the revolutionary Soviet director and theorist Serge Eisenstein, which he supposedly completed during his Berlin exile in the 1930s. In DeLillo's account of its history, the film was shown at Radio City Music Hall in 1974 and received an enthusiastic response. According to the narrative, not much happens in this silent black-and-white film—a person who appears to be a mad scientist fires an atomic ray gun at prisoners or experimental subjects who are aimlessly roaming around a dark underground room. As the radiation takes effect, the victims morph into deformed monsters. There is no plot—the film consists of a series of images and episodes spliced together in what seems to be an arbitrary way. In fact, Eisenstein never made such a film. DeLillo uses this fictive device to signal some of the major themes and, more important, distinctive stylistic features of his work by effectively translating Eisenstein's signature montage technique onto the written page to create a multilayered text in which connections appear to be random but nonetheless are significant. DeLillo might well be expressing his own ambition when he describes Eisenstein's motivation. "All Eisenstein wants you to see in the end, are the contradictions of being. You look at the faces on the screen and you see the mutilated yearning, the inner divisions of people and systems, and how forces will clash and fasten, compelling the swerve from evenness that marks a thing lastingly" (444). "The inner division of people and systems"—this is the force driving DeLillo's narrative. As the pages accumulate, the nuances of "underworld" spread like a rhizome that cannot be controlled: unconscious—personal and collective, organized crime, CIA, KGB, FBI, prisons, subways, catacombs, political revolutionaries (the Weather Underground), underclasses, Plato, Pluto, Plutonium, Hades, nuclear testing, sewers, and waste—above all, waste. Everywhere you turn, waste accumulates—the shit just keeps getting deeper.

Rather than a single narrative drawing together characters and events, *Underworld* tracks countless trails that unfold, intertwine, and unravel between October 3, 1951, the day the Giants and the Dodgers played the epic third game to determine the National League pennant race—and the day the Soviet Union conducted a nuclear test that is commonly considered to mark the beginning of the Cold War—and the collapse of the Soviet Union in 1992. Most commentators read DeLillo's magnum opus as an allegory of the way the Cold War shaped American life for more than four decades. From this point of view, the decisive game between the Giants and Dodgers represents the deadly game between the U.S. and the S.U., whose outcome depended on stealing signals other than those the catcher sends the pitcher. This interpretation is not incorrect, but it is incomplete and hardly does justice to either the breadth or the depth of DeLillo's analysis.

The title of the epilogue points to the far-reaching ramifications of *Underworld*'s plots and counterplots—*Das Kapital*. This is, of course, the title of Karl Marx's most extended account of capitalism. By citing Marx, DeLillo underscores the importance of the contest between capitalism and communism for his novel. In the euphoria following the collapse of the Berlin Wall on November 10, 1989, Khrushchev's declaration of November 18, 1956, "We will bury you," seemed a distant memory. The United States appeared to have emerged victorious, and the Soviet Union seemed to have been relegated to the trash heap of history. By the early 1990s, it was evident that this ostensible victory had been more economic than military. The collapse of the wall was not merely a victory for the brand of consumerism that had fueled the American economy after World War II; it also signaled the emergence of new media, information, and communications technologies that would quickly create different forms of power far more complex and elusive than those that were the foundation of the military-industrial complex. The opening lines of the section titled *Das Kapital* effectively capture the drift of events:

Capital burns off the nuance in a culture. Foreign investment, global markets, corporate acquisitions, the flow of information through transnational media, the attenuating influence of money that's electronic and sex that's cyberspaced, untouched money and computer-safe sex, the convergence of consumer desire—not that people want the same things, necessarily, but they want the same range of choices. . . .

Some things fade and wane, states disintegrate, assembly lines shorten their runs and interact with lines in other countries. This is what desire seems to demand. A method of production that will custom-cater to cultural and personal needs, not to cold war ideologies of massive uniformity. And the system pretends to go along, to become more supple and resourceful, less dependent on rigid categories. But even as desire tends to specialize, going silky and intimate, the force of converging markets produces an instantaneous capital that shoots across horizons at the speed of light, making for a certain furtive sameness, a planning away of particulars that affects everything from architecture to leisure time to the way people eat and sleep and dream. (785–786)

While others were confidently proclaiming "the end of history" and announcing an American empire that would dominate the new millennium, DeLillo was expressing doubts about the sustainability of the new world order.

What DeLillo understood before most others was that the Cold War— even the balance of terror—had been a stabilizing arrangement. The dissolution of the Soviet Union did not insure a secure world governed by one superpower but ushered in a radically unstable world in which power is decentralized, distributed, and dispersed in ways that make it much harder to identify, contain, and control individuals and state and nonstate agents. In such a world, it is only fitting that a marginal rather than a central character expresses the telling insight. Marvin Lundy, who lives on the outskirts of town, just off the interstate, and traffics in baseball memorabilia, much of which he reluctantly admits is counterfeit or has been stolen, proves to be considerably more astute than the pundits pontificating on TV. He had a half-brother, Avram Lubarsky, who was a dedicated communist and hated capitalism with a passion. Avram served in the Red Army and was wounded in the Battle of Stalingrad. After the war, Marvin married a prim and proper Englishwoman named Eleanor, and they spent their honeymoon traveling through Eastern Europe in search of Avram. The deeper into Czechoslovakia they went, the more the pollution they found, and the worse the toilets became. When Marvin developed an intestinal bug, his shit stank so much that his new bride became disgusted and insisted they leave the country. Late one night, passing through pathologically clean Switzerland on the return trip, Marvin overhears Russ Hodges call Bobby Thompson's home run on the Armed Forces Network. Years later, looking back on his experience in the former Soviet Union, he finds himself unexpectedly nostalgic for the Cold War and concerned about the new era that is beginning.

> You need the leaders of both sides to keep the cold war going. It's the one constant thing. It's honest, it's dependable. Because when the tension and rivalry come to an end, that's when your worst nightmares begin. All the power and intimidation of the state will seep out of your personal bloodstream. You will no longer be the main—what do I want to say? . . . point of reference. Because other forces will come rushing in, demanding and challenging. The cold war is your friend. You need it to stay on top. (170)

Marvin's words prove prescient—the end of the Cold War led to a new form of capitalism that created a period of sustained instability. Just as America's industrial capacity led to victory in World War I, so victory in World War II was made possible by the development of new media, information, and communication technologies. With the end of the First World War, factories shifted from producing materials for military purposes to churning out consumer goods to satisfy pent-up demand for more and more new stuff. With this development, industrial capitalism gave way to consumer capitalism, which constantly requires new markets. When the people of Eastern Europe and the Soviet Union finally dared to cross once heavily guarded borders, they were running toward the consumerist utopia they had seen on pirate TV and read about in smuggled magazines as much as they were running away from years of personal and political repression. It is no exaggeration to say that most of these people were more interested in the freedom to buy than the freedom to vote.

There were, however, other changes occurring that proved even more important, though they were less obvious at the time. The media, information, and communications technologies developed to support the war against Germany and Japan were redeployed for commercial rather than military purposes, and with this development another form of capitalism began to emerge. Just as consumer capitalism displaced industrial capitalism, so, during the late decades of the twentieth century, finance capitalism came to dominate the world economy. As digital technologies emerged and connectivity spread, swapping signs and numbers became more profitable than producing, buying, and selling stuff. By the early 1990s, the world was wired and money was never sleeping—with the fall of the wall, capital went global.

DeLillo recognized that the end of the Cold War marked the beginning of an era of increasing uncertainty, instability, and insecurity in which everything always seems to be drifting toward the edge of chaos. The best-known line of *Underworld*, which is repeated several times, is "Everything's connected."

> There were people here who didn't know where their work ended up, how it might be applied. They didn't know how their arrays of numbers and symbols might enter nature. It could conceivably happen in a flash.
>
> Everything connected at some undisclosed point down the systems line. This caused a certain select disquiet.
>
> But it was a splendid mystery in a way, a source of wonder, how a brief equation that you tentatively enter on your screen might alter the course of many lives, might cause the blood to rush through the body of a woman on a tram many thousands of miles away, and how do you define this kind of relationship? (408–409)

This is a very important comment because it underscores DeLillo's belief that connectivity is *systemic*. Though designed to control all kinds of processes that threaten to disrupt life, systems, DeLillo insists, harbor a disruptive mystery that can provoke wonder as well as anxiety. Far from being merely a danger, he regards this unsettling mystery as the only remaining hope in a world that is increasingly flat.

In an essay entitled "In the Ruins of the Future," published in the *Guardian* on December 22, 2001, DeLillo reflects on the impact of 9/11 and clarifies the kind of destabilizing systems he has in mind.

> Technology is our fate, our truth. It is what we mean when we call ourselves the only superpower on the planet. The materials and methods we devise make it possible for us to claim our future. We don't have to depend on God or the prophets or other astonishments. We are the astonishment. The miracle is what we ourselves produce, the systems and networks that change the way we think and live. But whatever great skeins of technology lie ahead, ever more complex, connective, precise, micro-fractional, the future has yielded, for now, to the old slow furies of cutthroat religion.

In *Underworld*, as in all of his other works, DeLillo is preoccupied with "the systems and networks that change the way we live and think." Indeed, it would not be too much to suggest that he is actually a systems theorist writing in the guise of a novelist.[9] In keeping with theories of emergent complex adaptive systems that scientists were developing during the years he was writing *Underworld*, DeLillo recognizes that systems are isomorphic across the media in which they function; that is to say, natural, sociopolitical, economic, and cultural systems have a common structure and operational logic. Though designed to control and regulate all kinds of flows, these systems inevitably produce a resistant surplus or remainder that either transforms or destroys them. System and excess are bound in a complex parasitic relationship, in which each presupposes yet seeks to destroy the other. Paradoxically, the condition of the possibility of a system is simultaneously the condition of its impossibility. DeLillo's interest in system and excess is not simply analytic but is, more important, critical. By using theoretical insights to develop a penetrating criticism of capitalism in all of its forms, he provides a cautionary tale for life in the twenty-first century.

## Andy 1

*mor[e] auto biography*

In our family, there was no clear line between religion and baseball. My father was a talented pitcher whose right arm had gotten him off the farm and into college. Born in 1907, he grew up tending livestock before dawn, walking three miles to a one-room schoolhouse, and spending long afternoons behind a horse-drawn plow on the family farm a few miles outside Gettysburg. By the time he reached high school, he found baseball, or baseball found him. Perhaps it was the years of physical labor—though all his teammates were also farm boys—that made his right arm so strong. He was fast and also wild—and not just his pitches. He always said it was Eddie Plank who made the difference.

Eddie, nicknamed "Gettysburg Eddie," was a local boy who made good. He pitched for the Philadelphia Athletics, and toward the end of his career for the St. Louis Terriers of the Federal League, and he ended his career with the St. Louis Browns. He was the first lefthander to win two hundred games and in 1946 was elected to the Hall of Fame. My most vivid memory of our family visit to Cooperstown with my father, when I was eleven, is my brother and me standing in front of Eddie Plank's plaque and listening to my father tell the story of his relationship with him. Eddie had heard about my father and came to see him play. Duly impressed, he encouraged my father to continue pitching, and my father, needless to say, was flattered by words of praise from his hometown hero. When a minor-league contract with a farm team of the Philadelphia Athletics came a few weeks later, my father had no doubt who had arranged it. He was tempted but declined, deciding that education was more important than athletics. I still wonder why a kid who had never been off the farm made that decision.

Sports, however, continued to play an important part of his life and, by extension, in mine as well. Dad pitched his way through college, playing for

4.2  Noel A. Taylor.

*Source:* Mark C. Taylor.

Shippensburg and earning money during the summer by working part-time in factories and playing for company teams in the semiprofessional leagues that were popular during that era. My father's glove hangs in our family room, and I still have one of his all-wool summer-league uniforms.

4.3  Noel A. Taylor's glove.

*Source:* Mark C. Taylor.

4.4  Noel A. Taylor's uniform.

*Source:* Mark C. Taylor.

Baseball was in our family DNA. By the time I was born, my father was teaching science at a New Jersey high school and coaching the baseball team. On game days, he would let me skip school and tag along as the team batboy. I was in locker rooms, team meetings, and on the bench before I knew how to read. What I most remember about those days is how competitive my father was and how much he hated to lose. That too seems to be in the Taylor DNA. He won the state championship only once and always remained very proud of that accomplishment. As a token of their appreciation, the team incongruously gave him a cigarette lighter inscribed "To Coach Noel Taylor from the Championship Team of 1949." Imagine—a cigarette lighter as a memento for a state baseball championship!

As soon as he thought I was old enough, he bought me my first baseball glove. I can still picture it vividly, but, alas, I have long since lost it. The glove was autographed by Andy Pafko. I was already following professional baseball by that time. With the Yankees, Giants, and Dodgers all playing in New York at the time, it was the heyday of baseball in suburban New Jersey. I hadn't heard of Pafko but soon learned about him. My dad told me that he had just been traded to the Dodgers from the Cubs (1951) and was a good all-round player. I decided that Andy Pafko was my favorite player and instantly became a Dodgers fan—not a popular decision in our family at that time. I wrote a fan letter to Andy to tell him about my new glove, and a few days later an autographed postcard arrived in the mail.

This card is still on the bookcase in my study. My stint with the Dodgers was short; before the 1953 season Andy was traded to the Milwaukee Braves, where he played until 1959. Where Andy went, I followed—I became an ardent Braves fan from 1953 through 1959. I can still name the players at each position, and even the numbers, all the numbers. Why, I wonder, can I recall all those numbers when I forget so much else? Pitchers—Warren Spahn (21), Lew Burdette (33), Gene Conley (22), who also played for the Boston Celtics (6), Bob Buhl (22); catchers—Del Crandall (1), Joe Torre (15); first base— Joe Adcock (9) and Frank Torre (14); second base—Red Schoendienst (2); shortstop—Johnny Logan (23); third base—Eddie Matthews (41); left field— Andy (48); center field—Wes Covington (43); right field—Hank Aaron (44).

4.5  Cigarette lighter.

*Source:* Mark C. Taylor.

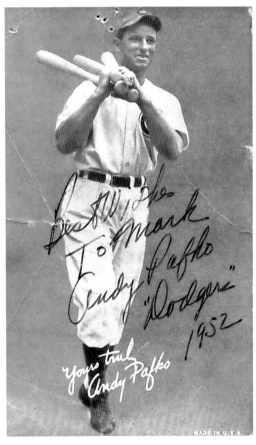

4.6  Andy Pafko.

*Source:* Mark C. Taylor.

**4.7 and 4.8** Polo Grounds.

*Source:* Mark C. Taylor.

My dad's favorite player was, predictably, a pitcher—Bob Feller, and he, like me, went where his guy went. Dad was a Cleveland Indians fan and followed the American League more than the National League. He preferred Yankee Stadium to the Polo Grounds or Ebbets Field, but when the Braves came to town, he condescended to take me to the Polo Grounds to see them play the Giants. I still have programs, photographs, and autographs from those games.

## Part 2

*Underworld* is as rich and complex as the territory it maps. People, things, and events proliferate in narratives and counternarratives that simultaneously connect and disconnect, until everything becomes somewhat chaotic. The only thing that seems to tie it all together is waste. With every turn of the page, there is more waste—wasted lives, wastelands, wasted bodies, limbs, sewers, dumps, landfills, junk, trash, garbage, shit—all kinds of shit—and, of course, radioactive nuclear waste. There are also other less recognizable and predictable forms of waste—games, art, and religion. In ways that are not immediately obvious, all of this has something to do with capital and its aftermath. Though the Cold War is over when DeLillo begins a second time, the problem is still containment—not the containment of the Soviet Union but the containment of waste.[10] The main character of the novel, Nick Shay, whom we will soon meet again, is a waste manager working for a company named Waste Containment. His story, like everything else in this messy novel, is long and complex. DeLillo spins his yarns around a ball and a bomb—a ball and a bomb connected by a game.

More precisely, a ball that's a bomb and a bomb that's a ball. The ball is the ball Bobby Thompson hit out of the Polo Grounds on that fateful October day. Even at the time, it was clear that this game was about more than baseball. As Marvin Lundy observes:

> It's like they knew. They sensed there was a connection between this game and some staggering event that might take place on the other side of the

world. . . . Not the day before or the day after. Because this was an all-or-nothing game between the two hated rivals of the city. People had a premonition that this game was related to something much bigger.     (172)

"An all-or-nothing game between the two hated rivals"—not a bad description of the United States and the Soviet Union during the Cold War. Reflecting typical American hubris that would come to full expression during the last decade of the twentieth century, Thompson's home run quickly became known as "the shot heard round the world." DeLillo threads his narratives between the lines of Russ Hodges's call of the game. The mysterious movement of the ball establishes an implausible connection that keeps all the characters in play and keeps the reader turning pages. In DeLillo's hands, a ball is never simply a ball but is thoroughly overdetermined and lodges itself in the country's collective memory. Once again, Marvin knows the value of the tokens he trades.

> "And the ball has a history by this time that I've been inching along, where different things match and join. But I can't locate the man or even—what?"
> "Ascertain," Brian said.
> "His correct name. By this time, forget the footage—I'm using rumors and dreams. There's an ESP of baseball, an underground what, a consciousness, and I'm hearing it in my sleep."     (179)

Rumors and dreams—there are many underworlds in which different balls circulate and other tests occur.

Theories can be played out, and games can be theorized. For Cold War strategists, game theory provided scenarios that became war games played in deserts of the American west.[11] Characters become players in a game that defines their positions and actions by the movement of the ball/bomb. In a fascinating essay published in his book *Parables for the Virtual: Movement, Affect, Sensation*, Brian Massumi draws on Michele Serres's seminal work, *The Parasite*, to suggest that a more effective way to understand some games is to assume the perspective of the ball rather than the of the players or teams. The ball, Massumi argues,

> catalyzes the play as a whole but is not itself a whole. It attracts and arrays the players, defining their effective role in the game and defining the over-all state of the game, at any given moment, by the potential movement of the players with respect to it. The ball moves the players. *The player is the object of the ball*. True, the player kicks the ball. But the ball must be considered in some way as an autonomous actor because the global game-effects its displacements produce can be produced by no other game element. When the ball moves, the whole game moves with it. Its displace-ment is more than a local movement: it is a global event.[12]

On October 3, 1951, ball and bomb collided in a global event that changed the game for half a century.

A ball that's a bomb and a bomb that's a ball. In making his sales pitch, Marvin incongruously associates Thompson's home-run ball with the nuclear bomb.

> " . . . the whole thing is interesting because when they make an atomic bomb, listen to this, they make the radioactive core the exact same size as a baseball."
>
> "I always thought it was a grapefruit."
>
> "a regulation major league baseball no less than nine inches in circum-ference, going by the rule book."                    (172)

Marvin's comment raises intriguing questions. Uncertainty about the ball's authenticity casts doubts on the bomb's reality. In a world of fakes and counterfeits, where words deceive and images lie, it is never possible to be sure what is real and what is not. It is, after all, possible that the Russians faked the nuclear test to trick the United States into excessive spending for national defense. Later in the novel, DeLillo even goes so far as to suggest that the Soviet Union might not have really collapsed but might have staged a fake fall, so that America would let down its guard. In a certain sense, it doesn't matter if the ball is authentic or if the bomb is real because belief in the possibility of the real is what keeps everything in play. Politics, like economics, is a confidence game in which each side attempts to con the other. The balance of terror rested on the policy of deterrence, which in turn was based on the prospect of mutually assured destruction: each side believed the other had the capacity to launch a devastating nuclear attack. The bomb, like the ball, "must be considered in some way an autonomous actor because the global game-effects its displacements produce can be produced by no other game element." Since the bomb can never be used, its reality is virtual, but this virtuality does not make its effects any less real; to the contrary, the bomb's impossible presence renders it hyperreal.

The question of whether the ball is real or fake arises repeatedly, but nowhere with more of an edge than in a conversation between Nick and his boss, Simeon Biggs, known as Big Sims, while they are watching a game between the Giants and Dodgers years after Thompson's home run. The dilapidated Polo Grounds, with its peeling paint, falling trash, and the centerfield Chesterfield sign is long gone, and Nick, Brian Glassic, Sims, and a woman working on a documentary film for the BBC are enjoying drinks and dinner, safely sealed off from the clutter, noise, and confusion of the crowd, in the Stadium Club at Dodger Stadium. The ballpark resembles Powers's sealed VR Cavern more than a real stadium. Brian, Nick's business partner and erstwhile lover of his wife, expresses dismay at being isolated from the noise and frenzy of the crowd. "We need video helmets and power gloves. Because this isn't reality. This is virtual reality. And we don't have the proper equipment" (92). As they eat and drink more than they should, the conversation turns to the epic game decades earlier.

> "Nick owns the baseball. The Bobby Thompson home-run ball. The actual object."
> Sims took his time lighting the cigar.
> "Nobody owns the ball."
> "Somebody has to own it."

"The ball is unaccounted for," Sims said. "It got thrown away decades ago. Otherwise we'd know it."                                          (96)

Nick protests and insists that the ball is real, but to no avail; Sims will have none of such sentimental nonsense. Balls or bombs, it's all a pile of crap.

"Buying and selling baseballs. What heartache. And you never told me," Sims said.

"It was some time ago."

"I would have talked you out of it."

"So you could buy it yourself," Glassic said.

"I deal in other kinds of waste. The real stuff of the world. Give me disposable diapers by the ton. Not this melancholy junk from yesteryear."                                          (99)

Waste, waste, and more waste. There are, of course, many kinds of waste—human as well as nonhuman—and it can take many forms or be completely formless. Of the various kinds of waste that fascinate DeLillo, two are particularly noteworthy—the trash, garbage, and refuse rotting in underground landfills and the radioactive nuclear waste decaying in underground caverns beneath the Nevada desert. What if Sims is right? What if this waste *is* the real stuff of our world?

## Part 3

*Underworld* is big—too big—and messy. By any reasonable measure, it is excessive—827 pages! It seems to fall apart more often than hang together. Characters connect and disconnect without rhyme or reason; things appear, disappear, and reappear randomly, and there are coincidences, far too many unexplainable coincidences. Shit happens—good shit, bad shit, all kinds of shit—and as it keeps happening, the reader gradually begins to realize that *Underworld* is actually a heap of trash, a pile of garbage that resembles a dump or a not-so-sanitary landfill where "everything is changing shape, becoming something else" (33). As pages turn and stuff keeps piling up, readers are left to sort through the historical and cultural debris of the latter half of the twentieth century in the hope of finding patterns where there seems to be nothing but noise. To create art from garbage is the alchemy of the word.

In DeLillo's cosmology, creation is not *ex nihilo*; rather, the world is created from garbage. In the beginning is garbage! "Garbage comes first, then we build a system to deal with it" (288). Cities, architecture, logic, science, mathematics, art, and music have their origin and foundation in garbage.

> Civilization did not rise and flourish as men hammered out hunting scenes on bronze gates and whispered philosophy under the stars, with garbage as a noisome offshoot, swept away and forgotten. No, garbage rose first, inciting people to build a civilization in response, in self-defense. We had to find ways to discard our waste, to use what we couldn't discard, to reprocess what we couldn't use. Garbage pushed back. It mounted and spread. And it forced us to develop the logic and rigor that would lead to systematic investigations of reality, to science, art, music, mathematics.
>
> (287)

This is an extremely important insight—the structures and systems that constitute civilization have as a condition of their possibility an unassimilable remainder that always threatens to undo them as if from within. *Underworld* presents the counternarrative of the excess that civilization cannot bear yet cannot survive without. For DeLillo, "waste is the secret history, the underhistory, the way archaeologists dig out the history of early cultures, every sort of bone heap and broken tool, literally from under the ground" (791).

It was, of course, Freud who first drew the analogy between psychoanalysis and archaeology. His lifelong fascination with Rome and obsession with collecting archaeological artifacts led him to compare the structure of the human psyche to the accumulating debris in what he describes as "the Eternal City."

> It is hardly necessary to remark that all these remains of ancient Rome are found dovetailed into the jumble of a great metropolis, which has grown

up in the last few centuries since the Renaissance. There is certainly not a little that is ancient still buried in the soil of the city or beneath its modern buildings. This is the manner in which the past is preserved in historical sites like Rome.

Now let us, by a flight of imagination, suppose that Rome is not a human habitation but a psychical entity with a similarly long and copious past—an entity, that is to say, in which nothing that once has come into existence will have passed away and all the earlier phases of development continue to exist alongside the latest one.[13]

For Freud, the contents of the unconscious remain unconscious through acts of repression. DeLillo admits a Freudian dimension to his work in an interview with Kim Echlin entitled "Baseball and the Cold War," published shortly after *Underworld* appeared. "In this book," he explains,

> "under" can apply to suppressed or repressed memories or even consciousness. Nick Shay does not want to acknowledge a very strong truth in his life, the fact that his father simply abandoned the family, and he devises an entire mythology about it, a mob hit. Aside from that, I think that all the unders spring originally from my sense of the physical meaning of the word applied to the burial of nuclear waste. This is when I first hit upon the idea of calling the book *Underworld*.[14]

If *Underworld* is, inter alia, the cultural unconscious of America during the latter half of the twentieth century, then Freud's method for decoding dreams provides helpful clues for deciphering it. To interpret this text is to decode the counternarrative of our lives. Freud develops a method for deciphering the unconscious but always admits that understanding can never be complete. In an inconspicuous footnote in *The Interpretation of Dreams*, he writes, "There is at least one spot in every dream at which it is unplumbable—a navel, as it were, that is the point of contact with the unknown."[15] This unknown is the unassimilable remainder that leaves every system and structure—psychic and otherwise—open.

In Freud's account, dreams are constituted through a process of distortion, in which disturbing thoughts are disguised so that they can slip by the psychic censor and enter consciousness. Psychoanalysis reverses the activity of the dream-work by interpreting manifest dream content in terms of latent dream thoughts. "The essence of the decoding procedure," Freud writes, "lies in the fact that the work of interpretation is not brought to bear on the dream as a whole but on each portion of the dream's content independently, as though the dream were a geological conglomerate in which each fragment of rock required a separate assessment." The fragments of this "geological conglomerate" are not fixed and stable but constantly shift as layers of psychic debris pile up and more and more connections are made. Freud argues, "the new connections are, as it were, loop-lines or short-circuits, made possible by the existence of other and deeper-lying connecting paths." The most suggestive term he uses for these shards is "nodal points." In his well-known account of "The Dream of the Botanical Monograph," Freud writes,

> This first investigation leads us to conclude that the elements "botanical" and "monograph" found their way into the content of the dream because they possessed copious contacts with the majority of the dream-thoughts, because, that is to say, they constituted "nodal points" upon which a great number of dream-thoughts converged, and because they had several meanings in connection with the interpretation of the dream. The explanation of this fundamental fact can also be put in another way: each of the elements of the dream's content turns out to have been "overdetermined"— to have been represented in the dream-thoughts many times over.[16]

The dream, then, forms something like a subterranean web or network composed of proliferating nodes linked by "loop-lines" that create "deeper-lying connecting paths." The spatial imagery of depth/surface implies a corresponding temporal structure: infantile/mature, ancient/contemporary, primitive/modern. In this spatiotemporal scheme, to dig down beneath the surface is to go back in time.

The temporal organization of *Underworld* is as complex as its spatial structure. DeLillo's counternarrative is not straightforward but consists of multiple narratives and countercounternarratives joined by tangled loop-lines. The events he recounts all take place during the four decades from the summers of 1951 and 1952 and the summer-spring of 1992. The novel is divided into six parts that are framed by a prologue set in 1951 and an epilogue set in 1992. Like a psychoanalyst's attempt to interpret the present life of a patient in terms of the past, DeLillo tells his tale in reverse. This counternarrative is interrupted by three sections that come after the odd-numbered parts and are separated from the rest of the text by empty black pages. In these textual supplements, DeLillo tells the sad story of Cotter's father, Manx Martin, who stole Thompson's home-run baseball from his son and sold this priceless memento for a paltry thirty-six dollars. What occurs in this three-part story follows a chronological order from past to present and is only marginally related to what is going on in the rest of the work.

| Prologue | October 3, 1951 |
| | The Triumph of Death |
| Part 1 | Spring-Summer 1992 |
| | Elegy for Left Hand Alone |
| Supplement | Manx Martin 1 |
| Part 2 | Mid-1980s–Early 1990s |
| Part 3 | Spring 1978 |
| | The Cloud of Unknowing |
| Supplement | Manx Martin 2 |
| Part 4 | Summer 1974 |
| | Cocksucker Blues |
| Part 5 | Selected Fragments Public and Private in the 1950s and 1960s |
| | Better Things for Better Living Through Chemistry |
| Supplement | Manx Martin 3 |

Part 6

Epilogue

Fall 1951–Summer 1952
Arrangement in Gray and Black
1992
*Das Kapital*

There is no straightforward way to understand this convoluted temporal structure any more than there is one way to interpret the nodal points in *Underworld*. By creating a narrative that consists of counternarratives interrupted by a countercounternarrative, DeLillo has created a work that performs or enacts the alternating rhythms between past and present. It is as if he were attempting to reverse the flow of time by rewinding the tape of history. But this task proves impossible because the counternarrative keeps running into the resistance of eddies created by the inexorable rush of time. Accumulating piles of rotting garbage signal the inevitable increase of entropy. As things decay and regulatory systems break down, the world rushes faster and faster toward the edge of chaos, where everything eventually returns to the prime matter from which it originally emerged. To reverse the flow of time would be to decrease entropy and, correlatively, to increase negentropy.[17] If waste could be managed effectively, the end might be deferred, at least for a while. But time always triumphs, and at the end of the day we are all recycled as worm meat.

DeLillo's relentless exploration of the trash heap of cultural history poses a direct challenge to the central tenets of modernism. While many modern writers, artists, and architects have long been preoccupied with wiping the slate of history clean, no one expresses this modernist agenda more clearly and forcefully than Le Corbusier. In *Après le Cubisme*, he and Amédée Ozenfant declare the New Age of Purism.

Not fifty years have passed since the birth of industry. Already formidable works have been realized. . . . They bring us the perception of a clear, airy, general beauty. Not since Pericles has thought been so lucid. . . . Actual spirit is a tendency to rigor, precision, to better utilization of forces and materials, to the least *déchet*, in sum, a tendency to purity. This is also the definition of art.

As the tendency to purity, art, according to Le Corbusier, wipes away *le déchet*: loss, waste, offal—refuse, rubbish, garbage, cut off parts of butchered animals. As we will see below, this is what Georges Bataille aptly labels *la part maudite*, "the accursed share." "Purism," Le Corbusier insists, "wants to conceive clearly, execute loyally, exactly, without *déchet*; it turns away from troubling conceptions."[18]

Corbusier dreams of building *la ville radieuse*, in which everything is clean, neat, tidy, and where there are only straight lines, right angles, and white structures. As Nietzsche has taught us, however, all forms of purity are nihilistic because they necessarily destroy what they cannot tolerate. The demand for order eventually runs out of control and leads to the very chaos it is designed to contain. The history of the twentieth century is, in large part, a revelation of the dark side of the utopian dreams of modernism. Modernism's new age calls for a new order—*Neue Ordnung*.[19] Le Corbusier celebrates what he calls "the 'White World'—the domain of clarity and precision, of exact proportion and precise materials, culture standing alone—in contrast to the 'Brown World' of muddle, clutter, and compromise, the architecture of inattentive experience."[20] White versus brown—purity versus danger . . . light versus darkness . . . order versus chaos . . . art versus shit. But what if purity is dangerous, light is dark, order is chaos, and art is shit?

What repels Le Corbusier and his fellow modernists attracts DeLillo and his fellow postmodernists. Rather than seeking the Radiant City, DeLillo hangs out in dumps, landfills, slums, prisons, heroin dens, subways, tunnels where the homeless live, and the desert—especially the desert. It is too easy to set up a simple opposition between a modernist utopia and a postmodernist dystopia because the liminal spaces DeLillo explores are too complex to be contained by such sharp boundaries. His uncanny counternarrative takes place in what Michel Foucault aptly labels "heterotopias." While Foucault and his followers usually associate heterotopias with sites like prisons, asylums, brothels, and hospitals, there is no better example of such other spaces than dumps. In her suggestive book *Designing America's Waste Land-scapes*, Mira Engler points out that Foucault's heterotopias

> relate to all everyday places in a curious way. They contain the everyday
> and yet they subvert, contest, and often threaten those places, thus pro-
> viding an excuse for their own removal and rejection. Most importantly,
> Other Spaces shed light on our everyday places. They both affirm and
> contradict the everyday or normal *and provide us with the distance needed
> to look critically at our common landscapes and habits.* [Foucault] writes,
> "On the one hand they perform the task of creating a space of illusion that
> reveals how all of real space is more illusory, all the locations within which
> life is fragmented." . . . Waste sites—landfills and sewage plants—easily fit
> Foucault's category of Heterotopias of Deviation. Sequestered in remote,
> fringe locations, they too contain and treat undesirable material culture or
> conditions and are most successful in playing the social roles of landscape
> mirrors, supplements and critics.[21]

Heterotopias of Deviation are designed to be sites of containment, but they are never secure. Boundaries inevitably prove to be porous, and contamination spreads regardless of how carefully borders are patrolled.

One of the most intriguing aspects of heterotopias is how often they are surrounded with a religious aura. Nick, who devotes his life to the treatment of all kinds of waste, goes so far as to claim, "Waste is a religious thing" and as such has "a numinous glow" (88, 809). While the association of waste with religion and the sacred might initially seem puzzling, if not sacrilegious, DeLillo's use of the word "numinous" suggests the plausibility of such connection. In his classic study *The Idea of the Holy*, Rudolph Otto explains that the holy or, in more contemporary terms, the sacred surpasses rational comprehension because it bears a "surplus" or "excess" of meaning. To express this elusive excess, Otto explains, "I adopt a word coined from the Latin *numen*. *Omen* has given us 'ominous,' and there is no reason why from numen we should not similarly form a word 'numinous.'"[22] The trace of "ominous" lingers in "numinous." Whatever is numinous is dangerous

*O Ho numinous*

because it cannot be clearly defined, effectively contained, controlled, or managed. It eludes simple oppositions like productive/destructive and cannot be classified as rational or irrational; as such, it is beyond good and evil.

Like the sacred, waste is irreducibly ambivalent—this is what lends both of them their mystery and makes them so fascinating. Simultaneously attractive and repulsive, powerful and dangerous, creative and destructive, waste and the sacred mark the site where life and death meet. There can be no creation without destruction, no life without death, no renewal without decay. Far from merely repulsive, the dangerous aspect of waste and the sacred is their draw. Like moths circling the flame, we are attracted to what can destroy us. "The more ominous" waste is, DeLillo claims, the more "magical" it becomes (286). While attending a conference on "The Future of Waste," which takes place in the desert, Nick expresses his fascination with waste while voicing misgivings about American corporations:

> Corporations are great and appalling things. They take you and shape you in nearly nothing flat, twist and swivel you. And they do it without overt persuasion, they do it with smiles and nods, a collective inflection of the voice. You stand at the head of the corridor and by the time you walk to the far end you have adopted the comprehensive philosophy of the firm, the *Weltanschauung*. I use this grave and layered word because somewhere in the depths there is a whisper of mystical contemplation that seems appropriate to the subject of waste. (282)

DeLillo's repeated association of waste with religion is neither a parody, nor is it intended to be ironic; to the contrary, he recognizes an unexpected religious dimension of waste and a wasteful aspect of religion. Religion does not merely provide protection by controlling or claiming to control dangerous forces and repressing aberrant desires; it can also expose people to danger by actually soliciting the return of the repressed. This destabilizing dimension of religion is much more interesting but less often noticed. Far from a secure structure, religion can draw us toward what disturbs and disrupts every management system designed to establish human control in a world that is increasingly turbulent. While God might be the highest being or center of the universe for believers, the lowly sacred is encountered, if at all, at the periphery—along the edge, margin, frontier.[23] From time immemorial, religions east and west have taught that whoever searches for the sacred must err in the wasteland of the desert.

## Andy 2

On October 3, 1951, I was in first grade and remember being excited by the Dodgers-Giants playoff. Who could have known that the final game of that series would come to mark Andy's place in baseball history? I have seen films of "The Shot Heard Round the World" so many times that I no longer am sure where my memory begins and where the grainy newsreel images and Ralph Branca's (13) pitch, Bobby Thompson's (23) swing, the brief glimpse of Andy standing at the wall, Thompson rounding third with Leo Durocher (2) jumping up and down and throwing his hat in the air end. Thompson's walk-off home run was all the more dramatic because the Giants' situation had seemed so hopeless. Favored to win the pennant in 1951, by mid-August they were 13½ games behind the Dodgers, and then they inexplicably won thirty-seven out of their last forty-four games, tying the Dodgers on the last game of the season and forcing a three-game playoff. With the series deadlocked at 1–1 and the Dodgers leading 4–2 in the top of the ninth, Willie Mays (24) on deck, two men on base, and ominous clouds threatening rain, Thompson stepped to the plate. Though this was the first sports series ever telecast coast to coast, Russ Hodges's radio call for WMCA-AM is what everybody remembers.

> Bobby Thomson . . . up there swingin' . . . He's had two out of three, a single and a double, and Billy Cox is playing him right on the third-base line . . . One out, last of the ninth . . . Branca pitches . . . Bobby Thomson takes a strike called on the inside corner . . . Bobby hitting at .292 . . . He's had a single and a double and he drove in the Giants' first run with a long fly to center . . . Brooklyn leads it 4–2 . . . Hartung down the line at third not

taking any chances . . . Lockman with not too big of a lead at second, but he'll be runnin' like the wind if Thomson hits one . . . Branca throws . . . [audible sound of bat meeting ball] There's a long drive . . . it's gonna be, I believe . . . THE GIANTS WIN THE PENNANT! THE GIANTS WIN THE PENNANT! THE GIANTS WIN THE PENNANT! THE GIANTS WIN THE PENNANT! Bobby Thomson hits into the lower deck of the left-field stands! The Giants win the pennant, and they're goin' crazy, they're goin' crazy! HEEEY-OH!!! [ten-second pause for crowd noise] I don't believe it! I don't believe it! I do not believe it! Bobby Thomson . . . hit a line drive . . . into the lower deck . . . of the left-field stands . . . and this blame place is goin' crazy! The Giants! Horace Stoneham has got a winner! The Giants won it . . . by a score of 5 to 4 . . . and they're pickin' Bobby Thomson up . . . and carryin' him off the field![24]

Andy and Bobby knew it was gone the moment the ball left the bat. As Thompson loped around the bases, Pafko slumped against the wall. That single stroke of the bat bound Pafko, Thompson, and Branca together in America's collective memory.

Few people realize that two years later, Thompson was traded to the Braves, and he and Pafko played side by side in the outfield until Thompson went to the Cubs in 1957. Nor did people know at the time that the fix was in. The Giants' late-season turnaround was no accident. Starting July 20, they installed a telescope in the centerfield clubhouse to steal the catcher's signals. They rigged a wire to transmit the signal to the leftfield bullpen, where teammates signaled the pitch that was coming to the batter. In a 2001 *Wall Street Journal* article, several players admitted that the Giants stole the sign from Rube Walker (10), who was playing for the injured Roy Campanella (39). Though he always denied it, Bobby Thompson undoubtedly knew a fastball was coming.[25]

I have never forgotten that series and often think of Andy Pafko. A few years ago, for reasons I do not understand, I decided I wanted a baseball autographed by Andy. Searching the Internet, I found a sports memorabilia company that had one, and I bought it. Who knows whether it's real or fake,

or if he actually signed it? I don't really care—the counterfeit is as good as the original, if you believe in it. I have a baseball from my high school playing days, still covered with traces of infield dirt, on my desk in my study. Dirt, yes, once again dirt—I collect dirt. A dirty baseball—a memento, a relic of a past that lies buried beneath layers and layers of mental debris I will never clear away. What would the story of my life look like if it were read through that baseball?

## Part 4

So much ends and begins in the desert. A place of wandering and exile, of temptation and tribulation, of loss and sometimes recovery. If you know what you're looking for when you go to the desert, you'll never find it, and if you find it, you will never know what it is. The desert takes time, always *takes* time—lots of time. If you are patient enough to linger, eventually you will be exposed to elements you cannot control that are critical for life. In DeLillo's artful hands, the desert becomes more than a place—it is a character, perhaps the leading character, in *Underworld*.

When we first meet Nick in the summer of 1992, he is safely sealed in a robotically manufactured Lexus driving across the desert to find Klara Sax, an older woman with whom he had an affair when he was only a teenager. Nick had a rough childhood—his father, who was a small-time bookie, disappeared when he and Matt were kids, and Nick spent far too much time trying to convince himself that his father had been abducted and had not abandoned his family. Without a father and left to roam Bronx streets alone, Nick got involved with the wrong crowd and wound up unintentionally shooting a guy in a cellar where junkies hung out. He was sentenced to prison and did time but after a few years was reassigned to a rehab program run by the Jesuits in the hinterlands of northern Minnesota. He eventually got his life on track and by 1992 is approaching the end of a respectable career as a senior manager for the Waste Containment Corporation. He works in "a great bronze tower," which his colleague Brian insists "resembles a geometric turd"; wears crisp white shirts; has a wife, Marian, and an aimless son, daughter, and granddaughter. They live in a neat and tidy neighborhood in Phoenix, where people keep their hair and grass closely clipped; everyone "separates [their] household waste according to the guidelines" and recycles religiously. Nick watches his weight, eats healthy foods, and regularly runs along the drainage ditches that separate city from desert (163, 803). By any reasonable measure, his life has turned out much better than might have been expected.

By the end of the book, however, it is clear that Nick regards his success as failure. Plans and purposes that once seemed clear become obscure, and, in the fog of sleepless nights, he muses,

> At Waste Containment I've become a sort of executive emeritus. I go to the office now and then but mostly travel and speak. I visit colleges and research facilities, where I'm introduced as a waste analyst. I talk to them about the vacated military bases being converted to landfill use, about the bunker system under a mountain in Nevada that will or will not accommodate the thousands of steel canisters of radioactive waste for ten thousand years. Then we eat lunch. The waste may or may not explode, seventy thousand tons of spent fuel, and I fly to London and Zurich to attend conferences in the rain and sleet.
>
> I rearrange books on the old shelves and match and mix for the new shelves and then I stand there looking. I stand in the living room and

look. Or I walk through the house and look at the things we own and feel the old mortality that clings to every object. The finer and rarer the object, the more lonely it makes me feel, and I don't know how to account for this.

(804)

Things have value by virtue of the life lived through them, and when that life is over they become mere objects waiting to be carted off to the dump. This dreary prospect is what surrounds our most precious objects with an aura of melancholy—like a baseball from a game that once seemed so important.

With time running out, Nick grows restless. The more secure his life becomes, the more he wants something else, something more, something different, something other—something he senses but cannot name. "Most of our longings," either Nick or DeLillo says (it no longer is clear who is speaking), "go unfulfilled. This is the word's wistful implications—a desire for something lost or fled or otherwise out of reach" (803). It is not until the final night before Matt arrives for the funeral of their mother that Nick thinks he knows what he wants. "I'll tell you what I long for, the days of disarray, when I didn't give a damn or a fuck or a farthing" (806). In the end, Nick longs for nothing as much as the very disorder he had spent his entire life trying to contain, control, and manage—not stability but instability, not security and securities but insecurity and insecurities, not system but excess.

Perhaps carefree disarray or the memory of it is what draws Nick into the desert in search of Klara. His decision to seek out Klara is uncharacteristically impulsive. When a business trip ends earlier than expected, he rearranges his plans.

Let's just say the desert is an impulse. I decided in a flash to switch planes and get a car and hit the back roads. There is something about old times that's satisfied by spontaneity. The quicker you decide, the more fully you discharge the debt of memory. I wanted to see her again and feel something and say something, a few words, not too many, and then to head back into the windy distance. It was all distance. (63–64)

Nick and Klara first met when he was seventeen and she was thirty. He had a summer job driving a truck delivering soda, and she was the desperate housewife of a high school teacher who was Nick's brother's chess tutor. Klara seduces Nick, and their relationship lasts the entire summer. In the intervening years, she has become a well-known artist, but Nick had never seen her again and, though he had read about her from time to time, he had not followed her career. Nick knew Klara was working on a big project somewhere in the desert but had no idea exactly where it was. He just begins driving in the direction of Phoenix and hopes for the best, when out of nowhere he meets a New York taxi that looked like "a pop-art object" (65). He asks the driver if she has ever heard of Klara Sax and is startled to discover that she is, incongruously, a member of the volunteer army of art students assisting Klara with her work. Klara and her team have taken over a military base reminiscent of Slab City, but without the Salton Sea nearby. The day Nick arrives unannounced is Klara's seventieth birthday, and she is being interviewed by a French film crew making a documentary about her art. Klara explains to the interviewer that she and her assistants are reconditioning and repainting more than 230 decommissioned military aircraft, many of which were designed to transport and drop nuclear bombs. As the conversation nears completion, Klara underscores the continuity of her work from her early paintings to this massive undertaking in the desert. With words that sound like Michael Heizer trying to explain his desert *City* to one of his critics, she explains,

"This is an art project, not a peace project. This is a landscape painting in which we use the landscape itself. The desert is central to this piece. It's the surround. It's the framing device. It's the four-part horizon. This is why we insisted to the Air Force—a cleared area around the finished work." . . .

"But the beauty of the desert."

"It's so old and strong. I think it makes us feel, makes us as a culture, any technological culture, we feel we mustn't be overwhelmed by it. Awe and terror, you know. Unconducive"—and she waved a hand and laughed—"to industry and progress and so forth. So we use this place to test our weapons. It's only logical of course. And it enables us to show our mastery. The desert bears the visible signs of all the detonations we set off. All the craters and warning signs and no-go areas and burial markers, the sites where debris is buried."

The interviewer asked a series of questions about young conceptual artists working with biological and nuclear waste and then called for a short break.                                                              (70–71)

During the pause, Nick asks Klara's handlers if she might have time to meet. Though their lives could not have taken more different courses, they have both ended up in the same business—waste management. While Nick oversees systems that control the ever-increasing flow of waste that contemporary society produces, Klara recycles the accumulating debris of the military-industrial complex. When asked about other artists, Klara acknowledges that the closest analogy to her project is Simon Rodina's Watts Towers in Los Angeles. From 1921 to 1954, Rodina, who was an Italian immigrant construction worker, created an astonishing complex from trash he and others gathered in the surrounding neighborhood. When Klara first encountered the towers, DeLillo reports, "she didn't know what this was exactly. It was an amusement park, a temple complex and she didn't know what else. A Delhi bazaar and Italian street feast maybe. A place riddled with epiphanies, that's what it was" (492). The budget cuts in California now threaten Watts Towers. Legislators and local officials think supporting the arts in a time of austerity brought on by financial excess is a waste of money.

"A place riddled with epiphanies"—this is also an apt description of Klara's art as well as the desert where she works. She insists "this is an art project, not a peace project" because she understands that the world has become a more dangerous place since the end of the Cold War. The bombs these planes carried had been a mutual deterrent, and the policy of containment had worked. But the price of survival had been the creation of something the human imagination could not comprehend, much less control.

I've seen them in every kind of light and I've thought hard about the weapons they carried and the men who accompanied the weapons and it is awful to think about. But the bombs were not released. You see. The missiles remained in the underwing carriages, unfired. The men came back and the targets were not destroyed. You see. We all tried to think about war but I'm not sure we knew how to do this. The poets wrote long poems with dirty words and that's about as close as we came, actually, to a thoughtful response. Because they had brought something into the world that out-imagined the mind. They didn't even know what to call the early bomb. The thing or gadget or something. And Oppenheimer said, It is merde. I will use the French. J. Robert Oppenheimer. It is merde. He meant something that eludes naming is automatically relegated, he is saying, to the status of shit. You can't name it. It's too big or evil or outside your experience. It's also shit because it's garbage, it's waste material. But I'm making a whole big megillah out of this.                                    (76–77)

The name of the unnamable, DeLillo suggests, is *merde*—shit. "Holy Shit!"

Matt, who was studying chess with Albert Bronzi while his teacher's wife was fucking his brother, understands the implications of this desert vision. He is a systems analyst developing weapons systems in a research facility named the Pocket, which is modeled on the site in Los Alamos where Oppenheimer led the team that created the first atomic bomb. Latter-day shamans attempting to tap forces they could not control, Matt and his colleagues were playing with fire—not the fire of smoking psychedelic mushrooms but the fire of a much more ominous mushroom that appeared as a cloud of smoke. The more successful his team was, the more Matt doubted the entire enterprise. When he tries to explain his misgivings, his fiancée, Janet, responds, "You make it sound like God. Or some starker variation thereof. Go to the desert or tundra and wait for the visionary flash of light, the critical mass that will call down the Hindu heavens, Kali and Shiva and all the grimacing lesser gods" (458). Janet's words echo Oppenheimer's reaction to the first detonation of his invention at 5:30 AM on July 15, 1945, "now I have become death, the destroyer of the world." Confronted with such awful power, the only language that seems appropriate is religious; the line Oppenheimer quotes is drawn from the *Bhagavad-Gita*.

> If the radiance of a thousand suns
> Were to burst at once into the sky
> That would be like the splendor of the Mighty one . . .
> I become Death,
> The destroyer of Worlds.

Waste . . . garbage . . . shit . . . bomb . . . art . . . religion . . . capital . . . a thousand suns. What thread could possibly tie all of this together?

## Part 5

We know *how* the story ends but not *when* it will end. The Omega Point will be reached when the sun consumes itself. In *Point Omega*, DeLillo explains why Elster retreated to the desert. "The sun was burning down. This is what he wanted, to feel the deep heat beating into his body, feel the body itself, reclaim the body from what he called the nausea of News and Traffic. This was the desert, out beyond cities and scattered towns. He was here to eat, sleep and sweat, here to do nothing, sit and think."[26] The sun is burning down, always burning down until it burns itself out. In his richly suggestive book *The Accursed Share* (*La part maudite*), Georges Bataille argues that this irreversible process involves an alternative economy that he labels "the solar economy."

> I will speak briefly about the most general conditions of life, dwelling on one crucially important fact: Solar energy is the source of life's exuberant development. The origin and essence of our wealth are given in the radiation of the sun, which dispenses energy—wealth—without any return. The sun gives without ever receiving. Men were conscious of this long before astrophysics measured that ceaseless prodigality; they saw it ripen the harvests and they associated its splendor with the act of someone who

gives without receiving. . . . In former times value was given to unproduc-
tive glory, whereas in our day it is measured in terms of production: Pre-
cedence is given to energy acquisition over energy expenditure.[27]

The notion of the solar economy appears to stand in marked tension
with the foundational principles of traditional economic theory. The focus
of all previous economic theories, Bataille maintains, has been too limited,
and thus it is necessary to expand the analysis by placing human activity
in a broader context. Toward this end, he draws a distinction between the
restricted economy, which is characteristic of modern industrial, consumer,
and financial capitalism, and the general economy, which "is concerned with
the movement of energy on the earth—from geophysics to political economy,
by way of sociology, history and biology" (AS, 10). The restricted economy is
a closed system whose primary purpose is production and exchange. By carefully regulating flows of energy, material, labor, and capital, managers seek to
maximize profits and minimize losses. The restricted economy is thoroughly
utilitarian—it is a system of reciprocal exchange in which every investment is
calculated to yield a reasonable return. Within this scheme, reason is nothing
other than this principle of calculated return. When investors are "rational,"
the system works efficiently and tends toward equilibrium.

The general economy, by contrast, implies a very different understanding
of humankind's place in the cosmos. Bataille argues that to understand the
general economy

> requires thinking on a level with a play of forces that runs counter to ordi-
> nary calculations, a play of forces based on the laws that govern us. In
> short, the perspectives where such truths appear are those in which more
> general propositions reveal their meaning, propositions according to
> which *it is not necessity but its contrary, "luxury," that presents living matter
> and mankind with their fundamental problems.* (AS, 12)

This way of thinking, Bataille insists, requires nothing less than a "Coperni-
can revolution."

If the general economy is a system, it is open and not closed; rather than scarcity, the general economy presupposes superabundance.

> Human life cannot in any way be limited to the closed systems assigned to it by reasonable conceptions. The immense travail of recklessness, discharge and upheaval that constitutes life could be expressed by stating that life starts only with the deficit of these systems; at least what it allows in the way of order and reserve has meaning only from the moment when the ordered and reserved forces liberate and lose themselves for ends that cannot be subordinated to anything one can account for.[28]

Excessive consumption creates waste that is, contrary to conventional wisdom, a sign of life's infinite exuberance. In contrast to prudent investment strategies that inform agents in the restricted economy, the distinguishing feature of the general economy is expenditure without expectation of return. This is not a system of reciprocal exchange that tends toward equilibrium; to the contrary, nonreciprocal expenditure gives so freely that things drift toward disequilibrium. Utility yields to prodigality that appears completely irrational. Those who play by the rules of this game court the very risk and danger that reasonable people spend their lives trying to avoid.

In developing the distinction between the restricted and general economy, Bataille draws on Kant's account of the purposelessness or uselessness of art, Nietzsche's contrast between the Apollonian and Dionysian principles, Durkheim's discussion of the creative effervescence released in religious rituals, and Mauss's study of gift giving. The idea that integrates these disparate lines of analysis is the notion of waste, which is "an ostentatious squandering" of wealth (AS, 73). In its pure form, wasteful expenditure is useless and reaps no profit, nor does it release tension and thereby reestablish order, balance, or equilibrium. Pure expenditure is without rhyme or reason—it is completely gratuitous.

> The living organism, in a situation determined by the play of energy on the surface of the globe, ordinarily receives more energy than is necessary

for maintaining life; the excess energy (wealth) can be used for the growth of the system (e.g., an organism); if the system can no longer grow, or if the excess cannot completely absorbed its growth, it must necessarily be lost without profit; it must be spent, willingly or not, gloriously or catastrophically.

Every system or organizing structure inevitably produces an excess or surplus it cannot use. This is the "accursed share" that "finally can only be wasted" (AS 21, 11). As these comments suggest, the relationship between the restricted and general economy is even more complex than Bataille realizes. Instead of clearly defined opposites, these contrasting economies are folded into each other in such a way that each is the condition of the possibility and impossibility of the other. The restricted economy inevitably becomes excessive and produces waste that fuels the general economy. While the general economy temporarily defers systemic collapse by processing waste, at Point Omega, the two economies implode.

In ways that are not immediately obvious, the restricted and general economies issue in contrasting expressions of the religious imagination. Elsewhere, I have defined religion as "an emergent, complex, adaptive network of symbols, myths, and rituals that, on the one hand, figure schemata of feeling, thinking and acting in ways that lend life meaning and purpose and, on the other, disrupt, dislocate and disfigure every stabilizing structure."[29] When religion provides stabilizing structures, it functions as a restricted economy, and when it disturbs stabilizing structures, it functions as the general economy. Though Bataille never denies that religion often stabilizes individuals, societies, and cultures, he is much more interested in the ways in which religious beliefs and practices elude regulation and upset management systems. He offers a broad range of examples of wasteful expenditure that tend to become excessive or even run out of control: rituals and festivals (e.g., potlatch, animal and human sacrifice), flamboyant display (fashion and jewelry), play, games of chance, eroticism, violence, war, and, most important, art and religion. The function of the restricted economy is to avoid waste by transforming expenditure into profitable production:

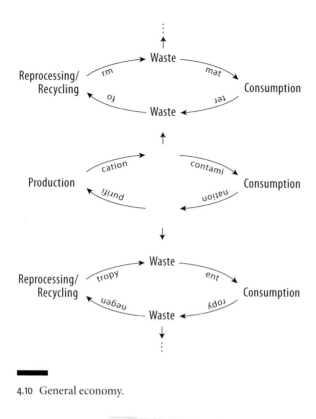

4.10 General economy.

a worthless baseball is bought, sold, and resold; art is commodified and financialized; war enriches private investors; and believers cut deals with their gods in which devotion is rewarded with redemption.

But not all religion involves profitable exchange, and not all art can be so easily commodified.[30] Consider, for example, Redemption Mountain at the edge of Slab City; Klara Sax's 230 painted airplanes in the middle of the desert; Michael Heizer's *City*, sunk in a pit surrounded by sculptures resembling Mayan or Aztec sacrificial pyramids with their tips knocked off; expensive land art in the Berkshires that no one ever sees; or an 827-page book. Bataille might well have been describing the uselessness of these works when he writes:

a society can also be led to consume all its products. Hence it must somehow destroy the surplus resources it has at its disposal. Idleness is the simplest means for this purpose. The man of leisure destroys the products necessary for subsistence no less fully than does fire. But the worker who labors at the construction of a pyramid destroys those products just as uselessly: From the standpoint of profit the pyramid is a monumental mistake; one might just as well dig an enormous hole, then refill it and pack the ground. (AS, 119)

From any reasonable point of view, digging a hole in the middle of the desert that no one is ever likely to see or writing a hundred-page essay or an eight-hundred-page book that few people will ever read is a waste of time, money, and even a life—unless waste is what art, religion, and perhaps even life are all about.

Not all waste can be recycled, and what cannot be assimilated, mastered, or managed assumes the aura of the sacred. Bataille develops his theory of religion by recasting Nietzsche's distinction between the Dionysian and the Apollonian as the difference between the sacred and the profane. Returning to the contrast between the nonutilitarian and the utilitarian that Kant formulated to distinguish high from low art, respectively, Bataille defines the sacred as nonutilitarian, excessive, extravagant, and ostentatious; the profane, by contrast, is utilitarian, instrumental, and prudent. The distinguishing feature of the profane is discontinuity, which, Bataille argues, is coterminous with the distinction separating subjects and objects. "The object . . . has a meaning that breaks the undifferentiated continuity, that stands opposed to immanence or to the flow of all that is—which it transcends. It is strictly alien to the subject, to the self still immersed in immanence. It is the subject's property, the subject's thing, but is nonetheless impervious to the subject."[31] The differentiation of the subject emerges through language and is secured by reason. Reason is an Apollonian activity that "withdraws from the *continuum*" by defining differences it seeks to establish through the principle of noncontradiction. So understood, the domain of profane established by reason is insistently dualistic.

The sacred, by contrast, is "continuous being, lost in the world like water is lost in water" (TR, 29). Instead of separation and opposition, the sacred involves "*intimacy*, the immanence between man and the world, between the subject and the object" (TR, 44). The purpose of religion, especially its rituals, is to recover lost unity.

> Man is the being that has lost, and even rejected, that which he obscurely is, a vague intimacy. Consciousness could not have become clear in the course of time if it had not turned away from its awkward contents, but clear consciousness is itself looking for what it has itself lost, and what it must lose again as it draws near to it. Of course what it has lost is not outside it; consciousness turns away from the obscure intimacy of consciousness itself. Religion, whose essence is the search for lost intimacy, comes down to the effort of clear consciousness which wants to be a complete self-consciousness: but this effort is futile, since consciousness of intimacy is possible only at a level where consciousness is no longer an operation whose outcome implies duration, that is, at a level where clarity, which is the effect of the operation, is any longer given. (TR, 57)

In contrast to religious traditions in which God is transcendent or even an alien other, Bataille regards the sacred as "the immanence or the flow of all that is" (TR, 29). While the profane world is defined by clear and precise categories, the sacred contaminates everything deemed proper by dissolving boundaries designed to contain it. In a manner reminiscent of Dionysus and his follower Pan, the sacred is fraught with ambiguity and provokes ambivalence that prompts panic. "What is sacred attracts and possesses an incomparable value, but at the same time it appears dangerous for that clear and profane world where mankind situates its privileged domain" (TR, 36). The danger of the sacred is the possibility that its "immanent immensity, where there are neither separations nor limits," will dissolve all distinctions and thereby overwhelm individuals and shatter regulatory systems (TR, 42).

Having appropriated Nietzsche's account of tragedy to develop a theory of religion, Bataille proceeds to use his understanding of religion to interpret art. By soliciting the return of the repressed underside of orthodox modernism, he elaborates an interpretation of art that illuminates DeLillo's *Underworld*. One of the central categories in this critical reassessment of art is *informe*, which usually is mistranslated "formless." In his brief entry for the "critical dictionary," originally published in *Documents*, Bataille attempts to define the undefinable *informe*.

A dictionary begins when it no longer gives the meaning of words, but their tasks. Thus *informe* is not only an adjective having a given meaning, but a term that serves to bring things down in the world, generally requiring that each thing have its form. What it designates has no rights in any sense and gets itself squashed everywhere, like a spider or an earthworm. In fact, for academic men to be happy, the universe would have to take shape. All of philosophy has no other goal: it is a matter of giving a frock coat to what is, a mathematical frock coat. On the other hand, affirming that the universe resembles nothing and is only *informe* amounts to saying that the universe is something like a spider or spit. (VE, 31)

In contrast to pure forms and stable structures, in-form(e)s are impure waste, shit, piss, spit, sperm, blood, garbage, trash, refuse. Bataille designates such stuff "matter" and describes his philosophical position as "base materialism." It is impossible to locate this matter and the materialism it entails on the grid of traditional philosophy. "Matter," Bataille explains, "can only be defined as the *non-logical difference* that represents in relation to the *economy* of the universe what *crime* represents in relation to the law" (VE, 129). Matter is nonlogical because it eludes the principle of noncontradiction that traditionally defines logic. Not just any matter, *informe* is the prime matter from which everything emerges and to which it eventually returns. When waste is understood as *informe*, it appears to be "a religious thing—or nothing." DeLillo warns us that the temples of waste have been expanding at an unsustainable rate for more than half a century.

Part 6

Since the end of the Cold War, shit has been piling faster and faster until it now seems that our own excesses rather than communism will bury us. This insight helps to explain why DeLillo titled the epilogue *Das Kapital*. In her informative book *Gone Tomorrow: The Hidden Life of Garbage*, Heather Rogers notes,

> In the nineteenth century, Karl Marx had already warned that new super-efficient industrialized manufacturing could easily out-pace consumption: "The production of . . . surplus value based on the increase and development of the productive forces, requires the production of new consumption." Back in postwar America, the chief of the J. Walter Thompson advertising agency understood this same threat: "We must cut down the time lag in expanding consumption to absorb this production."[32]

*[handwritten margin note: The dual nature of capitalism + the problem + the specter.]*

Capitalism cannot survive without steady growth, and, therefore, markets must expand constantly. During World War II, the nation's industrial capacity was deployed to support the war effort. This resulted in a dearth of consumer goods, which, in turn, led to pent-up demand. The end of the war ushered in what Vance Packard aptly labeled the "era of prodigality," which created pressure for sustained growth. During the decade immediately after the war, domestic demand kept pace with the renewed production of consumer goods, but by the late 1950s, demand declined, and other outlets had to be developed.

Markets can expand both spatially and temporally. With the engines of production running at full speed and American consumers consuming less, American businesses sought new markets for their goods in other countries. The United States' ambitious plan to rebuild Europe was in large measure motivated by economic interests. But spatial expansion has unavoidable limits, and when they are reached, it is necessary to develop new strategies to keep the system running. In the postwar years, spatial expansion gave way to temporal acceleration—product cycles were introduced to entice consumers to buy what they did not really need. For example, in 1958, Detroit started introducing new models every year. Packard points out,

> American motorists by 1960 were trading in their "old" car by the time it reached an average age of two and a quarter years. The Ford Motor Company in one of its advertisements said this showed how smart and shrewd the average motorcar owner was becoming. At that age, it pointed out, the car starts showing minor ailments and dents. Further, it stated, "the car is two years old in style. Its fine edge is gone."[33]

In this system, the mission of the burgeoning advertising industry was to create desire where there is no need. Tapping every available resource, Madison Avenue enlisted the services of artists like Salvador Dali, Andy Warhol, Robert Rauschenberg, James Rosenquist, and others to peddle the consumer goods flooding the market. Products dissolved into fashionable images that were artfully marketed with greater and greater speed.

The strategy worked. During the 1950s, Americans consumed more than twice as much as they did before the war, and by the 1960s the U.S. was outproducing the S.U. in consumer durable goods by twenty to one. As DeLillo makes clear in his account of the famous Kitchen Cabinet debate, which took place between Vice President Richard Nixon and Soviet Premier Nikita Khrushchev at the opening of the American Exhibition in Moscow on July 24, 1959, the war had shifted from the battleground to the market. While most Americans thought Nixon got the better of Khrushchev, what DeLillo labels "the dark underside of consumerism" was growing. In the mid-fifties, the marketing consultant Victor Lebow wrote in *The Journal of Retailing*, "Our enormously productive economy . . . demands that we make consumption our way of life, that we convert the buying and use of goods into rituals, that we seek our spiritual satisfactions, our ego satisfactions in consumption. . . . We need things consumed, burned up, worn out, replaced, and discarded at an ever increasing rate."[34] In this latter-day potlatch, art and commerce intersect in the obsession with the new. The strategy of planned obsolescence is, in effect, the commercial implementation of the avant-garde challenge, "Make it New!" When consumption becomes a way of life that is deemed spiritual, "the throwaway society" is born. The more the churn, the more the profit, the more the profit, the more the waste, and, thus, the more the waste, the more the profit. This is the world DeLillo describes in his account of a desert conference on "The Future of Waste," run by Whiz Co., the "firm with an inside track to the future." Jesse Detweiler, whom Sims declares to be "the visionary in our midst, the waste theorist whose provocations had spooked the industry," proudly reports, "I take my students into garbage dumps and make them understand the civilization they live in. Consume or die. That's the mandate of the culture. And it all ends up in the dump. We make stupendous amounts of garbage, then we react to it, not only technologically but in our hearts and minds. We let it shape us. We let it control our thinking" (288).

But not all waste was material. As more and more people bought into the religion of consumerism, debt exploded. Having forgotten the lessons their parents learned during the Great Depression, people went on a borrowing spree. Though not the most obvious excess of the 1950s and 1960s, reckless borrowing and spending have proven to be the most pernicious. Delayed gratification became a thing of the past, and if people didn't have the money to buy what they wanted, they just borrowed. Businesses were more than willing to facilitate this pact with the devil by introducing installment plans and, most fatefully, introducing the plastic credit card in 1959. During the 1950s, consumer debt rose three times faster than income. A *Business Week* report issued at the time summarized all relevant financial forces in five simple words: "Borrow. Spend. Buy. Waste. Want."[35] As always, the very success of capitalism proved to be its own undoing. It was not long before the captains of industry figured out that buying and selling debt and dealing in complex financial instruments were more profitable than producing and marketing consumer goods. With this development, financial capitalism displaced consumer capitalism as the primary engine of the American economy.[36] It took half a century for the excesses of this new form of capitalism to bring the global economy to the brink of collapse.

By the end of *Underworld*, the tape has been rewound, and we are back at the beginning—1992. The Berlin Wall has fallen, communism has failed, Wall Street is soaring, and capitalism reigns triumphant, or so it seems. "Everything's connected," and network culture is emerging at warp speed. DeLillo begins *Das Kapital* by describing this new world of "foreign investment, global markets, corporate acquisitions, the flow of information through transnational media" (785). Money is no longer as good as gold or even as good as paper; it has dematerialized and "is becoming very esoteric. All waves and codes. A higher kind of intelligence. Travels at the speed of light" (386). As Marx had predicted in *The Communist Manifesto*, "all that is solid melts into air," or, in a more contemporary idiom, evaporates in the ether of worldwide webs.

*Underworld* ends with a burial and a death—the burial of nuclear waste in the hinterlands of Kazakhstan and a death in the wastelands of the Bronx, where Nick and Matt had grown up. During the 1990s, the sheer power of raw capitalism was nowhere more evident than in the former Soviet Union. Russian oligarchs and entrepreneurs maneuvered to take over as many previously state-owned industries as possible. With competition in the waste management business reaching a fever pitch, Nick and Brian travel to the Kazakh Test Site with the Russian Viktor Maltsev to join geologists, game theorists, energy experts, journalists, waste traders, venture capitalists, arms dealers, and uranium speculators. The purpose of the trip is to observe a demonstration of a new method for disposing of the most dangerous radioactive waste. Hurtling though the darkness in a rickety Soviet cargo plane, Nick and Victor reflect on their mission.

I tell Viktor there is a curious connection between weapons and waste. I don't know exactly what. . . . He says maybe one is the mystical twin of the other. He likes this idea. He says waste is the devil twin. Because waste is the secret history, the underhistory, the way archaeologists dig out the history of early cultures, every sort of bone heap and broken tool, literally from under the ground.

All those decades, he says, when we thought about weapons all the time and never thought about the dark multiplying byproduct.

"And in this case," I say. "In our case, in our age. What we excrete comes back to consume us."

We don't dig it up, he says. We try to bury it. But maybe this is not enough. That's why we have this idea. Kill the devil. And he smiles from his steeple perch. The fusion of two streams of history, weapons and waste.

We destroy contaminated waste by means of nuclear explosions.    (791)

A novel solution: nuclear explosions to deal with waste from nuclear explosions. The cycle is endless. At the Point Omega in the underground recesses of a distant desert, creation and destruction become one. In this instant, the sacred and the profane meet in the dark light of Shiva and Kali's shadows.

On the opposite side of the world, in the abandoned neighborhood where Nick's story began, another burial is taking place along a different wall. "Her name is Esmeralda. She lives wild in the inner ghetto, a slice of the South Bronx called the Wall—a girl who forages in empty lots for discarded clothes, plucks spoiled fruit from garbage bags behind bodegas" (810). The nuns who had taught Nick and Matt in elementary school, Sisters Grace and Edgar, serve the outcasts living in slums and underground tunnels by bringing them food, clothing, and medical supplies. But their efforts prove futile; decay spreads like a fatal virus, and violent crime is an everyday occurrence. The only ray of hope in this otherwise bleak underworld is provided by Ishmael Munzo, a graffiti artist who suffers from AIDS but still manages to help others. Like Klara Sax and Don DeLillo, Ishmael is a latter-day alchemist who transforms waste, garbage, and even shit into valuable works of art. He enthusiastically subscribes to Andy Warhol's credo, "Being good in business is the most fascinating kind of art."[37] Ishmael explains his strategy to the skeptical nuns, "I'm planning to go on-line real soon, Sisters. Advertise my junk cars. Go, like, global. Scrap metal for these trodden countries looking to build a military. . . . Some people have a personal god, ok. I'm looking to get a personal computer. What's the difference, right?" (813). For Sisters Grace and Edgar, there obviously is a big difference between the personal god and the personal computer, but they fail to convince Ishmael. Like Nick's son, Jeff, Ishmael believes "the real miracle is the web, the net, where everybody is everywhere at once" (808). Omnipresent, omniscience, omnipotent—what more might God be? In light of the foregoing discussion of *House of Leaves*, the association between the name Ishmael and Melville's *Moby-Dick* is particularly suggestive. Both Danielewski's haunted house and DeLillo's uncanny underworld are latter-day versions of Melville's whale, which today surfaces in labyrinthine worldwide webs we can never fully fathom.

Though Ishmael's god is different, he shares many of the sisters' values. No devotee of the modernist doctrine of art for art's sake, he uses the money he makes from his junk business and art to support homeless and parentless children in the neighborhood. When Esmeralda is brutally raped and murdered, Ishmael adds her image to the "Wall of Angels" he has created to memorialize forgotten children. As word of the child's death cycles and recycles through the 24/7 news cycle, Sister Edgar's faith turns into doubt. But just when despair threatens to consume her, a miracle occurs. Rumors of an astonishing sign start circulating—the image of Esmeralda, people report, is appearing on a nearby billboard advertising Minute Maid orange juice. Grace is skeptical, but Edgar is intrigued and insists they go to see for themselves. By the time they arrive, a crowd of more than a thousand has gathered. As everyone waits patiently for the image to appear, Grace declares that the whole thing is a scam perpetrated by the media. Edgar disagrees, and when a passing train illuminates the sign, she is convinced she sees Esmeralda's image. Throwing caution to the wind, Edgar rips off the latex gloves she has always used to protect her from germs and embraces the sickly Ishmael. Having seen God in the face of a child, her life is complete; "there is nothing left to do but die and this is precisely what she did, Sister Alma Edgar, bride of Christ, passing peacefully in her sleep" (824).

It is far from clear how this enigmatic sign and the events surrounding it are to be read. Is this a genuine religious vision or a cynical parody of such experiences? It is not insignificant that the revelation occurs in an *advertising* sign. This might, after all, be the mark of the profane rather than the sacred—the specter of the new religion of capitalism replacing the tried and true old-time religion? DeLillo scatters suggestive clues about this sign throughout the novel. This is not the first time Minute Maid orange juice appears. While waiting for Janet in the Tucson airport before beginning their trip into the desert, Matt "was thinking about his paranoid episode at the bombhead party the night before. He felt he'd glimpsed some horrific system of connections in which you can't tell the difference between one thing and another, between a soup can and a car bomb because they are made by the same people in the same way and ultimately refer to the same thing" (446). If everything is, in fact, connected, the question becomes exactly how the dots are joined. During his tour in Viet Nam, Matt's job had been literally to connect the dots—he studied aerial photographs to identify bombing targets for military pilots. Though he had enlisted because he wanted to serve his country, Matt, like so many others, had become disillusioned with the war.

> There were rumors about whole other wars, just to the east, or was it the west?
>
> The drums resembled cans of frozen Minute Maid enlarged by a crazed strain of DNA. And the substance the drums contained, so the rumor went, a cancer-causing agent.
>
> He heard the rumors and the mortars and felt the monsoon heat and heard the universal slogan of the war.
>
> Stay stoned, man. (463)

The cancer-causing agent was, of course, Agent Orange.

> And how can you tell the difference between orange juice and agent orange if the same massive system connects them at levels outside your comprehension?
>
> And how can you tell if this is true when you're already systemed under, prepared to half believe everything because this is the only intelligent response?
>
> People hid in dark places, where mushrooms grow, sprouting quickly.

The dots he marked with his grease pencil became computer bits in Da Nang, Sunday brunch in Saigon and mission briefings in Thailand, he guessed, or Guam.

When you alter a single minor component, the system adapts at once.

(465)

As connections spread, the signs of the times proliferate, and many apocalyptic visions are reported by different tricksters and shamans. Bomb and waste. Bomb and God. God and Waste. Everything's connected.

Sister Edgar was right, there *is* life after death, but is it not where she thought it would be. She dies and is reborn not in heaven but in cyberspace. It seems the Singularity arrived before Kurzweil and his followers realized.[38] While aimlessly surfing the Web, Jeff stumbles on a site devoted to miracles ("http:blk.www/dd.com/miraculum"), where he learns about the reported visions of Esmeralda. With a single keystroke, he unexpectedly meets his father's former teacher, Sister Edgar, who with a click "joins the other Edgar. A fellow celibate and more or less kindred spirit but her biological opposite, her male half, dead these many years" (826). DeLillo describes this new domain where humankind seems to be migrating.

> There is no space or time out here, or in here, or wherever she is. There are only connections. Everything is connected. All human knowledge is gathered and linked, hyperlinked, this site leading to that, this fact referenced to that, a keystroke, a mouse-click, a password—world without end, amen.
>
> But she is in cyberspace, not heaven, and she feels the grip of systems. This is why she's so uneasy. There is a presence here, a thing implied, something vast and bright. She senses the paranoia of the web, the net. There's the perennial threat of virus of course. Sister knows all about contaminations and the protective measures they require. This is different— it's a glow, a lustrous rushing force that seems to flow from a billion distant nodes.
>
> (825)

Liberated from the constraints imposed by bodily existence in the material world, Sister Edgar is free to surf her way through the infinity of the cloud. On a whim no more reasonable than the impulse that drew Nick into the desert, she decides to visit the H-bomb homepage, where she believes she has a vision within a vision.

> She sees the shock wave and hears the high winds and feels the power of false faith, the faith of paranoia, and then the mushroom cloud spreads around her, the pulverized mass of radioactive debris, eight miles high, ten miles, twenty miles, with skirted stem and smoking platinum cap.
>
> The jewels roll out of her eyes and she sees God.
>
> No, wait, sorry. It is a Soviet bomb she sees, the largest yield in history, a device exploded above the Artic Ocean in 1961, preserved in a computer that helped to build it, fifty-eight megatons—add the digits and you get thirteen. (825–826)

God, it seems, wears the mask of Shiva or Kali rather than of Jesus Christ. DeLillo does not, however, conclude his massive narrative on a destructive note—his last word is "Peace." When asked in a 1999 interview, "Is the end is about redemption?" he replies, "I think so to some degree."

> What happens between Sister Edgar and J. Edgar Hoover is an illustration of the final word in the novel. There is a reference to the different derivations of the word "Peace." I think in English, if you trace the word back in time, you find that it means a fitting together, a binding together. And that's what I had in mind with Sister Edgar and J. Edgar. They illustrate, I suppose, the idea of peace on a strictly human level. And the idea of that in a novel that's completely devoted to conflict between nations, races, men and women, the idea, a longing at least, for peace might be a way to end the book. And certainly the word "Peace" is not meant ironically, it's meant seriously. But it's all about longing, it's certainly not a realistic expectation. And that's why these two characters merge in cyberspace and become one.[39]

Novel as neχus—neχus as novel. Even though DeLillo insists he is not being ironic, his words betray him. Peace is never the last word, for, as the prophet Jeremiah proclaimed long ago, "Peace, peace, but there is no peace" (6:14). The more telling end of *Underworld* is a question posed a few lines before "Peace." "Is cyberspace a thing within the world or is it the other way around? Which contains the other, and how can you tell for sure?" (826). Is the world of counterfeits and fakes, realities more virtual than real, and consuming waste bigger on the inside than it is on the outside? This haunting question lingers long after the end of *Underworld*.

## Andy 3

*Underworld* is one of those books you intend to read but never seem to get around to it. It's *so* long and *so* weighty that there never seems to be enough time. It had been sitting on my bookshelf for several years, making me feel guilty, when one summer afternoon I picked it up and started reading. Finally opening the book, I wondered, what makes us read a book when we do? And what difference does it make when we read a book for our understanding of it? Is it merely a matter of chance? Or are there other currents silently circulating beneath the surface that draw us to a particular work at a particular time? Would we see something else if the timing were different? Do we choose the book or does the book choose us? What would it mean to be chosen by a book?

### PROLOGUE

### THE TRIUMPH OF DEATH

Death. Decay. Disaster. Pretty much what I expected from DeLillo. But, then, the unexpected. Baseball—baseball amid all the garbage. A young kid skipping school, just like I had done, to go to a baseball game, but he was alone and not with his father. A fourteen-year-old black youngster from Harlem rather than a white kid from the Jersey suburbs—Cotter Martin (How can you not hear Cotton Mather?) with no money and no ticket, crashing the gate and getting lost in the mob.

> He is part of an assembling crowd, anonymous thousands off the buses and trains, people in narrow columns tramping over the swing bridge of the river, and even if they are not a revolution, some vast shaking of the soul, they bring with them the body heat of a great city and their own small reveries and desperations, the unseen something that haunts the day—men in fedoras and sailors on shore leave, the stray tumble of their thoughts, going to a game. (11)

" . . . the unseen something that haunts the day . . . " This is the underworld that fascinates DeLillo and draws his readers into the tangled webs he spins. This is not just any game—it's the Giants and the Dodgers on October 3, 1951: "metropolis of steel and concrete and flaky paint and cropped grass and enormous Chesterfield packs aslant on the scoreboards, a couple of cigarettes jutting from each" (11). Once again cigarettes—baseball and cigarettes. The Polo Grounds—exactly like I remember.

Weaving his narrative between the lines of Russ Hodges's call of the game, DeLillo introduces not only his cast of characters but also the celebrities— J. Edgar Hoover, Frank Sinatra, Jackie Gleason (*The Honeymooners* was set to premier two days later), Toots Shor, Walter Winchel. Cotter is the kid looking for an empty seat in the lower deck of left field as the story unfolds; Andy is in the middle of the action. In the second inning, with the Giants' first-baseman Whitey Lockman (25) on first, "Thompson hits a slider on a line over third. Lockman swings into an arc as he races toward second, looking out at left field. Pafko moves to the wall and plays the carom" (16). All the while, trash and debris are falling down on Andy.

> Paper is falling again, crushed traffic tickets and field-stripped cigarettes and work from the office and scorecards in the shape of airplanes, windblown and mostly white, and Pafko walks back to his position and alters

stride to kick a soda cup lightly and the gesture functions as a form of recognition, a hint of some concordant force between players and fans, the way he nudges the white cup, it's a little onside boot, completely unbegrudging—a sign of respect for the sly contrivances of the game, the patterns that are undivinable. (37)

But are these undivinable patterns in the game and in the trash? If so, what game? What trash? Whose trash? After all, J. Edgar Hoover's lackeys went through people's trash to get dirt on them. Now DeLillo is going through Hoover's trash—real and fabricated—looking for clues to get dirt on him.

In the ninth, it was again Pafko, Thompson, and Lockman. Don Mueller singles to right, "Lockman hits the second pitch on a low line over third . . . slicing toward the line and landing fair and sending up a spew of dirt and forcing Pafko into the corner once again" (36). The stage is set for Thompson—"one out, one in, two runs down, men on second and third." Carl Erskine (17) and Branca are warming up in the bullpen, and Dodger manager Chuck Dressen (7) decides to yank Newcombe (36). Even though Branca had lost the first game and Thompson had homered off him, Dressen brings him in to shut down the Giants.

Two pitches later, the game is over, and DeLillo's story is just beginning. When the ball lands near Cotter, he scrambles to retrieve it. No sooner does he have it in his grasp than he finds himself at the bottom of a pile struggling to hold on to it. As he works himself free and races out of the stadium and back to Harlem, thousands of fans stream out of the stadium and onto the city streets.

Amid the debris that continues to fall, a single piece of paper catches Hoover's eye. It is an image of death, perhaps the apocalypse, that has, ironically, been torn from the pages of *Life*—Pieter Bruegel the Elder's *The Triumph of Death*. The painting proves prophetic—gathering rain clouds were not the only ominous sign that fall afternoon. While Hoover was sitting with his buddies Sinatra and Gleason, one of his aides comes up and quietly whispers in his ear that the Soviet Union has secretly conducted their second nuclear test. Though not totally unexpected, Hoover knows immediately

4.11 Bobby Thompson home run.

*Source:* The Sporting News 100 Years of Sports Images, Sporting News Archive, Getty Images.

that this time the game has really changed. Gazing at Bruegel's horrifying painting sets off a chain of revealing associations in Hoover's mind:

> Death elsewhere, Conflagration in many places, Terror universal, the crows, the ravens in silent glide, the raven perched on the white nag's rump, black and white forever, and he thinks of a lonely tower standing on the Kazakh Test Site, the tower with the bomb, and he can almost hear the wind blowing across the Central Asian steppes, out where the enemy lives in long coats and fur caps, speaking that old weighted language of theirs, liturgical and grave. What secret history are they writing? There is the secret of the bomb and there are the secrets the bomb inspires, even things the Director cannot guess—a man whose own sequestered heart holds every festering secret in the Western world—because these plots are

only now evolving. This is what he knows, that the genius of the bomb is printed not only in its physics of particles and rays but in the occasion it creates for new secrets. For every atmospheric blast, every glimpse we get of the bared force of nature, that weird peeled eyeball exploding over the desert—for every one of these he reckons a hundred plots go underground, to spawn and skein. (50–51)

This underground is the underworld—or one of the underworlds—DeLillo plots.

The prologue to *Underworld* was originally published in 1992 in *Harper's Magazine* and in 1997 was incorporated into the novel with only minor changes. In 2001, "The Triumph of Death" was issued yet again as a novella entitled *Pafko at the Wall: The Shot Heard Round the World.* On the cover is a picture of a diminutive Andy Pafko standing against the seventy-foot wall, beside the "315 Ft." sign with arms folded, looking up at Thompson's homer disappearing into the stands.

Between the cover and the beginning of the text, DeLillo inserts a full two-page reproduction of the October 4, 1951, *New York Times.* The lead story is about the nuclear test: "Soviet's Second Atom Blast in Two Years Revealed by the U.S.; Details Are Kept a Secret." The *Times* report sounds eerily like a commentary about contemporary Iran: "News of the atomic experiment was made public by Joseph Short, White House Press Secretary, who declared that the event belied the persistent Communist propaganda, led personally by Premier Stalin, that the atomic energy development of the Soviet Union was being devoted exclusively to peaceful purposes and not to the manufacture of weapons." The headline directly across from this article reads: "Giants Capture Pennant, Beating Dodgers 5–4 in 9th on Thompson's 3-Run Homer." Directly below the banner headline is a picture of Bobby Thompson and Leo Durocher embracing. With the Korean War raging, the articles between these two make it clear that the Cold War has become very hot: "U.N. Units Advance on a 40-Mile Front; Truce Shift Upset." The article, datelined Tokyo, begins, "A massive United Nations offensive jumped off at dawn yesterday in Central and Western Korea against an estimated quarter

4.12　Don DeLillo, cover, *Pafko at the Wall.*

*Source:* Don DeLillo, *Pafko at the Wall,* copyright 1997 by Don DeLillo. Reprinted with the permission of Scribner, a Division of Simon and Schuster, Inc.

4.13  Roosevelt Junior High School Baseball Team, 1960.

*Source:* Mark C. Taylor.

of a million Communist troops." Beside this article, under a photograph of Dr. Phillip C. Jessup, ambassador at large, appearing before the Senate Foreign Relations Committee, the headline reads, "Jessup Denies Any Red Ties, Calls McCarthy Charge False." About this, at least, Hoover was right—the game has changed forever. And we are still trying to deal with the mess—not just the political mess but the waste, radioactive and otherwise.

## EPILOGUE TO THE EPILOGUE

### Das Kapital III

This is not, of course, the end of the story, and DeLillo cannot resist adding an afterword. Since 1992, it has begun to seem as if the world actually is "a thing within cyberspace." DeLillo's subsequent novel, *Cosmopolis* (2003), can be read as an epilogue to the epilogue of *Underworld*. Echoing Marx's warning about communism in *The Communist Manifesto*, DeLillo declares,

A SPECTER IS HAUNTING THE WORLD—
THE SPECTER OF CAPITALISM[40]

In the relatively brief course of its history, capitalism has taken three forms: industrial, consumer, and financial capitalism. While each type of capitalism breeds its own excesses, financial capitalism might prove to be the most destructive of all. In his 2002 Berkshire Hathaway report, Warren Buffett famously compared derivatives to an uncontrollable nuclear explosion waiting to detonate:

> I view derivatives as time bombs, both for the parties that deal in them and the economic system. . . . The derivatives genie is now well out of the bottle, and these instruments will almost certainly multiply in variety and number until some event makes their toxicity clear. Central banks and governments have so far found no effective way to control, or even monitor, the risks posed by these contracts. In my view, derivatives are financial weapons of mass destruction, carrying dangers that, while now latent, are potentially lethal.[41]

Though the game keeps changing, many of the most important patterns remain the same. Systems continue to create excesses they both need to remain productive yet cannot process effectively. In financial capitalism, the nature of the waste that must be managed has changed. It is no longer merely material waste—degrading consumer products—but also immaterial—degraded financial assets. Recent experience has made it painfully obvious that waste is no less toxic when the assets are virtual rather than real; indeed, it may be even more toxic.

A cross between *24* and *Money Never Sleeps*, *Cosmopolis* tells the story of one day in the life of Eric Parker, who is a somewhat older version of William Gaddis's eleven-year-old financial wizard JR.[42] Eric, who is a

*Cosmopolis*

twenty-eight-year-old multibillionaire asset manager, traffics in counterfeits of counterfeits. As he tries to make his way across congested midtown Manhattan to get his hair cut, he is repeatedly diverted by a string of bizarre experiences as surreal as the world he and his fellow "masters of the universe" have created for themselves and increasingly for others. With chaos reigning around him and entering into chance encounters that defy rational explanation, Eric, in a manner reminiscent of Nick speeding across the desert in his robotic Lexus, remains sealed in the cocoon of his excessively customized stretch limousine, surrounded by mobile computers and LCDs tracking the global flows of currencies and securities. Money has, indeed, become mysterious and never sleeps—currencies vaporizing in currents have become nothing more than bits of code circling the globe at the speed of light. Signs, signs, and more signs, until it's bits all the way down. Eric is mesmerized by the virtual reality surrounding him. "The glow of the screens. I love the screens. The glow of cyber-capital. So radiant and seductive." Though he is making billions of dollars for himself and others, he freely admits, "I understand none of it" (C, 78). He is, however, a believer—a true believer who has faith in things unseen. Eric is convinced that his analysts can detect order beneath all the chaos. While his god writes algorithms rather than scripture, the way he understands the world does not differ significantly from how the biblical prophets did. For informed exegetes who know the code, the message is clear. "Patterns, ratios, indexes, whole maps of information. This is our sweetness and light" (C, 14). But light can become blinding, and order can get out of control. Just as the waste manager Nick Shay longs for "the days of disorder" at the precise moment he seems to have achieved the success he had always been seeking, so Eric is ambivalent about systems and machines designed to generate profits by filtering noise. "There was something about the noise," DeLillo writes, "that he did not choose to wish away" (C, 14).

In 1998, one year after *Underworld* was published, the collapse of Long Term Capital Management brought financial capitalism to the brink of systemic collapse. Precisely one decade later, the weapons of mass destruction set off a chain reaction that spread across the global economy, bringing the world financial system perilously close to a complete meltdown. In the epilogue to *Underworld* and his later work *Cosmopolis*, DeLillo anticipates the catastrophic events that have recently unfolded.

Eric and his quants figured out how to game the system by turning derivatives and other complex financial products into valuable chips in the global casino. Connectivity increases volatility in all systems, and thus when everything is connected, everything becomes much less stable. When this happens, the investment game changes from producing, selling, and buying things to generating and swapping numbers that are backed by or grounded in nothing other than themselves. Cybercapitalism is all about risk—managing risk, distributing risk, taking risk, selling risk. Derivatives and other novel financial products were created to stabilize markets by distributing risk among investors who are more or less aggressive. But technology changed the game. Geeks, who were trained as physicists and astrophysicists and know nothing about finance, now devise impenetrable computer systems and program the global brain running the world economy. By repackaging and reselling abstract products on secondary and tertiary markets that lose touch with anything resembling the real economy, quants transform instruments devised to reduce risk into the riskiest investments of all. Derivatives have become speculative vehicles that far exceed their use as hedging instruments. Once again, the problem turns out to be the system's inevitable propensity to generate an excess that subverts it.

On the day we meet Eric, he has placed a huge and very risky bet on the Japanese yen. With global currency markets gyrating inexplicably, his analyst named, predictably, Michael Chin, remains confident, but Eric is not reassured.

> "I think the yen. I mean there's reason to believe we may be leveraging too rashly."
> "It's going to turn our way."
> "Yes. I know. It always has."
> "The rashness you think you see."
> "What is happening doesn't chart."

"It charts. You have to search a little harder. Don't trust standard models. Think outside the limits. The yen is making a statement. Read it. Then leap."

"We are betting big-time here."

"I know that smile. I want to respect it. But the yen can't go any higher."

"We are borrowing enormous, enormous sums."

"Any assault on the borders of perception is going to seem rash at first."

"Eric, come on. We are speculating into the void." (C, 21)

In this brave new world, the quick inherit the earth. Time becomes money in a completely new way, and the trick of the trade is to be the fastest kid on the street. In finance capitalism, as in consumer capitalism, markets expand by speeding up buying and selling cycles; this time, however, the products are virtual and effervescent rather than real and durable. Just as companies accelerated production cycles to increase profits, so financial firms hire quants to create algorithms for programmed trading at the speed of light. These algorithms cruise globally networked markets in search of price differentials that trigger trades that might last for no more than a few seconds. In this world, twenty seconds amounts to a long-term investment.

"The idea is time. Living in the future. Look at those numbers running. Money makes time. It used to be the other way around. Clock time accelerated the rise of capitalism. People stopped thinking about eternity. They began to concentrate on hours, measurable hours, man-hours, using labor more efficiently." . . .

"There's something I want to show you. . . . It's cyber-capital that creates the future. What is the measurement called a nanosecond?"

"Ten to the minus ninth power."

"That is what."

"One billionth of a second." (C, 79)

The people running these programs cannot possibly comprehend such speed, nor do they have any idea what they are buying and selling. Human beings, in other words, no longer control the systems they have created. In this emerging cosmopolis, Point Omega might turn out to be the mind of the market rather than the collective consciousness Teilhard de Chardin predicted. Not just Eric Parker but everyone is "speculating into the void."

As the nature of time changes, money is transformed and vice versa. In a vertiginous string of associations, DeLillo underscores the fungibility of money, art, and religion, which, as we have seen, is a recurrent theme in *Underworld*. Though their visions of the stuff of the cosmos might differ, financiers and artists are latter-day alchemists who attempt to create something out of nothing by transmuting pure code or prime matter into what is virtually as good as gold. Artists or, more precisely, some artists produce works that are commodities for the market or used as financial assets traded by private equity firms on global markets, and financial speculators cultivate what DeLillo describes as "the art of money-making." Entranced by the glow of the monitors, Eric admits that "he found beauty and precision here, hidden rhythms in the fluctuations of a given currency" (77, 78).

What much art and this latest incarnation or deincarnation of money share is a lack of referential value—they are grounded in nothing outside themselves. Eric's wife, Elise, appreciates the significance of this development when she muses, "money has taken a turn. All wealth has become wealth for its own sake. There's no other kind of enormous wealth. Money has lost its narrative quality the way painting did once upon a time. Money is talking to itself" (77). Abstractions of abstractions, signs of signs, everything circulating faster and faster until art for art's sake becomes money for money's sake. Eventually, we enter the "society of the spectacle" where the market is omnipresent, omnipotent, and omniscient; at this point money is God in more than a trivial sense.[43] "Never mind the urgent point, the thrust, the future. We are not witnessing the flow of information so much as pure spectacle, or information made sacred, ritually unreadable. The small monitors of the office, home and car become a kind of idolatry here, where crowds might gather in astonishment" (80). Signs of signs of signs. Faithful quants are like erstwhile believers hoping for a vision in an orange juice ad on a billboard in a ghetto. When everything is grounded in nothing, everything spins out of control, and whirl is king. Waiting in his sealed cocoon for the funeral procession of a popular rapper to pass, Eric has a vision of the dance of whirling Dervishes accompanying Sufi chants.

> Now music filled the night, ouds, flutes, cymbals and drums, and the dancers whirled, counterclockwise, faster at every turn. They were spinning out of their bodies, he thought, toward the end of all possessions.
>
> The chorus chanting vigorously now.
>
> Because whirl is all. Whirl is the drama of shedding everything. Because they are spinning into communal grace he thought. And because someone is dead tonight and only whirl can appease their grief.
>
> He believed these things. He tried to imagine a kind of fleshlessness. He thought of the whirlers deliquescing, resolving into fluid states, into spinning liquid, rings of water and fog that eventually disappear in air.      (C, 138–139)

The fluids are no longer bodily but are no less potent.

Once again "what we excrete comes back to consume us." In order to keep the system expanding, finance capitalism invents financial instruments that threaten to become its undoing. More is never enough, and wealth is generated by strings of bits, until excess itself becomes excessive. Bubble after bubble—ever different, always same. In the two decades since the collapse of the Berlin Wall, the amount of wealth created and destroyed by circulating signs has been obscene. Joseph Schumpter notwithstanding, destruction is not always creative. Any reasonable person has long known that the game is rigged and cannot go on forever. But when exuberance becomes irrational, no one wants to pick up the chips while the ante is still growing. The market has always been a game of chance in which, as Bataille teaches, risk is the draw. The greater the danger, the higher the high, until the inevitable occurs and the void consumes all. Eric's bet predictably turns bad, and he loses everything. Leaving the safety of his limo for the chaos of a different street, he finds himself pursued by a disgruntled employee, Richard Sheets, alias Benno Levin, who wants to kill him. Eric finds himself dangerously exposed in a dump that is closer to the Bronx of Nick, Matt, Esmeralda, and Sisters Edgar and Grace than his own Upper East Side.

The walls were down. This was the first thing he saw in the wobbly light. He was looking into a sizable space with wall rubble everywhere. He tried to spot the subject [i.e., Benno]. There was a shredded sofa, unoccupied, with a stationary bike nearby. He saw a heavy metal desk, battleship vintage, covered with papers. He saw the remains of a kitchen and bathroom, with brutally empty spaces where major appliances had stood. There was a portable orange toilet from a construction site, seven feet tall. . . . The toilet door opened and a man came out. (C, 186)

Orange . . . once again, orange and excess, garbage, waste, shit. Not realizing he had treated his erstwhile employee like shit, Eric asks Benno why he wants to kill him. Benno replies, "I'm helpless in their system that makes no sense to me. You wanted me to be a helpless robot soldier but all I could be was helpless" (C, 195). Though he is excluded from the system like so much waste thrown on a trash heap, Benno understands the game better than Eric. Driven by the "predatory impulse," masters of the universe try to find a way to win even by losing. The game becomes a contest to see who can become "the biggest loser." In diagnosing Eric's obsession, Benno compares the global economy run amok to a potlatch. "Even when you self-destruct, you want to fail more, lose more, die more than others, sink more than others. In the old tribes the chief who destroyed more of his property the other chief was the most powerful" (C, 194–195). By this measureless measure, Eric was very, very powerful.

Having reached the end of the line, with no money in his pockets and no lines of credit available, Eric unexpectedly happens on a mass of human flesh. Three hundred naked people are lying on the street waiting to be filmed by an artist, who might well have been Spencer Tunick.[44] One of the nude women turns out to be Eric's wife. Aroused when he sees her, they slip behind a fence and make love. With their deal consummated, Eric confesses to Elisa, "I lost all your money."

"I lose things all the time," she said. "I lost my car keys this morning. Did we talk about this? I don't remember . . . "

"First I stole the money, then I lost it."

She said laughingly, "Where?"

"In the market."

"But where?" she said. "Where does it go when you lose it?"

(C, 177–178)

"Where?" indeed. In the world of cybercapital, where does money go when you lose it? Was it ever there in the first place? Eric has no answers to these questions. Elisa then adds somewhat disingenuously, "What do poets know about money?" If, however, finance is an art and art is a financial asset, poets might know more about money than bankers and quants.

As *Cosmopolis* approaches its end, which, once again, "is not the end," Eric is still in a fix. Benno, who turns out to have been the person coming out of the orange toilet, has a gun pointed at his former boss's head. Convinced that he is going to die, Eric has another vision—this time he imagines technology saving him, just as it had saved Sister Edgar.

> O shit I'm dead.
>
> He'd always wanted to become quantum dust, transcending his body mass, the soft tissue over the bones, the muscle and fat. The idea was to live outside the given limits, in a chip, on a disc, as data, in whirl, in radiant spin, a consciousness saved from the void.
>
> The technology was imminent or not. It was semi-mythical. It was the natural next step. It would never happen. It is happening now, an evolutionary advance that needed only the practical mapping of the nervous system onto digital memory. It would be the master thrust of cybercapital, to extend human experience toward infinity as a medium for corporate growth and investment, for the accumulation of profits and vigorous reinvestment. (C, 206–207)

In this vision of the end, the Omega Point turns out to be "the Singularity."[45] Bodiless minds living forever and markets expanding *ad infinitum*. Who couldn't make money in that market? But the more real the virtual becomes, the less Eric wants it. Having lost everything he thought he desired, he realizes "the things that made him who he was could hardly be identified much less converted into data, the things that lived and milled in his body, everywhere, random, riotous, billions of trillions, in nervous neurons and peptides, the throbbing temple vein, in the veer of his libidinous intellect" (207). The random, riotous, libidinous . . . so much uncodable noise. This is what remains—remains unmasterable and unmanageable. And this excess is what makes life so terrifying, fascinating, and, yes, so hopeful.

Life is increasingly lived between the real and the virtual, the material and the immaterial. The complex systems that make life possible produce excesses, surplus, and waste that threaten to make life impossible. *Underworld* is the world where we are destined to dwell. Sorting through the debris left by the mess we have made of things, one is driven to wonder not only if redemption is any longer possible but what redemption might conceivably be in this dark underworld. Don DeLillo is Wallace Stevens's "The Man on the Dump" who leaves us with a question rather than answers.

> . . . Is it peace,
> Is it a philosopher's honeymoon, one finds
> On the dump?[46]

Or is it something else?

O

O

O

## AFTERTHOUGHT

Where does thinking begin? When does writing begin? Is it possible to think without thinking? Can one begin to write without knowing it? What if thought were always after thought—thought that is after an origin that forever withdraws and pursues an end that never arrives?

Many of our most intriguing thoughts arrive unexpectedly and can be understood—if at all—only looking back after much time has passed. Hegel was right when he said that the Owl of Minerva only takes flight at twilight. And he was right when he insisted that art is a thing of the past. But he did not understand his own insight about art because he could not comprehend the uncanny past that always haunts art. Nor can anyone else. The only art that matters is art that figures what thought can neither grasp nor avoid. Thinking always leaves a reminder that cannot be processed but must be pursued. Tracing this endless excess, art keeps thought in play. In this way, art gives thought the matter it forever seeks, and thought leaves the debris with which art works. When image and word, figure and concept, art and philosophy are woven together, what once was called the religious approaches but never arrives.

## EARTH WORKS

For more than a year, I had been clearing forest, hauling away stumps, moving dirt, shaping land, planting grass, and placing rocks, large and small, outside the window of the barn where I write. In all honesty, I didn't know why—I understood neither what I was doing nor why I was doing it.[47] But it seemed important—more important than writing at the time. What I eventually realized was that in creating gardens, pools, streams, and sculptures that unexpectedly resembled something like an earthwork more than a landscape, I was already writing *Refiguring the Spiritual* and *Rewiring the Real*. And while writing these books, I realized that my next work would be *nexus*.

With what I thought was the last rock in place and my work for the summer drawing to a close, another thought arrived as if from nowhere. Would it be possible, I wondered, to frame a work in which the earth itself is the artist? As images of Beuys, Barney, Turrell, Goldsworthy, and Heizer circulated through my imagination, I developed a strategy. Though I had not yet read *Underworld*, I decided to try to combine earthworks and

4.14 Mark C. Taylor, Earth Work.

painting to create something like underworld art. I purchased six yards of canvas and cut a piece that measured twenty-two inches by forty-eight inches. At the edge of the clearing beside the newly created pond, stream, and rock garden, I dug a hole eight inches deep and placed the canvas on the bottom of it. Once again dirt and burial—grave matters.[48] But something had changed, and my concerns were different this time—not death but life, not despair but hope.

With materials appropriated from Beuys and gestures borrowed from Pollock, I covered the canvas with swirls and whorls of honey, cereal, flower, and grass seed.

I then proceeded to bury it and marked the site with four metal stakes. My plan was to dig it up precisely one later. Over the course of the year, the burial site became completely overgrown and would have been unrecognizable without the markers. When the first anniversary of the interment

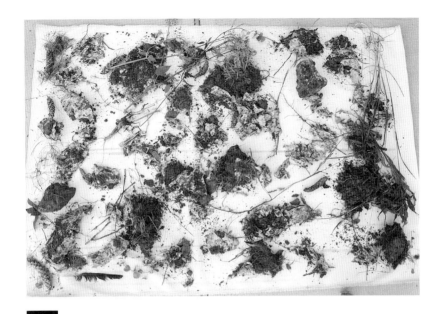

4.15 Mark C. Taylor, Earth Work.

4.16 Mark C. Taylor, Earth Work.

arrived, I hesitated and finally decided not to uncover it. Questions had begun to emerge—questions that went far beyond what I had first imagined.

Above all, or perhaps below all, the question of remains remains. What can be concealed and what cannot? What can be revealed and what cannot? What should be revealed and what should not? Imagine an artist who created a work and then buried it without telling anyone. Or an artist who created a monumental work in the desert and blew it up before anyone saw it. Imagine a writer who wrote a book, locked it up in a crypt, and threw away the key. Or a poet who spent her whole life writing and, on her deathbed, burned all her poems. Is it art if no one sees it, reads it, hears it? Does art that matters reveal or conceal? Perhaps reveal and conceal? What does it mean to show or to hide? What if hiding is showing and showing is hiding? I was not sure whether exposure would destroy or complete the art earth was working on.

Another year passed and, though my questions remained unanswered, I finally decided to dig up the canvas. What tipped the scales in favor of disclosure was reading *Underworld*. As I pondered DeLillo's work, I began to suspect that I had unknowingly begun the essay you are now reading when I buried the canvas. Without realizing it at the time, I was already thinking about many of the issues that circulate through *Underworld*: alpha, omega, materiality, immateriality, matter, form, noise, information, system, excess, closed, open, return, expenditure, investment, gift, order, chaos, purity, danger, repression, expression, thanatos, eros, tomb, womb, *Unheimlichkeit*, *Heim*, waste, art, profane, sacred. Thinking about what I had buried, I wondered what earth would have to say about all of this.

On June 14, 2010, the second anniversary of the burial, I began digging. I had no idea what to expect. The earth was moist and offered little resistance; I first dug a trench along what I thought was the edge of the canvas and then proceeded gingerly to strip away the dirt layer by layer until white fragments began to appear. I dug deeper until I was below the canvas and then carefully raised the remains. It quickly became apparent that the earth had done its work—the canvas had disintegrated, and rotting pieces were wrapped in a tangle of dirt, stones, and roots.

Form had become *informe*, little more than a pile of not-so-geometric turds returning to the humus from which humans emerge. It is telling that "human" and "humus" both derive from the same root: *dhghem*, earth, which in Greek is *khthon*, *chthonic*.[49] Brushing away dirt like an archaeologist uncovering ancient remains, I was surprised to discover the soil teeming with life: worms, ants, eggs, beetles, spiders, pinecones and needles, carrots, turnips, roots, roots, and more roots, even a crow's feather.

After pausing to assess the situation, I decided to cut a new piece of canvas exactly the same size as the original and to assemble all the fragments I found in something like an earthwork collage. The longer I studied the remains, the more I saw; each fragment appeared to be something like a small work of art, with shapes and shades never before seen. This work was not complete—particles of dirt crumbled, colors changed with the light and the moisture in the air. I realized that this work would never end.

As I gazed at the earth, a line from the Upanishads came to mind, not the line Oppenheimer recalled on that fateful day in the desert but a different line, which, at this moment, had a very different meaning.

Tat Tvam Asi
That Thou Art

I knew what I had to do. No one else would ever see this earth work; I would ponder it for a week and then, after returning the remains to their burial site, take the canvas to the dump. Religion . . . literature . . . technology. Waste . . . Art. Humus . . . Human . . . Humus. A complex neχus.

# 5
## CONCLUDING UNSCIENTIFIC POSTSCRIPT

Two Styles of the Philosophy of Religion

## THEOLOGICAL FOUNDATIONS

**IN 1946,** Paul Tillich published a seminal essay entitled "The Two Types of Philosophy of Religion," in which he maintained that every philosophy of religion developed in the Christian tradition takes one of two forms. While Alfred North Whitehead once suggested that everyone is born either a Platonist or an Aristotelian, Tillich argues that every philosophy of religion is either Augustinian or Thomistic: the former he labels the ontological type, the latter the cosmological type. The distinction between the two types of the philosophy of religion is based on the differences between the two classical arguments for the existence of God, i.e., the ontological and cosmological arguments, which, though present since the Middle Ages, were particularly influential during the modern period. Tillich regards the teleological argument, or the argument from design, as a variation of the cosmological argument, which argues from effect (i.e., the world or its design) to cause (i.e., God as creator, governor and designer). The essay opens with a description of the most important differences between the two types.

> One can distinguish two ways of approaching God: the way of overcoming estrangement and the way of meeting a stranger. In the first way man discovers *himself* when he discovers God; he discovers something that is identical with himself although it transcends him infinitely, something from which he is estranged, but from which he never has been and never can be separated. In the second way, man meets a *stranger* when he meets God. The meeting is accidental. Essentially they do not belong to each other.[1]

Since Tillich's concern is the philosophy of religion, he focuses on the problem of the knowledge of God. In the ontological type, "the knowledge of God and the knowledge of Truth are identical, and this knowledge is immediate or direct." From this point of view, "*God is the presupposition of the question of God*" (13). One cannot ask about God if one does not already possess an implicit knowledge of God. This argument is obviously Platonic: knowledge of truth is the condition of the possibility of distinguishing between true and false and as such cannot be derived from experience. The ontological argument, Tillich maintains,

> is the rational description of the relation of our mind to Being as such. Our mind implies *principia per se nota*, which have immediate evidence whenever they are noticed: the transcendentalia, *esse, verum, bonum*. They constitute the Absolute in which the difference between knowing and the known is not actual. This Absolute as the principle of Being has absolute certainty. It is a necessary thought because it is the presupposition of thought. (15)

Tillich's argument hinges on the identification of God and Being, or, in his own terms, the power of Being. In a move that has far-reaching consequences, he claims that in the ontological type, epistemology and ontology are inseparable. "The Augustinian tradition," he confesses, "can rightly be called mystical, if mysticism is defined as the experience of the identity of subject and object in relation to Being itself" (14). If God is being or the power of Being, then everything that exists is, in some way, united with the divine. God, in other words, is immanent in self and world.

In the cosmological type, by contrast, the relation between the human and divine is mediated or indirect. God is not immanent but is transcendent to self and world. Since nothing is grounded in itself, everything that exists is a sign referring beyond itself first to other things and ultimately to the divine origin, which is the truth of all reality.

> For Thomas all this follows from his sense-bound epistemology: "The human intellect cannot reach by natural virtue the divine substance, because, according to the way of the present life the cognition of our intellect starts with the senses." From there we must ascend to God with the help of the category of causality. This is what the philosophy of religion can do, and can do fairly easily in cosmological terms. We can see that there must be pure actuality, since the movement from potentiality to actuality is dependent on actuality, so that an actuality, preceding every movement must exist. (18)

In the cosmological type, knowledge of God is a posteriori rather than a priori; God or truth, therefore, is the conclusion instead of the presupposition of argumentation. Because God remains transcendent, human reason alone cannot reach the complete truth of the divine. At the limit of human understanding, faith must supplement reason.

In contrast to the ontological type in which God is Being as such, in the cosmological type, God is *a* being. While Tillich consistently associates the cosmological type of the philosophy of religion with Aquinas, he traces this decisive shift in the understanding of the divine to the medieval Scottish Catholic theologian John Duns Scotus (c. 1266–1308).

The first step in this direction was taken by Duns Scotus, who asserted an insuperable gap between man as finite and God as the infinite being, and who derived from this separation that the cosmological arguments as *demonstrations ex finito* remain within the finite and cannot reach the infinite. They cannot transcend the idea of a self-moving, teleological universe. . . . The concept of being loses its ontological character; it is a word, covering the entirely different realms of the finite and the infinite. God ceases to be Being itself and becomes a particular being, who must be known, *cognitione particulari.* Ockham, the father of later nominalism, calls God a *res singularissima.*                                         (19)

Tillich leaves no doubt that his sympathies lie with the ontological type. Indeed, he goes so far as to argue that the cosmological type represents "a destructive cleavage" that establishes oppositions that inevitably lead to human estrangement. In this analysis, unity is not only primal but is always *present* beneath or behind every form of separation. "The ontological principle in the philosophy of religion," he concludes, "may be stated in the following way: *Man is immediately aware of something unconditional which is the prius of the separation and interaction of subject and object, theoretically as well as practically*" (22). Though not immediately obvious in this essay, Tillich's argument grows out of his appropriation of analyses previously developed by Schelling and Heidegger.

This insight suggests that Tillich's analysis can be extended to illuminate contemporary philosophical and theological debates. The difference between the ontological and cosmological types roughly corresponds to the conventional distinction between continental and analytic philosophy, respectively. To see how this is so, it is necessary to take a detour through late medieval philosophical theology. Tillich's passing reference to William of Ockham in the context of his discussion of Aquinas suggests an unexpected connection between medieval nominalism and modern analytic philosophy.

At first glance, no two thinkers seem more different than Aquinas and Ockham. While the former believes that God always acts rationally and, therefore, that the world is comprehensible, the latter insists that God is a *deus absconditus* and, thus, that knowledge is inescapably uncertain. Aquinas, however, distinguishes the natural and supernatural and, by extension, reason and faith. This distinction opens the way for Ockham's theological innovation, which eventually led to the theological, philosophical, and sociopolitical revolution that in turn produced the Protestant Reformation.[2] For Aquinas, faith and the supernatural supplement and complement but never contradict reason and nature. For Ockham, by contrast, the divine and the human as well as faith and reason are, in terms Kierkegaard would invoke centuries later, "infinitely and qualitatively different."

According to Ockham, God is above all else omnipotent will—He is absolutely free and as such is bound by nothing, not even divine reason. God, in other words, is free to act in ways that sometimes seem arbitrary and often remain incomprehensible. Within this theological schema, the ground of the universe is the productive will of God, and existence is His unfathomable gift. This originary will is arational rather than irrational; as the condition of the possibility of reason as well as unreason, the divine will is finally unknowable. Faith, therefore, cannot be a matter of knowledge; indeed, one must believe *in spite of* not *because of* reason. If the universe (or the world) is the product of God's creative will, unguided by the divine Logos, the order of things is contingent or perhaps even arbitrary. As Radically free, God can always undo what He has done, and thus there can be no final certainty or security in the world. In an effort to avoid this frightful prospect without forsaking his thoroughgoing voluntarism, Ockham distinguishes between God's *potentia absoluta* (absolute power) and *potentia ordinata* (ordained power). While God has the absolute power to do anything that is not self-contradictory, He freely chooses to limit Himself by ordaining a particular order for the world. In different terms, divine will posits the codes by which the world is ordered and establishes the rules through which it operates. These codes and rules, however, are not themselves determined by any ascertainable code or rule. Every worldly structure, therefore, presupposes something it can neither include nor exclude. This voluntaristic ontology leads to an empirical epistemology—since whatever exists depends upon God's free will, knowledge must be a posteriori and inductive rather than a priori and deductive. The only way to know anything about the world is to begin with sense experience. Such knowledge, however, always remains incomplete because it is ultimately "grounded" in the abyss of divine freedom. This *Abgrund* is neither simply immanent nor transcendent and, thus, is neither exactly present nor absent.

Ockham's anthropology is the mirror image of his theology. Accordingly, his view of human beings is based on two fundamental tenets: first, the anteriority and priority of the singular individual over both social groups and the whole; and second, the freedom and responsibility of every individual subject. Ockham's position on these issues leads to his most devastating critique of medieval theology and ecclesiology. The question over which he split with his predecessors is the seemingly inconsequential problem of the status of universal terms. For scholastic theology, the universal idea or essence is ontologically more real than individuals and epistemologically truer than particular empirical experiences. According to this doctrine, known as realism, humanity, for example, is essential, and individual human beings exist only by virtue of their "participation" in the antecedent universal form. Exercising his fabled razor, Ockham rejects realism and insists that universal terms are merely *names*, which are heuristic fictions useful for ordering the world and organizing experience but are not real in any ontological sense. This position eventually came to be known as nominalism (from *nomen*, Latin for "name"). For nominalists, only individuals are real. In the case of human beings, individuals are not constituted by any universal idea or atemporal essence but are formed historically through their own free decisions. The defining characteristics of human selfhood are individuality, freedom, and responsibility. According to nominalism, every whole, up to and including the human race, is nothing more than the sum of all the individuals that make it up.

Finally, Ockham's nominalism entails a new understanding of language and, most important, of the relation between words and things. Though usually overlooked, there is a tension between Ockham's empirical epistemology and his theology. On the one hand, language is intended to refer to and, therefore, represent specific entities, but, on the other hand, insofar as language is general, if not universal, and subjects as well as objects are singular, existing entities cannot be represented linguistically. Words and things fall apart, leaving us caught in a linguistic labyrinth from which there is no exit. In semiotic terms, signifiers, which appear to point to independent signifieds, actually refer to other signifiers. As linguistic beings, we traffic in signs, which, though appearing to refer to things, are actually signs of other signs. While seeming to represent the world, language is actually a play of signs unanchored by knowable referents. Words, then, are traces of what can never be represented and, as such, remain ghosts or phantoms of a real that has always already slipped away without becoming precisely absent.

Though the importance of his work is rarely acknowledged, many of the themes Ockham identified have been enormously influential throughout the Western tradition. Over the course of the following centuries, philosophers and theologians drew different and often conflicting conclusions from his guiding principles. In this context, it is important to stress that logical positivism and analytic philosophy, on the one hand, and, on the other hand, certain strands of continental philosophy both derive from Ockham's nominalism. To trace relevant aspects of this genealogy, I will consider critical texts written by Martin Heidegger and Rudolf Carnap. This comparison creates the possibility of recasting Tillich's two types of philosophy in different terms and thereby points toward a more promising alternative.

## ART AND SCIENCE

While the distinction between Anglo-American and continental philosophy is a recent invention, its roots lie buried in the late Middle Ages. Ockham wrote many of his most important treatises while at Oxford, and his influence continues even among those who do not realize it. His trenchant criticism of speculative theology and metaphysics, insistence on empirical verification of epistemological claims, and preoccupation with language left a deep impression on British and, by extension, American philosophy. The revival of Hegelianism and speculative philosophy in the United Kingdom during the early decades of the twentieth century triggered a critical response, which was largely responsible for creating a philosophical divide that has grown wider over the years. In an attempt to distinguish itself, analytic philosophy constituted continental philosophy as its own other and by so doing uncritically grouped philosophical positions that shared little more than their difference from positivistic and analytic philosophy—phenomenology, existentialism, neo-Thomism, hermeneutics, structuralism, deconstruction, and poststructuralism. Since geographical categories are ill suited to express philosophical and methodological differences, it is necessary to reformulate the terms in which philosophical debates have been cast for a century.

Instead of recycling the tired distinction between Anglo-American and continental philosophy, it is more helpful to contrast two *styles* of philosophizing: one that models itself on art and one that models itself on an interpretation of science that sets itself in opposition to art. This way of posing the issue is deliberately provocative because it suggests that there is nothing outside or beyond style. Furthermore, art and style are inseparable—there is no art without style and no style without art. It is, therefore, misleading to set up a hard and fast opposition between science and art. Just as there is a religious dimension to all culture, so there is an artistic dimension to all creative thinking, and just as religion is often most significant where it is least obvious, so style is often most influential where it remains unnoticed. The choice is not between style and nonstyle but between a style that represses its artistic and aesthetic facets and a style that expresses them stylistically. In order to explore the differences between these two alternatives and their far-reaching implications, I will examine the debate between two philosophers whose work has played a crucial role in framing the debate for almost a century: Rudolf Carnap and Martin Heidegger.[3] Though Heidegger (1891–1976) and Carnap (1889–1970) were both German as well as contemporaries, they lived in completely different worlds. Heidegger was born into a Catholic family and never strayed far from his native Black Forest. After preparing for the priesthood as a youth, he went on to the University of Freiburg, where he wrote his *Habilitation Schrift*, entitled *Duns Scotus's Doctrine of Categories and Meaning*. After the First World War, he returned to Freiburg and served as Husserl's assistant until he eventually assumed his mentor's chair. Over the years, Heidegger turned down many offers to move to more prestigious universities in order to remain at Freiburg and write in his beloved mountain hut in nearby Todnauberg. Carnap was born in Ronsdorf and grew up in Barmen. From 1910 through 1914, he also attended the University of Freiburg, where he studied philosophy, physics, and mathematics, and at Jena, where he took three courses with Gottlob Frege. Combining research in physics with his interest in Kant, he completed a dissertation, entitled simply *Space* (*Der Raum*), under Bruno Bauch in 1921. In 1926, Carnap was appointed an assistant professor at the University of Vienna and became increasingly involved in the Vienna Circle. With a flourishing artistic community, the burgeoning field of psychoanalysis, and its long history of musical innovation, Vienna was a thriving center of modernism during these years. After moving to Prague in 1931, Carnap was forced to flee Europe for the United States, where he taught at the University of Chicago from 1936 to 1952.

In 1929, Heidegger and Carnap published brief texts that proved decisive for later twentieth-century philosophy. Carnap and his colleagues Hans Hahn and Otto Neurath issued what is widely acknowledged as the manifesto of the Vienna Circle, "The Scientific Conception of the World: The Vienna Circle," and Heidegger delivered his inaugural lecture at the University of Freiberg—"What Is Metaphysics?" Both Carnap and Heidegger called for the overcoming of metaphysics, but neither their reasons nor their intentions could have been more different. For Carnap, the abstractions and complexities of speculative metaphysics were vacuous as well as sociopolitically suspect. He insisted that clarity and simplicity are the necessary characteristics of truth. Philosophy can only enter the modern era by appropriating what he described as a scientific method of investigation and empirical procedures for verification. For Heidegger, by contrast, modern science and technology, which are the culmination of what he labels the Western "onto-theological tradition," pose a threat to human life as well as the future of the planet. The only way to avert impending disaster is to develop a thoroughgoing critique of science and technology by recovering philosophy's original

Carnap   Heidegger

relationship to art. Three years after Heidegger's lecture, Carnap responded in an article entitled "The Elimination of Metaphysics Through Logical Analysis of Language." The significance of these two essays far surpasses the initial exchange that led to their publication. In them, Heidegger and Carnap present contrasting positions that implicitly and explicitly shaped philosophical debate for decades.

Heidegger approaches his questioning of metaphysics from an unexpected direction by discussing the role of science in shaping the modern university: "What happens to us, essentially, in the grounds of our existence, when science becomes our passion?"[4] Far from a method of disinterested investigation capable of establishing objective truth, science, Heidegger maintains, is the product of the Western metaphysical tradition that has been characterized by the pernicious "forgetting of being." He argues, "Today only the technical organization of universities and faculties consolidates this burgeoning multiplicity of disciplines; practical establishment of goals by each discipline provides the only meaningful source of unity. Nonetheless, the rootedness of the sciences in their essential ground has atrophied."[5] By historically contextualizing science in terms of broader sociocultural currents, Heidegger extends the arguments of his mentor, Husserl. In his influential essay "The Origin of Geometry," which is appended to *Crisis of the European Sciences*, Husserl argues that even geometry, which is the "purest expression of the theoretical attitude," is constituted in what he labels the *Lebenswelt*. The crisis to which his title alludes occurs when people forget that mathematical ideas and scientific concepts are embedded in everyday attitudes and practices. The task of philosophy or, in Husserl's terms, phenomenology is to think what the tradition has left unthought through the phenomenological reduction, which exposes the originary constitution of every form of consciousness.

In his first book, *Edmund Husserl's* Origin of Geometry: *An Introduction*, Derrida clarifies the point of Husserl's analysis:

> By a *spiraling movement*, which is the major find in our text, a bold clearing is brought about within the regional limits of the investigation and

transgresses them toward a new form of radicality. Concerning the intentional history of a particular eidetic science, a sense-investigation of its contradictions of possibility will reveal to us exemplarily the conditions and sense of the historicity of science in general, then of universal historicity—the last horizon for all sense and Objectivity in general.[6]

Such critical reflection has important practical consequences because it "desedimentizes" tradition in a way that reactivates and revitalizes it. As we will see, there is a direct line from Husserl's phenomenological reduction and desedimentation through Heidegger's "de-structuring" (*Destrucktion*) or "dismantling" (*Abbau*) to Derrida's deconstruction. For Heidegger, the "essential ground" that science forgets is being itself. Far from disinterested, science's preoccupation with beings is an extension of Nietzsche's will to power in "the will to mastery" through which "man" seeks to "secure to himself what is most properly his." Within this scheme, the scientific attitude rests on two basic principles: representation and utilitarianism. In order to control the world, man must first objectify and then manipulate it. "This objectifying of whatever is," Heidegger argues,

is accomplished in a setting-before, a representing, that aims at bringing each particular being before it in such a way that man who calculates can be sure, and that means be certain, of that being. We first arrive at science as research when and only when truth has been transformed into the certainty of representation. What it is to be is for the first time defined as the objectiveness of representing, and truth is first defined as the certainty of representing, in the metaphysics of Descartes.[7]

When truth collapses into certainty with Descartes's turn to the subject, everything becomes a "standing-reserve" or resource programmed to serve human ends, and man finally seems to be at home in a world where everything is manageable. But at precisely this moment of apparent triumph, humankind's fortunes are reversed.

As soon as what is unconcealed no longer concerns man even as an object, but does so, rather, exclusively as standing-reserve, and man in the midst of objectlessness is nothing, but the orderer of the standing-reserve, then he comes to the very brink of a precipitous fall; that is he comes to the point where he himself will have to be taken as standing-reserve. Meanwhile man, precisely as the one so threatened, exalts himself to the posture of lord of the earth. In this way the impression comes to prevail that everything man encounters exists only insofar as it is his construct. This illusion gives rise in turn to one final delusion: It seems as though man everywhere and always encounters only himself.[8]

In a manner reminiscent of Hegel's analysis of the master-slave relationship in the *Phenomenology of Spirit*, the master affirms himself by negating the world around him. Through this unexpected reversal, the exercise of the will to power unleashes what Hegel, describing the reign of terror following the French Revolution, called "the fury of destruction," which ultimately destroys the world and with it humanity.

The only way to turn back from the all-consuming abyss opened by modern science and technology, Heidegger argues, is to turn toward a no less disturbing abyss that is buried deep in the ever-receding past. He devotes his entire philosophical enterprise to questioning what science forgets, ignores, or even represses. He names this elusive remainder *das Nichts*—(the) nothing. While science is preoccupied solely with "beings and beyond that—nothing," Heidegger asks, "What about this nothing?"

The nothing is rejected precisely by science, given up as a nullity. But when we give up the nothing in such a way don't we just concede it? Can we, however, speak of concession when we concede nothing? But perhaps our confused talk already degenerates into an empty squabble over words. Against it science must now reassert its seriousness and soberness of mind, insisting that it is concerned solely with beings. The nothing—what else can it be for science but an outrage and a phantasm?

If science is right, then only one thing is sure: science wishes to know nothing of the nothing.[9]

Heidegger is convinced that modern science and technology mark the closure, which is not the end, of the Western ontotheological tradition. Atomic and cybernetic technologies make explicit the destructive will to power that has always been implicit in metaphysics. The long march of history has been a pedagogy in forgetting whose trajectory cannot be reversed unless philosophy thinks what previously has been left unthought. From the naïve everyday perspective to the seemingly sophisticated point of view of science and mathematics, the unthought remainder, surplus, or excess, which is the condition of the possibility of thought as well as the impossibility of its completion, is nothing.

But what precisely "is" this nothing? The question, of course, negates itself in its very formulation. That is why Heidegger never asks it directly; rather, he asks indirectly, "How is it with nothing?" Nothing cannot be objectified, represented, or manipulated; it is never given yet always gives whatever is and is not. Nothing is apprehended, which is not to say comprehended, in moods like distraction, boredom, and above all anxiety. As we have seen, in contrast to fear, which always has a specific object, anxiety reveals nothing "in the slipping away of beings. . . . We 'hover' in anxiety. More precisely, anxiety leaves us hanging because it induces the slipping away of beings as a whole."[10] This void in the midst of whatever appears to be present renders all beings uncanny and undercuts the very possibility of complete knowledge and reasonable control. Where science sees causes that ground determinate entities, Heidegger glimpses the groundless ground—*der Abgrund*—from which everything emerges and to which all returns through a process he labels "nihilation." In an important passage that Carnap discusses at length, Heidegger argues:

[Nihilation] is neither an annihilation of beings nor does it spring from a negation. Nihilation will not submit to calculation in terms of annihilation and negation. The nothing itself nihilates.

Nihilation is not some fortuitous incident. Rather, as the repelling gesture toward the retreating whole of beings, it discloses these beings in their full but heretofore concealed strangeness as what is radically other— with respect to the nothing.

In the clear night of the nothing of anxiety the original openness of beings as such arises: that there are beings—and not nothing. But this "and not nothing" we add in our talk is not some kind of appended clarification. Rather, it makes possible in advance the revelation of beings in general. The essence of the originally nihilating nothing lies in this, that it brings Da-sein for the first time before beings as such.[11]

From Heidegger's point of view, the entities that science investigates and technology manipulates are neither self-contained nor self-grounded; to the contrary, they emerge from an elsewhere, which, while never present, is not absent. Nihilating nothing clears the space that allows differences to be articulated and identities to be established even if never secured. Truth, Heidegger maintains, does not involve the correspondence between word and thing, representation and fact, or signifier and signified; it is the primordial opening (*Aletheia*) between and among beings that is the condition of the possibility of all forms of correspondence. As such, truth can be neither represented nor comprehended but is revealed as the concealing that once was called the play of the gods and now is staged in the work of art.

With "seriousness and soberness of mind," Carnap confidently declares all such speculation meaningless nonsense. The goal of the Vienna Circle was "to set philosophy upon the sure path to science." In their 1929 manifesto, Carnap, Hahn, and Neurath declare:

It is the *method of logical analysis* that essentially distinguishes recent empiricism and positivism from the earlier version that was more biological-psychological in its orientation. If someone asserts "there is a God," "the poetic and primary basis of the world is the unconscious," "there is an entelechy which is the leading principle in the living organism," we do not say to him: "what you say is false"; but we ask him: "what do you mean by these statements?" Then it appears that there is a sharp boundary between two kinds of statements. To one belong statements as they are made by empirical science; their meaning can be determined by logical analysis or, more precisely, through the simplest statements about the empirically given. The other statements, to which belong those cited above, reveal themselves as empty of meaning if one takes them in the way that metaphysicians intend.

Logical positivism rests on two fundamental principles: (1) the strict adherence to the scientific method, which entails a rigorous empiricism, and (2) the insistence that all problems can be solved by logical and linguistic analysis. Absolutely convinced of the validity of their method, Carnap and his colleagues go so far as to proclaim, "The scientific world-conception knows *no unsolvable riddle*."[12] For science and philosophy to reach the lofty goal of total knowledge, they must free themselves from theology and metaphysics by dismantling traditional ways of thinking through a critical analysis of the language.

Though the details of analysis differ, variations of this philosophical approach share five important assumptions, several of the most important of which can be traced to medieval nominalist theology.

1. Meaningful linguistic claims are cognitive. This is not to imply that language is deployed in no other ways. It can, for example, be used to express intentions and feelings. Meaning, however, can only be determined by logical analysis and "the reduction to the simplest statements about the empirically given."

2. Meaningful statements are referential. They refer to actual entities, events, or states of affairs. A. J. Ayre points out that for logical positivists "the meaning of a proposition is its method of verification. The assumption behind this slogan is that everything that could be said at all could be expressed in terms of elementary statements. All statements of a higher order, including the most abstract scientific hypotheses, were in the end nothing more than shorthand descriptions of observable facts." This verification requires "introspectible or sensory experiences."[13]

3. Meaningful statements are representational. Words and statements represent objective facts to the cognitive subject.

4. Scientific and philosophical analysis presupposes logical/linguistic and ontological atomism. Statements are meaningful only insofar as "they say what would be said by affirming certain elementary statements and denying certain others, that is, only insofar as they give a true or false picture of the ultimate 'atomic' facts."[14]

5. Rigorous analysis reduces complexity to simplicity.

Before exploring the importance of these principles for theology and metaphysics, it is necessary to consider some of their implications for the philosophical position they are supposed to support. In logical and ontological atomism, terms and entities are taken to be singular; their identity is prior to and independent of their relations to other terms and entities. Since the singular alone is real, the whole is nothing more than the sum of its parts and as such is epiphenomenal.[15] Accordingly, this method of analysis privileges simplicity over complexity; more precisely, critical analysis always reduces complex structures and systems to their simple parts. For Carnap and those who share his faith, the task of philosophy at the end of metaphysics is largely negative. The application of scientific method to philosophical analysis "serves to eliminate meaningless words, meaningless pseudo-statements."[16] Any extension beyond critical and regulative analysis cannot be justified in terms of logical positivism's foundational principles.

As we have seen, the principle of verification plays a critical role in logical positivism as well as in radical empiricism. But when critically assessed, it is clear that this style of empirical verification leads to insurmountable difficulties. As Ockham and his followers realized centuries earlier, if reality, subjective as well as objective, is singular, it can be neither linguistically mediated nor conceptually represented. The generality of language cannot capture the constitutive specificity of real entities, events, states of affairs, or other subjects. Furthermore, if the principle of verification rests upon "the subject's introspectible or sensory experiences," it can hardly be normative. Protests to the contrary notwithstanding, experience is idiosyncratic or, in terms that would shake but not subvert logical positivism and radical empiricism, "private." Ayre correctly argues,

> the most serious difficulty lay in the privacy of the objects to which the elementary statements were supposed to refer. If each one of us is bound to interpret any statement as being ultimately a description of his own private experiences, it is hard to see how we can ever communicate. . . . It was maintained by Carnap and others that the solipsism which seemed to be involved in this position was only methodological; but this was little more than an avowal of the purity of their intentions. It did nothing to mitigate the objections to their theory.[17]

Contrary to every expectation, "scientific philosophy" ends up in the same solipsistic impasse as Sartrean existentialism.

Carnap finally conceded this problem, but his attempted solution creates further difficulties for his position. "In the theory of knowledge it is customary to say that the primary sentences refer to 'the given'; but there is no unanimity on the question of what it is that is given." In an effort to overcome solipsism, he proposes intersubjective criteria for verification. Instead of being grounded in private experiences, which cannot be communicated, verifiable statements of scientific philosophy must refer to physical realities and events that are publicly intelligible. This shift from private to intersubjective experience leads to the reinterpretation of meaning in terms of syntax: "The *syntax* of the word must be fixed, i.e., the mode of its occurrence in the simplest sentence form in which it is capable of occurring; we call this sentence form its *elementary sentence*." This revision leads to a further conclusion, which is decisive for his criticism of Heidegger: "Since the meaning of a word is determined by its criterion of application (in other words: by the relations of deductibility entered into by its elementary sentence-form, by its truth-conditions, by the method of verification), the stipulation of the criterion takes away one's freedom to decide what one wishes to 'mean' by the word."[18]

Carnap's argument does not resolve the problems with his position. First, as long as he remains committed to logical and ontological atomism, intersubjective experience and knowledge remain impossible. He asserts the necessity for intersubjective criteria of verification but does not explain how they are possible. Second, even if it were possible to establish such criteria, intersubjectivity would undercut the very positivity and objectivity to which Carnap remains committed. By associating meaning with "protocols" that determine the criteria of application, he effectively identifies meaning with use and, by extension, with convention. Insofar as meaning is intersubjective, it is established by consensus and as such is socially constructed. Far from objective and, thus, independent of any particular interpretive framework, criteria for adjudicating meaning are internal to historically contingent linguistic practices. In other words, there are no metarules, or, in Kierkegaard's terms, there is no Archimedean point with which to choose the rules by which we think and act. Protocols are not self-grounding but are constituted through originary decisions that can be neither explained nor justified in terms of the rules they institute. As Goethe and Freud insist, "in the beginning is the act."

Carnap does not seem to have been fully aware of these problems and proceeded with what he confidently believed was a thoroughgoing dismantling of "the metaphysical and theological debris of millennia."[19] The claims of metaphysics and theology, he argues, are "pseudo-statements" that are "entirely meaningless." As we have seen, a word is meaningless if no method of verification can be specified or if meaningful words are put together incorrectly. Since the word "God" refers to something beyond experience and is, therefore, "deliberately divested of its reference to a physical being or to a spiritual being that is immanent in the physical," it is inescapably meaningless.[20] Most of the other important terms used by metaphysicians and theologians, e.g., the Idea, the Absolute, the Unconditioned, the Infinite, essence, the I, etc., are similarly disqualified. In the second type of pseudostatement, meaningful words are combined in such a way that no meaning results. "The syntax of language," Carnap argues, "specifies which combinations of words are admissible and which are inadmissible."[21] Even though the rules of grammar and syntax are not violated, no meaning is conveyed.

To support his argument, Carnap turns to what he describes as the "metaphysical school, which at present exerts the strongest influence in Germany." He focuses on a few sentences from Heidegger's essay "What Is Metaphysics?" which I have already considered. Since the translation of the text of Heidegger that Carnap cites differs from the one I used, it will be helpful to quote this important passage again.

> What is to be investigated is being only and—*nothing* else; being alone and further—*nothing*; solely being, and beyond being—*nothing*. *What about this Nothing? . . . Does the Nothing exist only because the Not, i.e., the Negation exists?* Or is it the other way around? *Do Negation and the Not exist only because the Nothing exists? . . .* We assert: *the Nothing is prior to the Not and the Negation. . . .* Where do we seek the Nothing? How do we find the Nothing. . . . We know the Nothing. . . . *Anxiety reveals the Nothing. . . .* That for which and because of which we are anxious was "really"—nothing. Indeed: the Nothing itself—as such—was present. . . . *What about this nothing?—The Nothing itself nothings.*[22]

Heidegger's argument fails Carnap's test for meaning on two counts. First, his claims obviously do not refer to physical entities or actual events and, therefore, cannot be empirically verified. Given Carnap's criteria, every statement about nothing is necessarily a pseudostatement. But Heidegger's argument also fails the syntactic test—he violates linguistic conventions by using "the same grammatical form for meaning and meaningless word sequences." Carnap concentrates his criticisms on two sentences: "The Nothing nothings" and "The nothing only exists because . . . " In the first sentence, Heidegger makes two mistakes: first, he uses the word "nothing" as a noun, when "it is customary in ordinary language to use it in this form in order to construct a negative existential sentence," and second, he makes up a meaningless verb "to nothing" (in the previous translation, "to nihilate"). Far worse than attempting to extend the meaning through metaphorical use, Heidegger creates a new word that has no meaning. The second sentence, Carnap insists, is simply self-contradictory—to say that nothing exists—regardless of how this is understood—is nonsensical.

If Carnap is right, then why do so many seemingly intelligent people cling to their metaphysical and theological commitments? Such assertions, Carnap tentatively suggests, "serve for the *expression of the general attitude of a person towards life* (*Lebenseinstellung, Lebensgefühl*)." Suspending his usual criteria for judgment, he allows himself to speculate, "Perhaps we may assume that they originated from *mythology.* . . . The heritage of mythology is bequeathed on the one hand to poetry, which produces and intensifies the effects of mythology on life in a deliberate way; on the other hand, it is handed down to theology, which develops mythology into a system."[23] Following Freud, with whom he shares nothing else, Carnap insists that theologians and metaphysicians differ from artists in one important way: they believe in the reality of their fantasies. Such beliefs, he insists, pose a threat not only to scientific philosophy but to modernity itself.

While claiming that philosophy is always in the service of science, the agenda of Carnap and his colleagues is considerably more ambitious. They conclude "The Scientific Conception of the World" with a resounding declaration that echoes other modernist manifestos of the time: "We witness the spirit of the scientific world-conception penetrating in growing measure the forms of personal and public life, in education, upbringing, architecture, and the shaping of economic and social life according to rational principles. *The scientific world-conception serves life, and life receives it.*"[24] Above and beyond securing scientific knowledge, philosophy prepares the way for nothing less than the transformation of the world. In making such bold claims, Carnap echoed the ambitions of many modern artists.

During the first decades of the twentieth century, Vienna was a hotbed of modernism: art (Gustav Klimt, Oskar Kokoschka, and the Secessionists), music (Arnold Schoenberg), psychoanalysis (Freud), and architecture (Otto Wagner, Camillo Sitte, and Adolf Loss). Here as elsewhere in Europe, there were two conflicting strands of modernism, which bear a resemblance to the contrasting philosophical styles of Carnap and Heidegger. On the one hand, modern artists and especially architects appropriated modern science and technology to develop an aesthetic committed to rationality, clarity, transparency, utility, and functionalism; on the other hand, writers and artists, drawing on the work of Schopenhauer, Nietzsche, and Wagner, sought to fathom the irrational depths of human subjectivity in works that are deliberately obscure, polyvalent, and functionally useless. The most influential representative of the latter tendency is Klimt, whose paintings express Freud's eroticizing of the personality. By the time Carnap was developing his mature philosophy, this brand of expressionism was giving way to rationalism. This shift can be seen in the way Klimt's art changes from psychologically and sexually charged canvases to his more classical, almost Byzantine, later work. The change is also evident in the transformation of the organic and fluid forms of art nouveau into the crystalline and geometric forms of art deco. A parallel change occurs between Otto Wagner's early and late architecture. This rationalist trajectory leads to the purportedly styleless style of Walter Gropius, Mies van der Rohe, and their colleagues at the Bauhaus. Allergic to complexity and infatuated by simplicity, minimalist philosophers echo their architectural counterparts by quietly repeating the mantra "less is more." If logical positivism and radical empiricism share a vision of the transformative power of culture, then the difference between scientific philosophy and art might not be as great as its followers maintain. The issue is not so much art versus non-art but two different aesthetics that entail contrasting attitudes toward life.

In his provocative analysis of a seminal but long neglected book, *On Growth and Form*, Stephen Jay Gould writes: "As a subtle thinker, D'Arcy Thompson understood that emphases on diversity and unity do not represent two different theories of biology, but different aesthetic styles that profoundly influence the practice of science."[25] Philosophy and science are, like everything else, matters of style. In Vienna, no one was more vocal about the necessity to strip away superfluous excesses and meaningless details than the Austrian architect Adolf Loos, who was a contemporary of Carnap and the members of the Vienna Circle. In his influential book *Fin-de-Siècle Vienna*, Carl Schoske writes,

Loos had participated in the Secession movement in its early days, sharing its revolt against historical style. In 1898, he formulated in the Secession's *Ver Sacrum* the most vigorous indictment of Ringstrasse Vienna for screening its modern commercial truth behind historical facades. The Secession artists and architects sought a redemption from historical styles by developing a "modern" style, to sheathe modern utility and new beauty. Loos sought to remove "style"—ornamentation or dressing of any sort—from architecture and from use-objects, in order to let their function stand clear to speak its own truth in its own form.[26]

Philosophy and art mirror each other. While art, science, and technology become functional, philosophy's purportedly scientific program implicitly appropriates aesthetic principles to advance its practical agenda. Just as formalist architecture serves utilitarian ends, so scientific philosophy seeks to transform personal and public life. In both cases, the dismantling of tradition—be it artistic, architectural, metaphysical, or theological—is the prerequisite for the emergence of modernity.

Insofar as analytic philosophy is devoted to simplicity, purity, clarity, and transparency, it remains distinctively modern and as such is now outdated. In his influential work, *Complexity and Contradiction in Architecture*, Robert Venturi, who is largely responsible for launching postmodern architecture, might well be commenting on philosophy when writes:

> Architects can no longer afford to be intimidated by the puritanically moral language of orthodox Modern architecture. I like elements which are hybrid rather than "pure," compromising rather than "clean," distorted rather than "straightforward," ambiguous rather than "articulated," perverse as well as impersonal, boring as well as "interesting," conventional rather than "designed," accommodating rather than excluding, redundant rather than simple, vestigial as well as innovating, inconsistent and equivocal rather than direct and clear. I am for messy vitality over obvious unity. . . .

But an architecture of complexity and contradiction has a special obligation toward the whole: its truth must be in its totality or its implications of totality. It must embody the difficult unity of inclusion rather than the easy unity of exclusion. More is not less.[27]

For Venturi, style is substance, and substance is style. Rejecting every form of minimalism designed to reduce complex wholes to ostensibly simple parts, Venturi proposes an aesthetic that cultivates the contradictions that transform the work of art into an endless process as well as a finished product.

## RELIGION WITHIN THE LIMITS OF STYLE ALONE

Throughout the history of Western theology and philosophy, religion has been alternatively associated with cognition (thinking), volition (willing), and affection (feeling). During the eighteenth century, many defenders and critics interpreted religious claims as primarily cognitive, i.e., they viewed them as statements about the existence or nonexistence of God, who was understood theistically or deistically, as well as about human existence and events in the world. To defend religious beliefs during a time when the modern scientific worldview was gaining influence, theologians and philosophers appropriated empirical criteria of meaning and verification to recast the traditional cosmological and teleological arguments for the existence of God. Starting from the evidence of the existence of the world and its design, apologists argued to God as their necessary cause. By the end of the eighteenth century, however, it had become clear that this strategy was ineffective because, as Hume demonstrated, the very empiricism used to defend belief actually undercut its foundation. If faith were to be rationally justified, some argued, its defense would have to be practical rather than theoretical. One of Kant's primary motivations in his critical philosophy was to develop a persuasive argument for religion within the limits of reason alone by recasting belief in terms of moral activity rather than scientific or quasi-scientific knowledge. But his analysis of the relation between thinking and willing left unresolved problems that he eventually addressed in his third critique. Through an interpretation of aesthetic judgment, Kant extends the principle of autonomy from theoretical and practical reason to the work of art understood as both the process of production and the product produced. For many of Kant's followers, the *Critique of Judgment* raised the prospect of interpreting religion through art and vice versa.

While Heidegger and Carnap agree that religion can be understood in terms of art, they understand this relationship very differently. For Carnap, art, more specifically poetry, lacks referential value, and, therefore, its statements are pseudostatements, which, in the final analysis, are meaningless; for Heidegger, philosophy that is no longer bound by the assumptions of ontotheology discloses the poetic character of all thought—even scientific thought. Far from a limited genre, *poiesis* is the creative activity through which thinking as well as being emerge. Heidegger articulates the crucial insight upon which his thinking turns in *Kant and the Problem of Metaphysics*, which was published the same year he delivered his lecture "What Is Metaphysics?" To understand how he moves from Kant's critical philosophy to an interpretation of philosophy in terms of the work of art, it is necessary to turn to the third critique.

Kant's reformulation of the principle of autonomy through the notion of "inner teleology" leads to a new interpretation of the work of art. In contrast to all forms of utility in which means and ends are externally related, inner teleology involves what Kant describes as "purposiveness without purpose," in which means and ends are reciprocally related in such a way that each becomes itself in and through the other and neither can be itself apart from the other. He illustrates this idea by describing the interplay of whole and part in the work of art.

> The parts of the thing combine of themselves into the unity of a whole by being reciprocally cause and effect of their form. For this is the only way in which it is possible that the idea of the whole may conversely, or reciprocally, determine, in its turn the form and combination of all the parts, not as cause—for that would make it an art product—but as the

epistemological basis upon which the systematic unity of the form and combination of all the manifold contained in the given matter become cognizable for the person estimating it.[28]

Unlike art produced for the market, which is utilitarian and as such has an extrinsic purpose, fine art is produced for no external end but is created for its own sake. Never referring to anything other than itself, so-called high art is art about art and is, therefore, both self-referential and self-reflexive.

While seeming to be completely autonomous, the structures of self-referentiality and self-reflexivity are considerably more complicated than they initially appear. All such structures seem to be closed but, on closer inspection, prove to be open because they presuppose as a condition of their possibility something, which might be nothing, that they can neither incorporate nor assimilate. The interruption of the self-referential circuit of reflexivity exposes aporiae that provoke thinking *sensu strictissimo* and are the condition of creativity. The pivot upon which this analysis turns is the interplay of the imagination and representation in the production of self-consciousness. In self-consciousness, the subject turns back on itself by becoming an object to itself. Self-as-subject and self-as-object are reciprocally related and thus are coemergent and codependent. As such, the structure of self-relation constitutive of self-conscious subjectivity presupposes the activity of self-representation. Self-awareness, in other words, is impossible apart from the self's representation of itself to itself. Though not immediately obvious, precisely at the point where self-consciousness seems to be complete, it approaches its constitutive limit. Dieter Henrich identifies the crucial issue in commenting on Fichte's reading of Kant:

> We might cast this question another way: Will ontological discourse always make use of the premise that something can be said about the mind that is not of the mind, and that the mind can say something that is of the mind about what is not of the mind, so that the two discourses can never be derived from one another—or even form a third discourse, thereby precluding any fully intelligible linear formulation?[29]

Henrich implies that the impossibility of explaining self-consciousness through linear models does not necessarily mean that the self-reflexivity of self-consciousness is circular. When consciousness turns back on itself, it discovers a lacuna without which it is impossible but with which it is incomplete. The pressing question, then, is: Where does what the self-conscious subject represents to itself come from? If self-as-subject and self-as-object are codependent, neither can be the originary cause of the other. The activity of self-representation, therefore, requires a more primordial presentation, which must originate elsewhere. This elsewhere is the limit that is impossible to think but without which thinking is impossible. "Thinking," as Jean-Luc Nancy explains in another context, "is always thinking on the limit. The limit of comprehending defines thinking. Thus thinking is always thinking about the incomprehensible—about this incomprehensible that 'belongs' to every comprehending, as its own limit."[30] This limit is the edge of chaos where order simultaneously emerges and dissolves. To understand what occurs along this border, it is necessary to consider the dynamics of representation in more detail.

The problem of representation—*Vorstellung*—runs through all three critiques. In the first critique, Kant argues: "A concept [*Begriff*] formed from notions [*Notio*] and transcending the possibility of experience is an idea [*Idee*] or concept of reason."[31] In the exercise of practical reason, ideas that lie beyond experience and hence remain regulative are actualized as they become practically effective in moral activity. But the postulates of practical reason can no more be experienced than ideas and, therefore, yield no knowledge, even though they are rational. An idea or postulate, Rodolphe Gasché explains, "is a representation by a concept of the concepts that serve to represent representation with consciousness."

Representation here translates the German *Vorstellung*, a term Kant uses to designate the operation by which the different faculties that constitute the mind bring their respective objects before themselves. Yet when Kant claims that in spite of the impossibility of intuitively representing (and thus knowing) the ideas, they nonetheless play a decisive role for in the realm of cognition, or that in the moral realm they acquire an at least partial concretization, he broaches the question of the becoming present of the highest, but intuitively unpresentable representation that is the idea. This is the problem of the *presentation*, or *Darstellung* of the idea, and it is rigorously distinct from that of representation. The issue is no longer how to depict, articulate, or illustrate something already present yet resisting adequate discursive or figural expression but of how something acquires presence—reality, actuality, effectiveness—in the first place. The question of *Darstellung* centers on the coming into presence, or occurring, of the ideas.[32]

Coming into presence (*Darstellung*) is the condition of the possibility of re-presentation (*Vorstellung*). But how does such presencing or presentation occur?

In his analysis of Hegel's concept of experience, Heidegger suggests a possible answer to this question when commenting on the claim that "science, in making its appearance, *is* an appearance itself":

> The appearance is the authentic presence itself: the *parousia* of the Absolute. In keeping with its absoluteness, the Absolute is with us of its own accord. In its will to be with us, the Absolute is being present. In itself, thus bringing itself forward, the Absolute is for itself. For the sake of the will of the *parousia* alone, the presentation of knowledge as phenomenon is necessary. The presentation is bound to remain turned toward the will of the Absolute. The presentation is itself a *willing* [emphasis added], that is, not just a wishing and striving but the action itself, if it pulls itself together within its nature.[33]

This telling comment makes it clear that in developing his analysis, Heidegger takes Hegel's *Wissenschaft* rather than Carnap's positivism as the model of science. His remarkable insight complicates Hegelianism in a way that opens it up *as if* from within. Far from a closed system, which, as a stable structure, would be the embodiment of reason or even the Logos, the

Hegelian Absolute here appears to be an infinitely restless will that wills itself in willing everything that emerges in nature and history. Heidegger explains the implications of this reading of systematic thinking when he interprets the inconceivability of freedom in Kant's philosophy in a way that points toward his own account of the groundless ground of Being: "The only thing that we comprehend is its incomprehensibility."[34] All comprehension, it seems, emerges from and, therefore, returns to what remains incomprehensible. As if rewriting Freud's analysis of the unconscious, Heidegger insists that there is at least one spot in consciousness at which "it is unplumbable—a navel, as it were, that is its point of contact with the unknown."[35]

While Kant clearly and consistently distinguishes the theoretical and practical uses of reason, he always insists on the "primacy of practical reason." Cognition presupposes volition, but willing does not necessarily presuppose thinking. The imbrication of thinking and willing lies at the heart of the imagination. In his analysis of aesthetic judgment in the third critique, Kant offers a definition of the imagination that proved decisive for many later writers, artists, philosophers, and theologians: "If, now, imagination must in the judgment of taste be regarded in its freedom, then, to begin with, it is not taken as reproductive as in subjection to the laws of association, but as productive in exerting an activity of its own (as originator of arbitrary forms of possible intuitions)."[36] The imagination involves two interrelated activities, which Kant describes as productive and reproductive. In its productive modality, the imagination figures forms that the reproductive imagination combines and recombines to create the schemata that organize the data of experience into comprehensible patterns. The argument hinges on the relation between *Darstellung* and *Vorstellung*. Theoretical and practical reason are impossible apart from representations; the activity of representation, in turn, presupposes antecedently given data that can be re-presented. The question then becomes: how does *Darstellung* happen, or how do representations *emerge*? According to Fichte, presentation is an act that "occurs with absolute spontaneity," and, therefore, *Darstellung* is "grounded" in freedom. Such freedom is anarchic—it is not the freedom *of* subjectivity but the freedom *from* subjectivity through which both subjectivity and objectivity are given. From this point of view, being is donation.

While autonomy is self-grounded, an-archy is groundless. It "is not the diffraction of a principle, nor the multiple effect of a cause, but is the an-archy—the origin removed from every logic of origin, from every archae-ology."[37] Heidegger describes the an-archy of freedom glimpsed in the presentational activity of the imagination as an abyss. In *Kant and the Problem of Metaphysics*, he explains: "In the radicalism of his questions, Kant brought the 'possibility' of metaphysics to the abyss. He saw the unknown. He had to shrink back. It was not just that the transcendental power of the imagination frightened him, but rather that in between [the two editions of the first critique] pure reason as reason drew him increasingly under its spell."[38] This abyss or *Abgrund* from which all determination emerges is the groundless ground that is indistinguishable from nothing. Such an unfath-omable ground is the no-thing on which everything depends and every foundation founders. Contrary to expectation, it is Hegel who explains the relationship between nothingness and freedom: "In its highest form of explication nothingness would be freedom. But this highest form is negativ-ity insofar as it inwardly deepens itself to its highest intensity; and in this way it is itself affirmation—indeed absolute affirmation."[39] Negativity is affir-mative insofar as it is the condition of the creative emergence of everything that exists. Just as God creates freely *ex nihilo*, so the productive imagination creates freely out of nothing. This "is" the nothing that nothings or nihilates by giving the gift of being itself. Nothing, which is the condition of the pos-sibility of whatever exists, is never present and, therefore, cannot be repre-sented; nor, of course, is it absent. Far from subverting thought, this nothing keeps thinking in play.

At this point, the differences between Carnap's argument, which takes a dated understanding of the natural sciences as a model for philosophy, and Heidegger's use of art to reinterpret philosophy and technology become evi-dent. In contrast to so-called scientific philosophy, which presupposes that meaningful statements are referential and, thus, representational, Heidegger argues that the task of philosophy is to think that which eludes reference and resists representation. So understood, philosophy does not abandon critical thinking; to the contrary, when philosophical analysis is pushed to its limit, one encounters contradictions that are the conditions of the possibility of thinking itself. As Gasché points out,

> Aporia is thus not something negative. It is what allows the limits constitutive of philosophical thinking to be drawn, but, as limits that are neither pure nor undivided, they are crossable and consequently impossible limits. Far from being a flaw, the fundamental aporia of death in *Being and Time* represents the condition from which philosophical thought draws its very possibility; at the same time, however, this enabling condition undermines the claims that philosophical discourse makes for itself.[40]

What Carnap's scientific philosophy regards as the source of error is, for Heidegger, the origin of truth. While setting itself over against theology and art, "scientific" philosophy, Heidegger argues, actually extends the will to power characteristic of Western metaphysics. To subvert the will that would construct the world in its own image, he argues, it is necessary to return to the origin of the work of art by asking: what is the work of art?

Art, understood as *poiesis*, is the activity of figuring form in and through which determinate objects as well as the words and concepts with which they are apprehended are articulated. The correspondence between word and thing, which traditionally has been identified with truth, requires differentiation, which, in effect, presents whatever is present. Heidegger labels such presencing "unconcealment"—*Aletheia*, which, he argues, is truth.

> *Aletheia*, as opening of presence and presencing in thinking and saying, originally comes under the perspective of *homoiosis* and *adaequatio*, that is, the perspective of sense and correspondence of representing with what is present. But this process inevitably provokes another question: How is it that *aletheia*, unconcealment, appears to man's natural experience and speaking *only* as correctness and dependability? Is it because man's ecstatic sojourn in the openness of presencing is turned only toward what

is present and the existent presenting of what is present? But what else does this mean than that presence as such, and together with it the opening granting it, remain unheeded? Only what *aletheia* as opening grants is experienced and thought, not what it is as such.[41]

So interpreted, truth is an event that can be neither experienced nor thought properly. Instead of the accurate representation of an object to a subject, truth is the opening between subject and object that makes both representation and correspondence possible. This interpretation of truth involves an understanding of language that is completely different from that of logical positivists and linguistic analysts. For Heidegger, language does not represent antecedent entities but forms entities that can, in turn, be represented. This formative activity is the *poiesis* that defines the work of art. Language, therefore, is essentially poetic, and *poiesis* is the unconcealment that is the event of truth.[42] As our consideration of the interplay between *Vorstellung* and *Darstellung* suggests, such unconcealment is inseparable from concealment; there is no showing that is not at the same time hiding. The work of art *performs* the impossibility of representation, which is the origin of being and thinking.

> There is much in being that man cannot master. There is but little that comes to be known. What is known remains inexact, what is mastered insecure. What is, is never of our making or even merely the product of our minds, as it might all to easily seem. When we contemplate this whole as one, then we apprehend, so it appears, all that is—though we grasp it crudely enough.
>
>    And yet—beyond what is, not away from it but before it, there is still something other that happens. In the midst of beings as a whole an open place occurs. There is a clearing, a lighting. Thought of in reference to what is, to beings, this clearing is in a greater degree than are beings. This open center is therefore not surrounded by what is; rather, the lighting center itself encircles all that is, like the Nothing we scarcely know.[43]

"The Nothing we scarcely know" is the nothing that nothings, the nothing that nihilates. Never reducible to syntax or semantics, the work of art presents what can never be represented. Another name or, more "properly," pseudonym for this Nothing is God.

> For the listener, who listens in the snow,
> And, nothing himself, beholds
> Nothing that is not there and the nothing that is.[44]

## QUESTIONS OF STYLE

If there is nothing outside or beyond style, we might say of modern philosophy what Venturi said of modern architecture: non-style has become modernism's preferred style. This insight points to a suggestive analogy—analytic philosophy : modern architecture :: continental philosophy : postmodern architecture. While modern analytic philosophy seeks secure foundations in clear concepts and verifiable facts, postmodern continental philosophy reveals the absence of ground in artful works that turn us toward what is always turning away. The most interesting philosophers realize what the best scientists also know: there is an undeniable poetic aspect to their work. And the best artists and writers know that there is an undeniable philosophical—even theological or a/theological—dimension to their work.

The difference between the two approaches I have been considering does not, then, involve the opposition of two types of philosophy of religion but the contrast of two ways of thinking, writing, and even living—one acknowledges and cultivates the poetic, artistic, and literary characteristics of creative work, and the other denies and represses them. As Freud has taught us, however, the repressed never disappears but remains to haunt those who try to deny it. When analysis becomes critical, it bends back on itself and solicits the return of the repressed. This revenant inevitably disrupts the structures and systems—psychological, religious, social, political, and economic—designed to contain it. What is repressed always remains irreducibly ambiguous because it not only repels but also attracts. Order, after all, becomes repressive, and disruption can be both liberating and transforming.

Heidegger underscores this insight in an important essay entitled "The Question Concerning Technology," where he quotes Hölderlin, one of his two favorite poets:

> But where there is danger, there grows
> Also what saves.[45]

Having argued that the will to mastery embodied in modern science and technology has turned destructive and threatens the entire planet, Heidegger now unexpectedly suggests that this mortal danger harbors hope. This twist in his thinking results from his realization that technology has not always been what it has become during the modern era. "There was a time," he writes,

> when it was not technology alone that bore the name *techne*. Once that revealing that brings forth the truth into the splendor of radiant appearance was also called *techne*.
>
> Once there was a time when the bringing-forth of the true into the beautiful was called *techne*. The *poiesis* of the fine arts was also *techne* . . .
>
> The arts were not derived from the artistic. Art works were not enjoyed aesthetically. Art was not a sector of cultural activity.
>
> What was art—perhaps only for that brief but magnificent age? Why did art bear the modest name *techne*? Because it was a revealing that brought forth and made present, and therefore belonged within *poiesis*. It was finally that revealing that holds complete sway in all the fine arts, in poetry, and in everything poetical that obtained *poiesis* as its proper name.

Far from being opposed, art and technology were once complementary expressions of human *poiesis*—art as *techne*, technology as art. Rethinking "the essence of technology" in terms of *poiesis* displaces the will to mastery with a style of thinking that creates the possibility of transforming both self and world. Heidegger continues,

> The same from whom we heard the words

> But where danger is, grows
> The saving power also . . .

> says to us:
> . . . poetically dwells man upon this earth.[46]

To dwell poetically would be to transform art into life and life into art.

As I have noted, elsewhere I have argued in words that are far from artful, "religion is an emergent, complex adaptive network of symbols, myths and rituals that, on the one hand, figure schemata of feeling, thinking and acting in ways that lend life meaning and purpose and, on the other, disrupt, dislocate and disfigure every stabilizing structure."[47] From this point of view, there are two interrelated moments in religion—one structures and stabilizes, and the other destructures and destabilizes. These two moments, which correspond to the two styles of philosophy we have been considering, are inseparable and alternate in a quasi-dialectical rhythm. One style seeks the clarity, precision, and verification that can provide certainty and security by repressing disruptive emergence; the other style deliberately traces the elusive excess, remainder, and supplement that both harbors disruption and promises transformation.

These alternative styles of philosophy, in turn, reflect different deployments of the imagination. Heidegger's account of the interplay between *Darstellung* (presentation) and *Vorstellung* (representation) points to two sides of the imagination, which the poet Coleridge, commenting on the philosopher Fichte, labels "primary" and "secondary."

> The *imagination*, then, I consider either as primary, or secondary. The primary imagination I hold to be the living Power and prime Agent of all

human Perception, and as repetition in the finite mind of the eternal act of creation in the infinite I AM. The secondary Imagination I consider as an echo of the former, coexisting with the conscious will, yet still as identical with the primary in the *kind* of its agency, and differing only in the *degree* and the *mode* of its operation.[48]

In these seminal lines, art, philosophy, and religion intersect in a way that makes it impossible to be sure where one ends and another begins. The implications of Coleridge's provocative claim become clear over a century later in the work of the person who is, in my judgment, the most important modern poet, Wallace Stevens. The bridge between these two poets is the philosopher who most deeply influenced Stevens: Nietzsche.

In his philosophical fragments and unscientific postscripts to postscripts, Nietzsche develops an aesthetic a/theology that, like Kierkegaard's philosophical vision, can be communicated only through aesthetic indirection. Both his supporters and critics repeatedly misunderstand and misrepresent Nietzsche's notorious declaration of the death of God because they overlook an important qualification. The god who dies, Nietzsche argues, is the *transcendent moral God*: "At bottom, it is only the moral god that has been overcome. Does it make sense to conceive a god 'beyond good and evil'? Would a pantheism in this sense be possible? Can we remove the idea of a goal from the process and affirm the process in spite of this?"[49] Though Nietzsche never mentions Kant, he appropriates his interpretation of the beautiful work of art in terms of "inner teleology" or purposeless process to argue that the world itself is, in effect, a work of art whose purpose is nothing other than itself. The death of the moral God creates the possibility of the birth of the divine artist whose creative activity is no longer transcendent but has become immanent in the activity of the imagination.

In his early work, *Birth of Tragedy*, Nietzsche writes,

throughout the book I attributed a purely aesthetic meaning—whether implied or overt—to all process: a kind of divinity, if you like, God as the supreme artist, amoral, recklessly creating and destroying, realizing himself indifferently in whatever he does or undoes, ridding himself by his acts of embarrassment of his riches and the strain of his internal contradictions.

This process has two sides—Apollonian and Dionysian—that correspond to the two rhythms of religion and express the correlative operations of the imagination. While the Apollonian is "the *principium individuationis*" that establishes "just boundaries," the Dionysian transgresses fixed limits and tends "toward the shattering of the individual." These two tendencies are neither separate nor opposed; to the contrary, Dionysus needs Apollo as much as Apollo needs Dionysus. Dionysus upsets and dislocates the stabilizing structures that Apollo fashions, and Apollo creates the order Dionysus disrupts. In this way, if Dionysus puts into play the productive imagination that operates in *Darstellung*, and Apollo taps the reproductive imagination as well as the two guises of the "supreme artist" that Nietzsche names God, then God and the imagination are one.[50]

It was left for Stevens to expand Nietzsche's notion of art and the artist to include creative activity as such. Heaven and earth meet in "An Ordinary Evening in New Haven."

> The endlessly elaborating poem
> Displays the theory of poetry
> As the life of poetry. A more severe,
> More harassing master would extemporize
> Subtler, more urgent proof that the theory
> Of poetry is the theory of life . . . [51]

The creativity that transforms life into art and art into life is not merely human, and the poetry that is the theory of life is not merely a literary genre but is the "substance" of all things visible and invisible. If, as Heidegger, quoting his other favorite poet, Rilke, insists, "Only a god can save us now," my wager is that the God that saves at this late moment is the imagination.[52] The artful logic of the poet remains the last word.

Proposita: 1. God and the imagination are one. 2. The thing imagined is the imaginer.

The second equals the thing imagined and the imaginer are one. Hence, I suppose, the imaginer is God.[53]

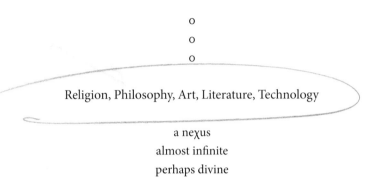

o

o

o

Religion, Philosophy, Art, Literature, Technology

a neχus
almost infinite
perhaps divine

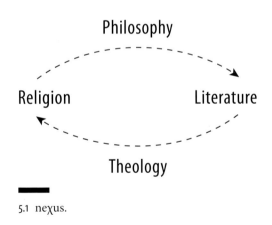

Philosophy

Religion           Literature

Theology

5.1 neχus.

# ACKNOWLEDGMENTS

**BOOKS ARE** always joint ventures. *Rewiring the Real*, as well as much else, would not have been possible without the generous support of Wendy Lochner, James Jordan, and Lisa Hamm, Columbia University Press; Nicholas Dirks, Columbia University; Emily Brennan and Chelsea Ebin, the Institute for Religion, Culture, and Public Life; Thomas Carlson, University of California, Santa Barbara; David Miller, Syracuse University; Mark Danielewski, and Richard Powers. A special word of thanks to past and present students at Williams College and Columbia University for exploring these ideas with me. And as always, my deepest appreciation to Margaret Weyers for her endless support, Jack Miles for our lifelong conversation, and Dinny for everything.

 Stone Hill

# NOTES

## neχus

*neχus* is the name of a multifaceted art complex that I am creating in the Berkshire Mountains. This will be the subject of my next work, which will not be only a book.

1. See Mark C. Taylor, *Disfiguring: Art, Architecture, Religion* (Chicago: University of Chicago Press, 1992); *About Religion: Economies of Faith in Virtual Culture* (Chicago: University of Chicago Press, 1999); *The Picture in Question: Mark Tansey and the Ends of Representation* (Chicago: University of Chicago Press, 1999); *Hiding* (Chicago: University of Chicago Press, 1997); *Grave Matters* (London: Reaktion, 2002); *Mystic Bones* (Chicago: University of Chicago Press, 2007); *Motel Real: Las Vegas Nevada* (Williamstown: Williams Museum of Contemporary Art and Massachusetts Museum of Contemporary Art, 1997). The art exhibition was *Grave Matters*, October 2001–March 2002, http://www.massmoca.org/event_details.php?id=51.
2. Søren Kierkegaard, *Stages on Life's Way*, trans. Howard Hong and Edna Hong (Princeton, N.J.: Princeton University Press, 1988), 8.
3. For further discussion of this point, see Taylor, *Disfiguring*, especially chapter 1.

4. Friedrich Schlegel, *Philosophical Fragments*, trans. Peter Firchow (Minneapolis: University of Minnesota Press, 1991), 97.

5. See Jean-Luc Nancy and Philippe Lacoue-Labarthe, *The Literary Absolute: The Theory of Literature in German Romanticism*, trans. Philip Barnard and Cheryl Lester (Albany: State University of New York Press, 1988).

6. See Mark C. Taylor, *The Moment of Complexity: Emerging Network Culture* (Chicago: University of Chicago Press, 2001).

7. See Jacques Derrida, "Of an Apocalyptic Tone Recently Adopted in Philosophy," trans. John Leavy, *Semeia* 23 (1982): 63–97.

8. See Paul Tillich, *The Theology of Culture*, ed. Roger Kimball (New York: Oxford University Press, 1964).

9. For a more detailed discussion of this essay, see Taylor, *After God* (Chicago: University of Chicago Press, 2007), chapter 1.

10. Heidegger offers this comment in the notorious *Der Spiegel* interview (May 31, 1976) in which he addresses his involvement with National Socialism. In anticipation of my analysis of William Gaddis's *The Recognitions*, a rarely noted detail in this interview is worth stressing. In the course of his remarks, Heidegger says that he, too, thinks art has lost its way. In the following exchange, he expresses surprising agreement with Horkheimer and Adorno's criticism of the "culture industry."

> *Spiegel:* The artist, too, lacks commitment to tradition. He might find it beautiful, and he can say: Yes, that is the way one could paint six hundred years ago or three hundred years ago or even thirty years ago. But he can no longer do it. Even if he wanted to, he could not. The greatest artist would then be the ingenious forger Hans van Meegeren, who would then paint "better" than the others. But it just does not work any more. Therefore the artist, writer, poet is in a similar situation to the thinker. How often we must say: Close your eyes.
>
> *Heidegger:* If the "culture industry" is taken as the framework for the classification of art and poetry and philosophy, then the parity is justified. However, if not only the industry but also what is called culture becomes questionable, then the contemplation of this questionableness also belongs to thinking's realm of responsibility, and thinking's plight is barely imaginable. But thinking's greatest affliction is that today, as far as I can see, no thinker yet speaks who is great enough to place thinking, directly and formatively, before its subject matter and therefore on its path. The greatness of what is to be thought is too great for us today. Perhaps we can struggle with building narrow and not very far-reaching footbridges for a crossing.

Han van Meergeren was the pseudonym for the Dutch painter and portraitist Henricus Antonius van Meegeren (1889–1947). When his work did not receive the critical acclaim he thought it deserved, van Meergeren started forging paintings of some of the most important artists in the Western tradition—Frans Hals, Pieter de Hooch, Gerard ter Borch, and Johannes Vermeer. During the Second World War, wealthy Dutch collectors attempting to prevent the Nazis from confiscating their artistic heritage purchased van Meergeren's fakes, thinking they were original. After the war, one of his forgeries was discovered in the collection of Hermann Göring, and Dutch authorities assumed that von Meergeren had sold works of art to the Nazis. To avoid the charge of treason, he confessed to forgery and was sentenced to one year in prison but died before he served his term. The von Meergeren case was much in the news during the years Gaddis was working on *The Recognitions*, and he used the Dutch forger as the model for the main character of his novel, Wyatt Gwyon.

## 1. COUNTERFEITING COUNTERFEIT RELIGION: WILLIAM GADDIS, *THE RECOGNITIONS*

1. William Gaddis, *The Recognitions* (New York: Penguin, 1993), 343. Throughout this chapter, citations to this work are given in the text.
2. See Hans Jonas, *The Gnostic Religion: The Message of the Alien God and the Beginnings of Christianity* (Boston: Beacon, 1963). More recent scholarship has raised questions about the accuracy of characterizing Gnosticism as dualistic. See, inter alia, Karen King, *What Is Gnosticism?* (Cambridge, Mass.: Harvard University Press, 2003); and Michael Williams, *Rethinking Gnosticism: An Argument for Dismantling a Dubious Category* (Princeton, N.J.: Princeton University Press, 1996).
3. Goethe, *Faust II*, lines 6834–6835. Stephen Moore, "A Reader's Guide to William Gaddis's *The Recognitions*," http://www.williamgaddis.org/recognitions/index. This is a superb resource, providing detailed notes for many of Gaddis's notoriously obscure references. Throughout this chapter, I have made use of material provided by this site.
4. For an elaboration of these points, see my book *Disfiguring: Art, Architecture, Religion* (Chicago: University of Chicago Press, 1992).
5. Gaddis is obviously also thinking about Richard Wagner, whose music echoes at critical points in the novel. No less important than Wagner's opera is his tangled relation to Nietzsche, whose work, we shall see, is never far from Gaddis's mind.
6. See Mircea Eliade, *The Forge and the Crucible: The Origins and Structures of Alchemy* (Chicago: University of Chicago Press, 1978).

7. William Gaddis, interview, *Paris Review*, no. 105 (Winter 1987): 78.

8. Ibid., 64.

9. Many of the names in the novel are selected to suggest mythological precursors. Camilla, Moore explains, was "the virgin queen of the Volscians who helped Turnus against Aeneas . . . and of whom Vergil says, 'over the mid sea, hung upon the swelling billow, she would keep on her way, nor wet her nimble soles on the surface of the water'. . . . Camilla was a devotee of Diana (in her capacity as goddess of the moon) and is the first woman mentioned in Dante's *Inferno*." Gwyon, "according to de Rougemont, 'was a Celtic divinity whose name . . . means the Fuhrer, who has in his custody the secret initiation into the way of divinization.' Also relevant are Gawain from the Grail romances and Gwion, a semi-legendary bard whose poetry hides 'an ancient religious mystery—a blasphemous one from the Church's point of view—under the cloak of buffoonery.' " Moore, "A Reader's Guide."

10. Immanuel Kant, *The Critique of Judgment*, trans. James Meredith (New York: Oxford University Press, 1973), 1:168–169, 181.

11. A chancre is a red, insensitive lesion that is the first manifestation of syphilis.

12. "*Perdu*" is the past participle of the French *perdre*, which means inter alia to lose, waste, ruin, destroy, undo, corrupt, deprave, disgrace, or dishonor. *Purdue Victory*, therefore, suggests a lost, ruined, wasted, or wrecked victory.

13. Leonard Primiano, "Halloween," *The Encyclopedia of Religion*, ed. Mircea Eliade (New York: Macmillan, 1987), 6:176–177.

14. Gaddis makes frequent allusions to Melville's *The Confidence-Man*. It is possible to read *The Recognitions* as a rewriting of both *The Confidence-Man* and *Moby-Dick*. One of the names of Melville's confidence man is Frank Goodman, who is neither frank nor good. Frank Sinisterra is, of course, both sinful and sinister. It is difficult to know where to stop because Gaddis might always be joking. Perhaps Frank Sinisterra is a con man like Frank Sinatra.

15. Arius, who was the leader of the post-Nicean opposition to the doctrine of *Homoousios*, insisted that Christ was a creature who was fully human but in no way divine. The strength of his following led to the convening of the Council of Constantinople for the purpose of reaffirming the principal tenets of the Nicean Creed. Radical Arians were known as "Dissimiliarians" because they espoused the view that the two natures of Christ are completely unlike each other. Gaddis dubs this alternative *Heteroousian*.

16. There is a colony of Barbary apes on the Rock of Gibraltar. According to legend, British domination of Gibraltar will end when the apes disappear.

17. For a consideration of how these issues play out in today's finance capitalism, see my book *Confidence Games: Money and Markets in a World Without Redemption* (Chicago: University of Chicago Press, 2004).

18. Gaddis, interview, 61.

19. Ibid., 65–66.

20. These divisions are mine and not Gaddis's. In fact, what I describe as the second section does not begin until page 700.

21. Gherardo Gnoli, "Mithra," *The Encyclopedia of Religion*, ed. Mircea Eliade (New York: Macmillan, 1987), 9:579.

22. Sir James Frazer, *The Golden Bough: A Study in Magic and Religion* (New York: Macmillan, 1980), 289–293. Gaddis refers to this section of Frazer's work on p. 23.

23. Here, as elsewhere, the novel folds back on itself. The charges listed on p. 701 repeat charges made on p. 9.

24. The paper bearing these calculations has a picture and report of a young Spanish girl whom the Catholic church is canonizing. This is, of course, the child buried next to Camilla in San Zwingli. In most Gnostic mythology, there are seven heavens. However, Basilides of Alexander, who used the word "*abraxas*" as a symbolic term before it became the name of the highest deity, insisted that there were 365 heavens. Moore, "A Reader's Guide."

25. Here, as in so many other places, Gaddis is astonishingly prescient. In the early 1950s, he already anticipated the world of televangelism, simulated news, and reality TV.

26. John Baldovin, "Easter," *The Encyclopedia of Religion*, ed. Mircea Eliade (New York: Macmillan, 1987), 4:557.

27. Moore, "A Reader's Guide."

28. G. W. F. Hegel, *Phenomenology of Spirit*, trans. A. V. Miller (New York: Oxford University Press, 1977), 27.

29. The devil's interval, according to Moore, is "the tritone, the interval of the augmented fourth. Its use was prohibited by early theorists." In a certain sense, *The Recognitions* itself is suspended in the devil's interval where mimicry and duplicity dissemble what once seemed real.

30. For a discussion of "about," see "About About," in my *About Religion: Economies of Faith in Virtual Culture* (Chicago: University of Chicago Press, 1999), 1–6.

31. It is possible that Gaddis borrows this name from J. D. Salinger's story, "For Esme, With Love and Squalor." Wyatt surely offered Esme more squalor than love.

32. Friedrich Nietzsche, *The Will to Power*, trans. Walter Kaufmann (New York: Random House, 1968), 98.

33. Friedrich Nietzsche, "The Anti-Christ," in *The Portable Nietzsche*, ed. Walter Kaufmann (New York: Penguin, 1980), 616.

34. The most telling reference to Dionysus occurs in the hilarious account of a masquerade ball for drag queens: "There was, in fact, a religious aura about this festival, religious that is in the sense of devotion, adoration, celebration or deity, before religion became confused with systems of ethics and morality, to become a sore affliction upon the very things it had once exalted. Quite as festive, these halls, as the Dionysian processions in which Greek boys dressed as women carried the ithyphalli through the streets, amid sounds of rejoicing from all sexes present, and all were" (311).

35. Gaddis, interview, 64–65.

## 2. MOSAICS: RICHARD POWERS, *PLOWING THE DARK*

1. Richard Powers, *Galatea 2.2* (New York: Farrar, Straus, Giroux, 1995), 141.

2. All quotations in this section are from Sigmund Freud, "The 'Uncanny,'" 221, 222. http://www.mit.edu/~allanmc/freud1.pdf.

3. Freud, *Civilization and Its Discontents*, trans. James Strachey (New York: Norton, 1961), 11. Hereafter, page numbers to this work are given in the text.

4. Richard Powers, *Plowing the Dark* (New York: Farrar, Straus, Giroux, 2000), 215. All remaining intertextual citations are to this work.

5. Richard Powers, "The Art of Fiction," *Paris Review* 175: 5.

6. John Leonard, "Mind Painting," *New York Review of Books* (January 11, 2001): 42.

7. Ibid., 43.

8. I have borrowed most of the elements in this list from ibid., 42–48.

9. Jeffrey Williams, "The Last Generalist: An Interview with Richard Powers," 17. http://clogic.eserver.org/2-2/williams.html.

10. Georges Bataille, *Lascaux; or, The Birth of Art* (Switzerland: SKIRA, n.d.), 11, 27.

11. Robert Reid, *Architects of the Web: One Thousand Days That Built the Future of Business* (New York: John Wiley, 1997), xxv.

12. Powers, "The Art of Fiction," 60.

13. Ibid., 6, 8.

14. See my book *The Picture in Question: Mark Tansey and the Ends of Representation* (Chicago: University of Chicago Press, 1999).

15. Herman Hollerith (1860–1929), a statistician, used punched cards to develop a mechanical calculator. This invention eventually led him to found IBM.

16. Douglas Hubbard explains: "*Monte Carlo methods* are a class *of computational algorithms* that rely on repeated *random* sampling to compute their results. Monte

Carlo methods are often used when *simulating physical* and *mathematical* systems. Because of their reliance on repeated computation and *random* or *pseudo-random* numbers, Monte Carlo methods are most suited to calculation by a *computer*. Monte Carlo methods tend to be used when it is unfeasible or impossible to compute an exact result with a *deterministic algorithm*." This method is often used to model situations in which there are multiple inputs and a high degree of uncertainty, like the degree of risk in business transactions. Douglas Hubbard, *How to Measure Anything: Finding the Value of Intangibles in Business* (New York: John Wiley & Sons, 2007), 46.

17. Ray Kurtzweil, *The Singularity Is Near: When Humans Transcend Biology* (New York: Viking, 2005).

18. George Bataille, *Visions of Excess*, trans. Allan Stoekl (Minneapolis: University of Minnesota Press, 1985), 220.

19. Powers, "The Art of Fiction," 13.

20. Jean Baudrillard, "The Precession of the Simulacrum," in *Simulations*, trans. Paul Foss, Paul Patton, and Philip Beitchman (New York: Semiotext[e], 1983), 8–9.


## 3. FIGURING NOTHING: MARK DANIELEWSKI, *HOUSE OF LEAVES*

1. For an account of the founding of Global Education Network and the philosophy behind it, see Mark C. Taylor, *The Moment of Complexity: Emerging Network Culture* (Chicago: University of Chicago Press, 2001), 233–270.

2. Mark Danielewski, *House of Leaves* (New York: Random House, 2000), 3. Hereafter, citations are given in the text. Though I taught this book for the first time in Real Fakes (spring 2004), I used the book in my seminar Architectures of Meaning, offered at the School of Architecture at Columbia in the fall of 2003. For their final project, I asked the students to read the book and design the *House of Leaves*.

3. For an analysis of what I describe as "network culture," see my *The Moment of Complexity*.

4. Larry McCaffery and Sida Gregory, "Haunted House—An Interview with Mark Danielewski," *Critique* 44, no. 2 (Winter 2003): 106.

5. References elsewhere in the text make it clear that Danielewski's comments about crack are a parody of Heidegger's analysis of the *Riss* in his influential essay "The Origin of the Work of Art." Derrida explores this text by Heidegger in his book *The Truth in Painting*.

6. Sigmund Freud, "The 'Uncanny,'" 221, 224–225. http://www.mit.edu/~allanmc/freud1.pdf.

7. This reference is to Melisa Tao Janis, "Hollow Newel Ruminations," in *The Anti-Present Trunk*, ed. Philippa Frake (Oxford: Phaidon, 1995), 293 (122). "Frake" is, of course, an almost homonym of "fake." If you search for *The Anti-Present Trunk* on Amazon.com, you get *House of Leaves*. At one point, Johnny describes the trunk holding Zampanò's manuscript, which was becoming overwhelming, as a *thing*.

> All those books, sketches, collages, reams and reams of paper, measuring tapes nailed from corner to floor, and of course that big black trunk right there in the center of everything, all of it just another way to finally say: no-no, no junk at all.
> "Throw it away, hoss," Lude said and started to cross to my desk for a closer look. I sprung forward, ordered by instinct, like some animal defending its pride, interposing myself between him and my work, those papers, this thing. (324)

8. Martin Heidegger, "The Thing," in *Language, Poetry, Thought*, trans. Albert Hofstadter (New York: Harper and Row, 1971). The texts cited in this section are all from pages 165–169 of this work.

9. Edgar Allan Poe, "MS. Found in a Bottle," in *Poe: Poetry and Tales* (New York: Library of America, 1984), 189–199.

10. Maurice Blanchot, *The Writing of the Disaster*, trans. Ann Smock (Lincoln: University of Nebraska Press, 1986).

11. *Sous rature*—under erasure—is a term Derrida uses repeatedly to describe his practice of crossing out words in his printed works. By preserving the words he nonetheless erases, Derrida enacts the Freudian practice of denegation, through which something is affirmed by a process of negating or repressing. Heidegger also crosses out the word *Sein* (Being) in his essay "On the Question of Being." See *Pathmakers*, ed. William McNeil (New York: Cambridge University Press, 1998).

12. Jacques Derrida, "Tympan," in *Margins of Philosophy*, trans. Alan Bass (Chicago: University of Chicago Press, 1982), x.

13. For an analysis of *Glas*, see my book *Altarity* (Chicago: University of Chicago Press, 1987), chapter 9.

14. I have considered Auster's *City of Glass* in my *Hiding* (Chicago: University of Chicago Press, 1997), chapter 1, "Skinsc(r)apes."

15. Ribbons is a pseudonym Auster uses.

16. John Leavey and Richard Rand are the English translators of *Glas*. Elsewhere, I have considered the theme of the bastard in *Glas*. See *Altarity*, 255–303.

17. Christian Norberg-Schulz, *The Concept of Dwelling: On the Way to Figurative Architecture* (New York: Rizzoli, 1984), 17.

18. I always tell students that if they can read a book while lying in the sun, it's not worth reading.
19. Helen Selonick.
20. Analia Sorribas.
21. Robin Hwang.
22. Adam Grogg.
23. *Hello* was Poe's first CD. Danielewski took the name Johnny for Johnny Truant from his sister's song "Angry Johnny."
24. Douglas Hoftstadter is, of course, the author of the influential *Gödel, Escher, Bach: An Eternal Braid* (New York: Basic Books, 1979). I have considered the importance of Hoftstadter's work for understanding complex adaptive systems in *The Moment of Complexity*.
25. This inconspicuous clue points to Danielewski's next book: *Only Revolutions: A Novel* (New York: Pantheon Books, 2006). Once again, graphic design is integral to the work. The novel is 360 pages long and is divided into two equal parts, one of which recount a cross-country joyride from the point of view of a young man named Sam and the other from the point of view of a young woman named Hailey. The two tales read front to back and back to front and meet precisely in the middle—page 180. This book is also color coded. Just as the word "house" is printed in blue in *House of Leaves*, so every "o," "O," and "o" is in green or gold throughout *Only Revolutions*. The interplay of gold and green suggests an alchemical process that once again might be a confidence game. See my *Confidence Games: Money and Markets in a World Without Redemption* (Chicago: University of Chicago Press, 2004).

## 4. "HOLY SHIT!": DON DELILLO, *UNDERWORLD*

JR, the kid who is the main character in Gaddis's novel with the same title, constantly uses the expression I take as this chapter's title.
1. A. R. Ammons, *Garbage* (New York: W. W. Norton, 1993), 8, 55, 27–29.
2. DeLillo's most recent novel, *Point Omega*, tells the story of James Elster, a "defense intellectual" who had worked for the military until he became disillusioned and retreated to the desert to reflect on his life. Like Danielewski, DeLillo uses film as a framing device. The narrative is suspended between two sections, "Anonymity" and "Anonymity 2," dated September 3 and September 4, respectively. In the first scene, an anonymous man is in a dark room at an art exhibition watching a conceptual work entitled *24 Hour Psycho* that is based on Alfred Hitchcock's influential

film *Psycho*. The man returns day after day, but nothing happens. With everything moving in slow motion, the opening section concludes with the lines, "Light and sound, wordless monotone, an intimation of life-beyond, world beyond, the strange bright fact that breathes and eats out there, the things that's not the movies." In the concluding episode, the anonymous man meets Elster's daughter at the exhibition. Jessie lives in Manhattan and frequents uptown and downtown museums. After a brief conversation, she gives him her phone number but not her name. By the end of the story, it seems there is nothing "that's not the movies." In the closing pages, DeLillo writes, "Real time is meaningless. The phrase is meaningless. There's no such thing."

The story proper begins on a philosophical note: "The true life is not reducible to words spoken or written, not by anyone, ever. The true life takes place when we're alone, thinking, feeling, lost in memory, dreaming, self-aware, the submicroscopic moments." Elster had retreated to the desert to find what might remain real in his life, when his meditations are interrupted by the unexpected arrival of Jessie, whose mother had sent her to stay with her father to get away from her boyfriend. The rest of the novella records the complex relationship between father and daughter. When tensions reach the breaking point, Jessie disappears in the desert without leaving a trace. In spite of the efforts of Elster and a young documentary filmmaker, Jim Finley, who is making a documentary about Elster's experience with the defense department, they never find Jessie. The narrative in this section begins where DeLillo ends by telling the story of what happened to Jessie Elster.

DeLillo borrows the title of this work from Teilhard Pierre de Chardin, a Jesuit trained as a paleontologist and geologist and who is best known for his participation in the expedition that discovered both Piltdown man and Peking man. His book, *The Phenomenon of Man*, presents a comprehensive account of the history of the cosmos from the time of creation to what he calls the Omega Point. The cosmic process culminates in what Teilhard calls the "Noosphere," where human consciousness becomes completely unified. For Teilhard, the evolutionary process ends with the material becoming immaterial and the real becoming virtual to create a planetary psychic unity. Elster, we will see, traces the reverse trajectory. At Point Omega, he declares, "We pass completely out of being. Stones." Might this be what Roger Caillois described as the "mysticism of matter"? What if Meister Eckhart were right: "The stone is God, but it does not know it, and it is the not knowing that makes it a stone." See Roger Caillois, *The Writing of Stones*, trans. Barbara Bray (Charlottesville: University of Virginia Press, 1985), xiv, xvi.

My fictional narrative in the first section of this essay picks up where DeLillo leaves off in *Point Omega*. All lines with single quotation marks in this section are from Don DeLillo, *Point Omega* (New York: Scribner, 2010). Though some of the names in this section are real, the events and conversations are fictitious unless otherwise indicated.

3. Quotations about Salton Lake are from Jeff Springer, *Plagues and Pleasures of Salton Sea*, http://www.youtube.com/watch?v=QhB2ZvHVFls.

4. In 2009, the Obama administration declared that Yucca Mountain is no longer an option for the disposal of nuclear waste and eliminated all funding for the site. No alternative site has been identified, and nuclear waste continues to accumulate at loosely guarded and unprotected locations throughout the country.

5. Quoted in Michael Kimmelman, "Art's Last, Lonely Cowboy," *New York Times* (February 6, 2005).

6. Derrida lifts this phrase from Hegel's *Phenomenology of Spirit* and makes it the focus of his argument in "The Pit and the Pyramid: Introduction to Hegel's Semiology." "A path, which we will follow, leads from this night pit, silent as death and resonating with all the powers of the voice which it holds in reserve, to a pyramid brought back from the Egyptian desert which soon will be raised over the sober and abstract weave of the Hegelian text, there composing the stature and status of the sign." *Margins of Philosophy*, trans. Alan Bass, (Chicago: University of Chicago Press, 1982), 77. For other examples of a pyramid with its tip knocked off, see the backside of the dollar bill and my *Altarity* (Chicago: University of Chicago Press, 1987), cover, 262; and *Hiding* (Chicago: University of Chicago Press, 1997), 229, 231.

7. Kimmelman, "Art's Last, Lonely Cowboy."

8. Wallace Stevens, "The Man on the Dump," in *The Collected Poems of Wallace Stevens* (New York: Knopf, 1981), 203.

9. For an elaboration of this point, see Tom LeClair, *In the Loop: Don DeLillo and the Systems Novel* (Chicago: University of Illinois Press, 1987). LeClair's book was published ten years before *Underworld* appeared and is based largely on the theoretical work of Ludwig von Bertalanffy's *General System Theory* (1968) and Talcott Parsons's sociology. LeClair's insightful analysis draws useful connections between DeLillo's novels and the work of Pynchon and Gaddis.

10. Containment was the strategy the United States used to counter the spread of communism in the years following the Second World War. The doctrine was first defined by George F. Kennan in 1946 and is most closely associated with President Harry Truman, but it was supported by every president down to Jimmy Carter.

11. The other game that DeLillo mentions in connection with the Cold War is chess, which Nick's brother Matt learned when he was young. During the Cold War, most game theorists used chess to develop models for military strategies. DeLillo stresses the political stakes of chess when he recalls the highly charged match between

Bobby Fischer and Boris Spassky. Sister Edgar, who had taught Nick and Matt when they were young, knew things about chess and much else that others did not. She adds a telling detail to the story of Cold War chess. "She knew that Bobby Fischer had all the fillings removed from his teeth when he played Boris Spassky in 1972—it made perfect sense to her—so the KGB could not control him through broadcasts made into the amalgam units packed in his molars" (251).

12. Brian Massumi, *Parables for the Virtual: Movement, Affect, Sensation* (Durham, N.C.: Duke University Press, 2002), 73.

13. Sigmund Freud, *Civilization and Its Discontents*, trans. James Strachey (New York: Norton, 1961), 17.

14. Don DeLillo, "Baseball and the Cold War," in *Conversations with Don DeLillo*, ed. Thomas DePietro (Jackson: University of Mississippi Press, 2005), 146.

15. Sigmund Freud, *The Interpretation of Dreams*, trans. James Strachey (New York: Avon, 1965), 143.

16. Ibid., 131, 314, 317–318.

17. The notions of entropy and negentropy, which originally were developed in thermodynamic theory and later appropriated in information theory, have proved fascinating for novelists and writers. Thomas Pynchon, for example, is obsessed with the idea of entropy, and Robert Smithson's work is a sustained exploration of entropy. As we will see below, since the end of the Second World War many visual artists have devised different ways of making art from trash.

18. Charles-Edouard Jeanneret and Amedee Ozenfant, *Aprés le cubisme* (Torino: Bottega d'Erasmo, 1975), 27, 32–33, 60. Not all modernists share Le Corbusier's purism. Joseph Itten, for example, admonished artists "to keep [their] eyes open, while out walking, for rubbish heaps, refuse dumps, garbage buckets, and scrap deposits as sources of material by means of which to make images (sculptures) which would bring out unequivocally the essential and antagonistic properties of individual materials." Cubists, surrealists, and Dadaists all used discarded found objects to create works of art. Quoted in Mira Engler, *Designing America's Waste Landscapes* (Baltimore, Md.: Johns Hopkins University Press, 2004), 154.

19. In 1940, Hitler used the term *Neue Ordnung* to define the new political, economic, and social order that he sought to impose on Europe.

20. Quoted in Robert Hughes, *The Shock of the New* (New York: Alfred Knopf, 1967), 191. Le Corbusier had fascist proclivities. He edited the journal *Prelude*, whose board included several well-known fascists. He wrote in the Italian Futurist Filippo Marinetti's profascist publication, *Stile futurista*, "The present spectacle of Italy, the state of her spiritual powers, announces the imminent dawn of the modern spirit. Her shining purity and force illumine the paths which had been obscured by the

cowardly and the profiteers." Quoted in Robert Fishman, *Urban Utopias* (New York: Basic Books, 1997), 240.

21. Engler, *Designing America's Waste Landscapes*, 36.

22. Rudolph Otto, *The Idea of the Holy*, trans. John Harvey (New York: Oxford University Press, 1958), 6–7.

23. For an elaboration of the distinction between God and the sacred, see "Denegating God," in *Nots* (Chicago: University of Chicago Press, 1993).

24. http://www.youtube.com/watch?v=lrI7dVj9ozs. See also http://en.wikipedia.org/wiki/Shot_Heard_%27Round_the_World_(baseball)#Russ_Hodges.

25. See Joshua Prager, *The Echoing Green: The Untold Story of Bobby Thompson, Ralph Branca, and the Shot Heard Round the World* (New York: Vintage, 2008).

26. DeLillo, *Point Omega*, 18.

27. Georges Bataille, *The Accursed Share*, trans. Robert Hurley (New York: Zone, 1988), 1:28–29. Hereafter citations are given in the body of the text as AS.

28. Georges Bataille, *Visions of Excess, Selected Writings, 1927–1939*, trans. Allan Stoekl, Carl Lovitt, and Donald Leslie (Minneapolis: University of Minnesota Press, 1985), 128. Hereafter citations are given in the body of the text as VE.

29. Mark C. Taylor, *After God* (Chicago: University of Chicago Press, 2007), 12.

30. I consider this issue in more detail in "The Financialization of Art," which is the first chapter of *Refiguring the Spiritual* (New York: Columbia University Press, 2011).

31. Georges Bataille, *Theory of Religion*, trans. Robert Hurley (New York: Zone, 1989), 29. Hereafter citations are given in the body of the text as TR.

32. Heather Rogers, *Gone Tomorrow: The Hidden Life of Garbage* (New York: The New Press, 2005), 112.

33. Vance Packard, *The Waste Makers* (New York: David McKay Company, 1960), 89.

34. Quoted in ibid., 25.

35. Ibid., 232.

36. For an extensive analysis of this development, see my book *Confidence Games: Money and Markets in a World Without Redemption* (Chicago: University of Chicago Press, 2004).

37. Andy Warhol, *The Philosophy of Andy Warhol* (New York: Harcourt, Brace, 1975), 92.

38. *Underworld* was published in 1997.

39. Maria Moss, "'Writing as a Deeper Form of Concentration': An Interview with Don DeLillo," in *Conversations with Don DeLillo*, ed. Thomas DePietro (Jackson: University of Mississippi Press, 2005), 156–157.

40. Don DeLillo, *Cosmopolis* (New York: Scribners, 2003), 89. Hereafter citations are given in the body of the text as C.

41. http://www.fintools.com/docs/Warren%20Buffet%20on%20Derivatives.pdf.

42. For a discussion of *JR*, see my *Confidence Games*.

43. Guy Debord, *The Society of the Spectacle* (Detroit, Mich.: Red and Black Press, 1967).

44. See http://www.spencertunick.com.

45. See Ray Kurzweil, *The Singularity Is Near: When Humans Transcend Biology* (New York: Penguin, 2006); Ashlee Vance, "Merely Human? So Yesterday," *New York Times* (June 13, 2010).

46. Stevens, *Collected Poems*, 203.

47. For my effort to make sense of this project, see "Cure of Ground," in *Refiguring the Spiritual* (New York: Columbia University Press, 2011).

48. See *Grave Matters* (London: Reaktion, 2002). This book of 150 photographs of modern writers, artists, and philosophers became the basis for an art exhibition I did at Mass MOCA from October to March in 2002–2003.

49. Other words that can be traced to this root are also suggestive: humble, humiliate, exhume, and homunculus.

## 5. CONCLUDING UNSCIENTIFIC POSTSCRIPT: TWO STYLES OF THE PHILOSOPHY OF RELIGION

1. Paul Tillich, "The Two Types of Philosophy of Religion," in *Theology and Culture*, ed. Robert Kimball (New York: Oxford University Press, 1959), 10. Though Tillich associates the ontological type with Augustine and the cosmological type with Thomas Aquinas, these categories are roughly parallel to Whitehead's distinction between Plato and Aristotle, respectively. Throughout this section, references to this essay are given in the text.

2. For an elaboration of this point, see my *After God* (Chicago: University of Chicago Press, 2007), chap. 2.

3. In what follows it will become clear that some artists and architects have insisted that to be effective in the modern world, art must become scientific. This point of view has inspired utopian fantasies that in some cases had devastating consequences.

4. Though Heidegger and Carnap were writing shortly after Max Planck, Werner Heisenberg, and others developed quantum theory and Einstein proposed his general theory of relativity, their work was not significantly influenced by these revolutionary scientific developments. The baffling world described in quantum mechanics, relativity theory, and string theory is in many ways more similar to Heidegger's philosophical and aesthetic vision than Carnap's logical positivism.

5. Martin Heidegger, "What Is Metaphysics?" in *Basic Writings*, trans. David Krell (New York: Harper and Row, 1977), 96.

6. Jacques Derrida, *Edmund Husserl's* Origin of Geometry: *An Introduction*, trans. John Leavey (Stony Brook, N.Y.: Nicholas Hays, 1978), 33–34, 47–48. Derrida's first book-length work, written for his diplome d'études superieures in 1953–1954, was also on Husserl and has now been published: *The Problem of Genesis in Husserl's Philosophy*, trans. Marian Hobson (Chicago: University of Chicago Press, 2003).

7. Martin Heidegger, "The Age of the World Picture," in *The Question Concerning Technology and Other Essays*, trans. William Lovitt (New York: Harper and Row, 1977), 127.

8. Martin Heidegger, "The Question Concerning Technology," in *The Question Concerning Technology and Other Essays*, trans. William Lovitt (New York: Harper and Row, 1977), 27.

9. Heidegger, "What Is Metaphysics?" 97–98.

10. Ibid., 103.

11. Ibid., 105.

12. Rudolf Carnap et al., "The Scientific Conception of the World: The Vienna Circle," in *The Emergence of Logical Empiricism from 1900 to the Vienna Circle*, ed. Sahotra Sarkar (New York: Garland, 1996), 306–307.

13. A. J. Ayre, introduction to *Logical Positivism*, ed. A. J. Ayre (Glencoe, Ill.: The Free Press, 1959), 13, 17.

14. Ibid., 11.

15. Again, it is important to stress that this line of argument is at odds with most contemporary *scientific* theories.

16. Rudolf Carnap, "The Elimination of Metaphysics Through Logical Analysis of Language," in *Logical Positivism*, ed. A. J. Ayre (Glencoe, Ill.: The Free Press, 1959), 77.

17. Ayre, introduction to *Logical Positivism*, 19.

18. Carnap, "The Elimination of Metaphysics," 62–63.

19. Carnap, "The Scientific Conception of the World," 317.

20. Carnap, "The Elimination of Metaphysics," 66.

21. Ibid., 67.

22. Ibid., 69.

23. Ibid., 79.

24. Carnap, "The Scientific Conception of the World," 317–318.

25. Stephen Jay Gould, *Hen's Teeth and Horse's Toes: Further Reflections on Natural History* (New York: Norton, 1983), 367.

26. Carl Schorske, *Fin-de-Siècle Vienna: Politics and Culture* (New York: Random House, 1979), 339.

27. Robert Venturi, *Complexity and Contradiction in Architecture* (New York: Museum of Modern Art, 1977), 16.

28. Immanuel Kant, *Critique of Judgment*, trans. James Meredith (New York: Oxford University Press, 1973), part 2, 21.

29. Dieter Henrich, *Between Kant and Hegel: Lectures on German Idealism*, ed. David Pacini (Cambridge, Mass.: Harvard University Press, 2003), 287.

30. Jean-Luc Nancy, *The Experience of Freedom*, trans. Bridget McDonald (Stanford, Calif.: Stanford University Press, 1993), 54.

31. Kant, *Critique of Pure Reason*, 314.

32. Rodolphe Gasché, "Ideality in Fragmentation," foreword to Friedrich Schlegel, *Philosophical Fragments*, trans. Peter Firchow (Minneapolis: University of Minneapolis Press, 1991), xix–xx.

33. Martin Heidegger, *Hegel's Concept of Experience*, trans. Kenley Dove (New York: Harper and Row, 1970), 48–49.

34. Martin Heidegger, *Schelling's Treatise on the Essence of Human Freedom*, trans. Joan Stambaugh (Athens: Ohio University Press), 162.

35. Sigmund Freud, *The Interpretation of Dreams*, trans. James Strachey (New York: Avon, 1965), 143.

36. Kant, *Critique of Judgment*, 86.

37. Nancy, *The Experience of Freedom*, 13.

38. Martin Heidegger, *Kant and the Problem of Metaphysics*, trans. Richard Taft (Bloomington: Indiana University Press, 1997), 118.

39. G. W. F. Hegel, *The Logic of Hegel*, trans. William Wallace (New York: Oxford University Press, 1968), 162.

40. Rodolph Gasché, *The Honor of Thinking: Critique, Theory, Philosophy* (Stanford, Calif.: Stanford University Press, 2007), 206–207.

41. Martin Heidegger, "The End of Philosophy and the Task of Thinking," in *On Time and Being*, trans. Joan Stambaugh (New York: Harper and Row, 1979), 71.

42. Though Heidegger does not make the point, his interpretation of language suggests an artistic and even aesthetic aspect of scientific discourse that Carnap overlooks.

43. Martin Heidegger, "The Origin of the Work of Art," in *Poetry, Language, Thought*, trans. Albert Hofstadter (New York: Harper Row, 1971), 53.

44. Wallace Stevens, "The Snow Man," in *The Collected Poems of Wallace Stevens* (New York: Knopf, 1981), 10.

45. Martin Heidegger, *Poetry, Language, Thought*, 118.

46. Martin Heidegger, "The Question Concerning Technology," in *Basic Writings*, ed. David Krell (New York: Harper and Row, 1977), 315–316.

47. Taylor, *After God*, 12.

48. Samuel Taylor Coleridge, *Biographia Literaria*, ed. J. Shawcross (New York: Oxford University Press, 1967), 1:202.

49. Friedrich Nietzsche, *Will to Power*, trans. Walter Kaufmann (New York: Random House, 1968), 36.

50. Friedrich Nietzsche, *Birth of Tragedy*, trans. Francis Golffling (New York: Doubleday, 1956) 9, 22, 42, 56, 65.

51. Wallace Stevens, "An Ordinary Evening in New Haven," in *The Collected Poems of Wallace Stevens* (New York: Knopf, 1981), 486.

52. Heidegger, *Der Spiegel* interview. See note 10 of the introduction to this book.

53. Wallace Stevens, *Opus Posthumous*, ed. Stanley Morse (New York: Vintage, 1990), 178.

# INDEX

apes, 2; Barbary, 26, 292n16; sacrifice of, 29–30, 45

Apollo, 214, 217, 285

apostolic succession, doctrine of, 13

Aquinas, Thomas, 252–54, 302n1

*Arcades Project* (Benjamin), 112

archaeology, 196–97, 278

*Architects of the Web: One Thousand Days That Built the Future of Business* (Reid), 80

architecture, 136–37, 271–72, 302n2; of house in *House of Leaves*, 147–50; non-style of, 281

Area 51, 168

Aristotle, 20, 302n1

Arius, 25, 292n15

art: Byzantine, 81, 103–4; Carnap on, 273; caves and relation to, 78, 83–84; *City*, 167, 174–76, 216; *Complex One*, 174, 176; counterfeits of counterfeits with, 33–36, 52–53; *Double Negative*, 175; information age and, 88; origin of, 34; Paris as synonymous with, 17; philosophy influenced by, 3, 270–71, 273; Powers with, 74–75, 81–82; as religious and spiritual inspiration, 4; as salvation, 16, 51–52; science and, 256–72; style's influence on, 10; theology influenced by, 3, 4, 57–58; as "thing of the past," 2–3, 245. *See also* high art; low art; Salvation Mountain

artificial intelligence, 63–64, 75

artists: as alchemist, 32–34; God and creative activity as one for, 4, 285–86; Kant influencing, 3–4; originality of, 22; Slab City and, 165–67, 173. *See also* *specific artists*

Association for the Advancement of Artificial Intelligence, 95–96

Augustine (saint), 9, 250, 302n1

Auster, Paul, 135–36

authorship: Johnny's, 115–17; Zampanò's, 116–20

Ayre, A. J., 264, 266

Bachelard, Gaston, 134

Barbary apes, 26, 292n16

Barney, Matthew, 5

Barnum, P. T., 112

baseball, *190*, 191; Pafko and, 188, *189*, 204–5, *206*, *234*; Roosevelt Junior High School team, *235*; Taylor, Noel Alexander and, 185, *186*, *187*; Thomson and, 182, 191, 194, 204–5, *232*, *233*; waste and, 191–95

Basilides of Alexander, 293n24

Bataille, Georges, 78, 212–19

Baudrillard, Jean, 6, 104–5, 112

"Bedroom in Arles," 89

*Begriffe* (concepts), 3

*Being and Time* (Heidegger), 121–22

Benjamin, Walter, 73, 112

Beuys, Joseph, 5, 245–46

*Biffures* (Leiris), 132

*Birth of Tragedy* (Nietzsche), 284–85

*Birth of Art, The* (Bataille), 78–79

black, 46, 150, 153–54, 201

Blanchot, Maurice, 5, 127

blood, Eucharist and, 37–38, 54–55

Boggs, J. S. G., 112

book covers, *137*

Borges, Jorge Luis, 130–32

brains: artificial, 63–64; poems about, 65–66. *See also* artificial intelligence

"Brain—is wider than the Sky—, The" (Dickinson), 65–66

Brin, Serge, 95
browsers, World Wide Web, 80–81
Bruegel, Pieter the Elder, 231–32
Bush, George W., 168
Byzantine art, 81, 103–4

calculator, mechanical, 294n15
Camilla myth, 292n9, 293n24
Camp Dunlap, 161
capitalism: as all-consuming success, 9;
    cyber-, 238; financial, 7–8, 85, 213, 236–
    40, 293n17; industrial and consumer,
    182–83, 236–40
Carnap, Rudolph, 10, 256, 262; on art, 273;
    early years of, 257–58; as opposed to
    obscurantism, 11; on science, 263–64,
    266–67; on syntax of language, 266–68
Carter, Jimmy, 299n10
causality principle, God and, 3–4
Cave Automatic Virtual Environment
    (CAVE), 81–82, 88
caves: allegory, 78–81, 92; art's relation to,
    78, 83–84; Jebel Hira, 78, 96; in Turkey,
    163–64
Celts, Samhain festival and, 23
center, centerless, 131–32, 138, 147
chancre, 292n11
chaos, 20, 37, 59, 187, 200
chapters, fragmented, 41–42
Chardin, Teilhard Pierre, 297n2
Chrichton, Michael, 95
Christianity: cave origins of, 78; as
    counterfeit of counterfeit, 38–39;
    God as eternal in, 20; Mithraism and,
    37–38, 40; Nietzsche on, 58–59, 60–61;
    paganism's influence on, 38–39, 42
Christmas. See Sol Invictus
Christmas, Doug, 166, 173

citizens, of Slab City, 162–66
*City* (sculpture), 167, 174–76, 216
*City of Glass* (Auster), 136
*Civilization and Its Discontents* (Freud), 69
classroom teaching technologies: new,
    111–13; Real Fakes course description,
    111–12, 295n2; with teleconferencing,
    111
Clement (bishop of Rome), 13, 15
Close, Chuck, 76
"Coastline Measure," 87
code: characters as, 144; color, 297n25;
    genetic, 75–76, 94; poetry of, 93
cognitive science, 76
Cold War, 182, 220, 299n11
Coleridge, Samuel Taylor, 4, 283–84
color coded, 297n25
colors. *See* black; white
comedy, 18–19, 40, 57
communications, modern, 5–6
communism, 191, 210, 299n10
*Communist Manifesto, The* (Marx), 223,
    236
*Complexity and Contradiction in
    Architecture* (Venturi), 271–72
*Complex One* (sculpture), 174, 176. *See
    also City*
*Concept of Anxiety, The* (Kierkegaard), 122
*Concept of Dwelling, The: On the Way
    to Figurative Architecture* (Norberg-
    Schultz), 136–37
*Confidence Games: Money and Markets
    in a World Without Redemption*
    (Taylor, M.), 7
*Confidence-Man* (Melville), 144
consumer capitalism, 236–40
containment: of communism, 191, 210,
    299n10; of waste, 191, 202, 207

continental philosophy, 10, 253, 256–57, 281

Cooper, Thelma Kathryn, 1, 65

cosmic tree, 154

cosmological philosophy, 9–10, 252–53

*Cosmopolis* (DeLillo), 9, 235–37, 243

Council of Constantinople, 24, 292n15

Council of Nicea, 24

"'Counterfeit Money'" (Derrida), 112

counterfeits, of counterfeits, 23–24, 28–29, 57–62; with art, 33–36, 52–53; Christianity as, 38–39; with mummy, 50–51; religion as, 12

counternarratives, 199–200

Cox, Billy, 204–5

crack, 295n5

craft, 3, 21. *See also* low art

creative activity, 4, 285–86

creativity: anthropology with originality and, 20; originality with, 16; in *The Recognitions*, 16

*Critique of Practical Reason* (Kant), 4

*Critique of Judgment, The* (Kant), 3, 21, 273

cubists, 300n18

culture: industry, 290n10; network, 8–9, 110, 114, 223, 295n3; of simulacra, 6–7, 55, 104–5, 112

cybercapitalism, 238

Dadaists, 300n18

Dali, Salvador, 221

Danielewski, Mark, 112; on *House of Leaves*, 119; influence of, 5, 7, 8; with knowledge of literary theory, 118–19; *Only Revolutions: A Novel*, 297n25; on writers, 109; writing style of, 113, 115, 119. *See also House of Leaves*

Danielewski, Tad Z. (father), 146–47

dark, light victorious over, 46

*Dark Night of the Soul, The* (St. John), 45

*Das Kapital* (Marx), 9, 180–81

death: All Saints Day with renewal and, 20–37; Easter with renewal and, 46–57; feast of Sol Invictus with renewal and, 37–46; of God, 284; knell, 135; as renewal, 19–20; "Triumph of," 231, 233

Debord, Guy, 6

debt, 208, 222–23

DeLillo, Don, 156, 299n9, 299n11; on capitalism, 9; on everything as connected, 182–83, 223, 227–28; with film as framing device, 297n2; Freud and influence on, 197; influence of, 5, 7, 8, 248; "In the Ruins of the Future," 184; with system and excess, 184–85; with waste and religion, 202–4. *See also Cosmopolis; Point Omega; Underworld*

Derrida, Jacques, 303n6; on centers, 147; death knell and, 135; on Hegel, 132–33; on Husserl, 259–60; influence of, 112, 132; literary absolute of, 5; on philosophy, 132; *sous rature* and, 131, 296n11; *Tympanum*, 132, 133, 134–35

*Der Spiegel* interview, with Heidegger, 290n10

Descartes, René, 260

desert, as underworld of waste, 206–11

*Designing America's Waste Landscapes* (Engler), 202

de Vega, Lope, 49

developmental theory, of Freud, 69

devil: Faust and, 31; incarnate, 30; interval of, 293n29; Lucifer, 26–27; Satan, 27, 58; in Western tradition, 16

Dickinson, Emily, 65–66

Dionysus, 48, 61, 134, 214, 217–18, 285, 294n34

Freud, Sigmund, 5, 66; developmental theory of, 69; *heimlich* and, 68; influence of, 197; on intoxicating drugs, 70–71; oceanic consciousness and, 69–70; on psychoanalysis and archaeology, 196–97; on sublimation, 17; on technology, 71–73; uncanny and, 67–69, 79, 89, 121–22; *unheimlich* and, 67–69

*Future of an Illusion, The* (Freud), 69–70

Gaddis, William, 74; on Faust, 31; on *Homoousios* or *Homoiousios*, 24–25; influence of, 5–7, 88; Melville influencing, 292n14; on modernism as plague, 21–22; on *The Recognitions*, 13–14, 18–19, 31; on religion as counterfeit, 12. *See also Agape Agape*; *JR*; *The Recognitions*

*Gain* (Powers), 75

*Galatea 2.2* (Powers): artificial intelligence influencing, 63–64, 75; epigram in, 65

games, video, 67

game theory, 75, 299n11

Gasché, Rodolphe, 275–76, 279

Gawain myth, 292n9

GEN. *See* Global Education Network

general economy, 213–15, *216*

*Generosity: An Enhancement* (Powers), neuroscience and psychopharmacology in, 76

genetic code, 75–76, 94

genius, Kant on originality and, 21

Germany. *See* Jena

*Ghosts* (Auster), 136

Gibraltar, 292n16

Gibson, William, 73

*Glas* (Derrida), 135–36

Global Education Network (GEN), 110, 295n1

Gnosticism, 293n24; dualism and, 14–15; Faust legend and, 15; Valentinus with, 14–15, 32

God: absolute and ordained power of, 254–55; causality principle and, 3–4; cosmological theology and, 252; creative activity and imagination one with, 4, 285–86; death of, 284; dualism of, 14–15; Eucharist and, 19; gold as good as, 16–17, 36; as house, 152; as nothingness, 280–81; with ontological theology, 252; originality of, 20; on Salvation Mountain, 163–64; with Samhain, 23

gods: Kali and Shiva, 211, 224; romanticism with disruptive, 4–5

Goethe, Johann Wolfgang von: influence of, 15, 267; romanticism and, 16

gold: as good as God, 16–17, 36; sublimation, 17; sun as, 36

*Gold Bug Variations, The* (Powers): genetic code influencing, 75; plot, 76

Goldsworthy, Andy, 5

*Gone Tomorrow: The Hidden Life of Garbage* (Rogers), 220

good, as God and gold, 16–17, 36

Good, I. J., 96

Google, 95, 142, 167

Gould, Stephen Jay, 270

graphic design, 113, 143, 297n25

Gropius, Walter, 270

Hahn, Hans, 258, 263–64

Halloween, 23, 117. *See also* Samhain

*Haunted*, 141

Hegel, Friedrich: on art as "thing of the past," 2–3, 245; Derrida on, 132–33;

influence of, 10; on nothingness and freedom, 278

Heidegger, Martin, 10, 256, 268; on abolition of distance and time, 123–24; on anxiety, 124; on culture industry, 290n10; early years of, 257–58; influence of, 10–11, 121; on nihilation, 262–63; with philosophy with art, 273; on science, 260–62, 276; on technology, 282–83; on thing as nothing, 124–25

*heimlich* (not strange), 68, 122. *See also* *unheimlich*

Heisenberg, Werner, 302n4

Heizer, Michael, 166–78; *City* sculpture, 167, 174–76, 216; *Complex One*, 174, 176; *Double Negative* sculpture, 175

*Hello*, 144–45, 297n23

Henrich, Dieter, 274–75

*Heteroousian*, 292n15

heterotopias, 201–2

*Hiding* (Taylor, M. C.), 67

high art, 3, 21, 217, 273–74

Hitler, Adolf, 300n19

Hodges, Russ, 204

Hoftstadter, Douglas, 297n24

Hölderlin, Friedrich, 4, 282

Hollander, John, 151

Hollerith, Herman, 88, 294n15

*Homoiousios* (like, similar), doctrine of, 24–25, 41, 60

*Homoousios* (identical), doctrine of, 24–25, 41, 60, 292n15

Horvitz, Eric, 95–96

hostages, 82

*House of Leaves* (Danielewski, M.), 8; adult reaction to, 113; *The Anti-Present Trunk* and, 296n7; anxiety in, 122–24;

architecture of house in, 147–50; Auster influencing, 136; black and white in, 150, 153–54; book cover, *137*; centerless center in, 131–32, *138*, 147; characterization of, 119–20; characters as code in, 144; cosmic tree uprooted in, 154; Danielewski on, 119; epigrams in, 120; *Glas* as prototype for, 135; history of, 139; *Idiot's Guide* website for, 143–44; image's relation to truth in, 113; interpretations of, 119; Johnny's authorship of, 115–17; labyrinthine format of, 113–14, 134, *138*, 148, *149*, 150, 151–52, 154–55; names in, 117–18; *The Navidson Record* in, 114–19, 135, 140–41; plot, 114–15; Poe influencing, 136; with Real Fakes class, 111–12; spatial domains in, 121, 139; student reaction to, 113–15, 141–44; terror in, 126–27; thing as nothing in, 124–25, 127–29, 136–37, 150–51; "Tympan" in, 133–34; as World Wide Web, 139; Zampanò's authorship of, 116–20

Hubbard, Douglas, 294n16

human freedom, 4, 266, 277

Hume, David: on causality principle, 3–4; influence of, 4

Hus, John, 26

Husserl, Edmund, 259–60

IBM, founding of, 294n15

*Idea of the Holy, The* (Otto), 202–3

identical. *See Homoousios*, doctrine of

illustrations, "Coastline Measure," 87

image, truth's relation to, 113

imagination: God as one with creative activity and, 4, 285–86; Kant with, 277; primary and secondary, 283–84 imitation, originality and, 21

industrial capitalism, 182–83, 236–40

industrial pollution, 75

information: age and, 88; technologies, 5–6

Internet, Mosaic and, 80–81

*Interpretation of Dreams, The* (Freud), 197–98

interval, devil's, 293n29

*In the Loop: Don DeLillo and the Systems Novel* (LeClair), 299n9

"In the Ruins of the Future" (DeLillo), 184

*Introductory Lectures* (Freud), 66

Irenaeus (saint), 14–15, 32, 34

Islam, cave origins of, 78

isolation, writing in, 83–84

Itten, Joseph, 300n18

Jabès, Edmond, 5

Janis, Melisa Tao, 296n7

Jebel Hira cave, 78, 96

Jena, 3

Jena, romanticism, 4

Jessup, Phillip, *235*

John (saint), 45

Johnny (fictional character): authorship of, 115–17. *See also House of Leaves*

*JR* (Gaddis), 6–7, 17

Kali, 211, 224

Kant, Immanuel: with ethical defense of religion, 4; on high art and low art, 3, 273–74; with imagination, 277; influence of, 3–4, 272–73; on originality and imitation, 21; romanticism and, 16

Kennan, George F., 299n10

*kenosis* (self-emptying), 62

Khrushchev, Nikita, 180, 221

Kierkegaard, Søren, 5; on anxiety, 122; influence of, 2–3, 10, 112

Kimmelman, Michael, 167–69

kitsch, 21

Klimt, Gustav, 270

Knight, Leonard, 163–64

Koons, Jeff, 112, 165

Kurtzweil, Ray, 94–95

labyrinth, in *House of Leaves*: format, 113–14, 134, 150, 154–55; names with centerless, *138*; of notes, 148, *149*, 151–52

Lacoue-Labarthe, Philippe, 5

Lafaye, 132

language, syntax of, 266–68

*Lascaux. See Birth of Art, The*; caves

Leavey, John, 296n16

Lebow, Victor, 221

LeClair, Tom, 299n9

Le Corbusier, 200–201, 300n18, 300n20

legislation, Yucca Mountain Development Act, 168, 299n4

Leiris, Michel, 132

Leonard, John, 75

Lichtenberg, Georg Christoph, 2

lies, self-negation of, 28–29

life: as human and computational, 90–93; the Singularity shift of, 96

light, Easter and symbolism of, 46–47

like. *See Homoiousios*, doctrine of

literary absolute, 5

*Locked Room, The* (Auster), 136

Loos, Adolf, 270

lose. *See perdu*

love, as necessity, 61

low art: craft as, 3, 21; high art distinct from, 3, 21, 217, 273–74; with kitsch, 21

Lucifer, 26–27. *See also* devil
Luther, Martin, 30

Malevich, Kasimir, 150
Mandelbrot, Benoit, 87
Mani, 47
Manichaeism, 47–48
*manii. See* sacramental loaves
Marinetti, Filippo, 300n20
market mechanisms, 75
Markoff, John, 95
Márquez, José, 67
Marx, Karl, 70, 180, 220, 223
mask, as reality, 51–54, 61–62
Massachusetts Museum of Contemporary
    Art, 2
Massumi, Brian, 192–93
melancholia, of things completed, 56, 58
Melville, Herman, 5, 144, 292n14
"Minotaur, The" (Borges), 130–31
miracles, 90, 153, 184, 225, 227
Mitchell, William J., 150
Mithraism: Christianity and, 37–38, 40;
    Sol Invictus with, 42
modernism: emergence of, 3; with Faust,
    15–16; music, 75–76; originality with,
    21; Paris as capital of, 17; as plague,
    21–22; in Vienna, 269–70
modernity, with originality, 20–21
Monte Carlo methods, 90, 294n16
Moore, Stephen, 47, 49, 292n9
Mosaic, 80–81
*Motel Réal: Las Vegas, Nevada*, 67
mother: with developmental theory, 69;
    uncanny related to, 69, 79, 89
"MS. Found in a Bottle" (Poe), 126–27, 136
Muhammed, 78, 96
Myspace, 110

mythological precursors, names as, 292n9
myths: Camilla, 292n9, 293n24; Gawain,
    292n9; Native American rituals and, 37

names: with centerless labyrinth, *138*; in
    *House of Leaves*, 117–18; multiplicity of,
    18, 24, 26, 31–32, 50, 55; as mythological
    precursors, 292n9
Nancy, Jean-Luc, 5, 275
narratives, counter-, 199–200
*Narrative of Arthur Gordon Pym, The*
    (Poe), 126, 136
National Center for Supercomputing
    Applications (NCSA), 80
Native Americans, myths and rituals, 37
*Navidson Record, The* (film), 114–19, 135,
    140–41
Nazis, 121, 290n10
NCSA. *See* National Center for
    Supercomputing Applications
necessity, love as, 61
negation, self-, 22, 28–29
negentropy, 200, 300n17
Nellis Air Force Base, 168
Netscape, 80
Neurath, Otto, 258, 263–64
neuroscience, 76
new: media, 5–6; old with, 21–22, 52; self-
    negation of, 22
*New York Trilogy* (Auster), 135, 136
Nietzsche, Friedrich, 14; on *amor fati*, 61;
    on Christianity, 58–59, 60–61; death of
    God and, 284; influence of, 17, 57–58;
    melancholia of things completed,
    56, 58; on nihilism, 201; with will to
    power, 10–11, 260
nihilation, 262–63
9/11, 184

Nixon, Richard, 221
nominalist theology, 264–65
Norberg-Schulz, Christian, 136–37
nothingness: freedom and, 278; God and, 280–81; in *House of Leaves*, 124–25, 127–29, 136–37, 150–51
not strange. *See heimlich*
Novalis, 4
nuclear bomb, 233
nuclear waste, 223, 299n4
numerology, three, 47

Obama, Barack, 299n4
object, paintings as image and unity of, 59–60
obscurantism, 11
oceanic consciousness, 69–70
Ockham, William of, 253–56, 265
old: new with, 21–22, 52; self-negation of, 22
One Can, 168
*On Growth and Form* (Gould), 270
*Only Revolutions: A Novel* (Danielewski, M.), 297n25
ontological philosophy, 9–10, 250–53
*Operation Wandering Soul* (Powers), 75
opiate, religion as, 70–71
Oppenheimer, J. Robert, 211, 249
ordained power, 254–55
"Ordinary Evening in New Haven, An" (Stevens), 285
originality: anthropology with creativity and, 20; of artists, 22; creativity with, 16; Kant on imitation and, 21; with modernism, 21; modernity with, 20–21; in *The Recognitions*, 16, 27–28; as theological issue, 20; of writers, 22
original sin, 27, 31

origins: of art, 34; of Eostur, 47
"Origin of Geometry, The" (Husserl), 259
Otto, Rudolph, 202–3
Ozenfant, Amédée, 200–201

Packard, Vance, 220–21
Pafko, Andy, 188, *189*; baseball and, *206*, *234*; pennant and, 204–5
paganism: Christianity influenced by, 38–39, 42; Easter influenced by, 47
Pahranagat Valley, 169
paintings: "Bedroom in Arles," 89; "The Dream," 89; forgeries, 290n10; "The Triumph of Death," 231, 233; *The Truth in Painting*, 136, 295n5; as unity of object and image, 59–60
*Parables for the Virtual: Movement, Affect, Sensation* (Massumi), 192–93
*Parasite, The*, 192–93
Paris, art synonymous with, 17
Patton, George S., 161
Paul (saint), 59
*perdu* (to lose), 292n12
*Phenomenon of Man, The* (Chardin), 297n2
philosophy: art influencing, 3, 270–71, 273; continental, 10, 253, 256–57, 281; cosmological, 9–10, 252–53; Derrida on, 132; ontological, 9–10, 250–53; religion as two types of, 250; task of, 259–60; as *wissenschaftlich*, 2
photography, 1, 2, 111, 114, 152; aerial, 226; banning of, 152, 173, 178; influence of, 75, 146, 191; Powers influenced by, 74; *Young Westerwald Farmers on Their Way to the Dance*, 74
physics, influence of, 75–76

"Pit and the Pyramid, The: Introduction to Hegel's Semiology" (Derrida), 299n6

plague, modernism as, 21–22

Planck, Max, 302n4

Plank, Eddie, 185

Plato, 8, 14, 78–81, 92, 302n1

*Plowing the Dark* (Powers): cave influences in, 79–81, 92; life as human and computational in, 90–93; reality in, 85–88; review, 75; Taimur's story in, 96–103; time in, 98–101; uncanny in, 89; virtual reality technology in, 7, 75, 80, 81, 84–88

Poe (singer): "Angry Johnny," 144, 297n23; father's influence on, 145–47; "5 and 1/2 Minute Hallway," 140–41, 147; *Hello*, 144–45, 297n23; "Terrified Heart," 147

Poe, Edgar Allen, 5, 126–27, 129, 136

poems: "The Brain—is wider than the Sky—", 65–66; "The Minotaur," 130–31; "An Ordinary Evening in New Haven," 285; "Sailing to Byzantium," 84, 103–4, 105

*Poetics of Space, The* (Bachelard), 134

poetry: coded, 93; as form of religion, 4, 59; on Wordsworth's, 151

poets, 4, 158. *See also specific poets*

*Point Omega* (DeLillo), 8–9, 212, 297n2

polarities: in *Plowing the Dark*, 97; in *The Recognitions*, 13

postmodernism, 3

Potter, Dennis, 8

power: absolute and ordained, 254–55; will to, 10–11, 260

Powers, Richard, 63, 67; with art, religion and technology, 74–75, 81–82; early writing career of, 73–74; *The Echo Makers*, 76; *Gain*, 75; *Generosity: An Enhancement*, 76; *The Gold Bug Variations*, 75, 76; influence of, 5, 7; *Operation Wandering Soul*, 75; photography influencing, 74; with science fiction, 73–77; with scientific theory, 7, 8; on structure of novels, 77; *Three Farmers on Their Way to the Dance*, 74, 75; *The Time of Our Singing*, 75–76; on Waite, 82–83. *See also Galatea 2.2; Plowing the Dark*

"Precession of the Simulacrum, The" (Baudrillard), 104–5

*Prey* (Chrichton), 95

primary imagination, 283–84

*Prisoner's Dilemma* (Powers), 66–67; game theory influencing, 75, 299n11

*Prose Edda*, 154

*Psycho* (film), 297n2

psychoanalysis, with archaeology, 196–97

psychological technology, 75

psychopharmacology, 76

Pynchon, Thomas, 300n17

quantum dust, 243

quantum theory, 302n4

"Question Concerning Technology, The" (Heidegger), 282–83

radioactive waste, 168–69

Rand, Richard, 296n16

Rauschenberg, Robert, 221

reading: books in sun, 141, 297n18; as different today, 110; as religious activity, 83

Real Fakes: course description, 111–12, 295n2; website for, 143. *See also House of Leaves* reality: cave allegory and, 78, 92; as elusive, 17–18; hide-and-seek play of, 152–53; mask as, 51–54, 61–62; in *Plowing the Dark*, 85–88; virtual reality replacing, 110; virtual reality technology and, 7, 75, 80, 81, 84–88

*Recognitions, The* (Gaddis), 6–7; All Saints Day in, 22–23; ape sacrificed in, 29–30; Christmas in, 37–46; as comedy, 18–19; counterfeiting counterfeits in, 23–24, 28–29, 33–36, 50–53, 57–62; with creativity and originality, 16; death in, 19–20; dualism in, 13, 18; Easter in, 46–57; epigram in, 14, 15–16, 41–42, 49; Faust influencing, 31; fragmented chapter in, 41–42; Gaddis on, 13–14, 18–19, 31; as last Christian novel, 12, 14, 19, 57; melancholia of things completed in, 56, 58; with multiplicity of names in, 18, 24, 26, 31–32, 50, 55; Nietzsche influencing, 57–58; originality in, 16, 27–28; origins of, 15; polarities in, 13; reality as elusive in, 17–18; reality as mask in, 51–54, 61–62; rituals in, 19–20; sacramental loaves in, 47–48; three in, 47; truth with title of, 13–14

*Reconfigured Eye, The: Visual Truth in the Post-Photographic Era* (Mitchell), 150

redemption, sun as, 36, 40, 43–44, 174

*Refiguring the Spiritual* (Taylor, M. C.), 10–11, 245

Reid, Robert, 80

religion: cave and influence in, 78; as counterfeit of counterfeit, 12; eighteenth century and changes in, 3–4; as intoxicating drug, 70–71; Kant's ethical defense of, 4; within limits of style alone, 272–81; poetry as form of, 4, 59; Powers with, 74–75, 81–82; purpose of, 218; with reading and writing, 83; two types of philosophy of, 250; virtual reality technology and ties to, 81; with waste, 202–4. *See also* Christianity; *specific religions*

religious inspiration, 4

renewal: All Saints Day with death and, 20–37; death as, 19–20; Easter with death and, 46–57; feast of Sol Invictus with death and, 37–46

representations. *See Vorstellungen*

*Republic, The* (Plato), 78

reviews: *Plowing the Dark*, 75; *Prey*, 95

Rheinardt, Adolf "Ad," 150

Ribbons, 296n15. *See also* Auster, Paul

Rilke, Rainer Maria, 11, 285–86

rituals: Native American myths and, 37; in *The Recognitions*, 19–20; of Sol Invictus, 43–46

Roden Crater, 139

Rodin, Sam, 163

Rogers, Heather, 220

romanticism: with disruptive gods, 4–5; in Europe, 4; with Goethe, 16; Jena, 4; with Kant, 16

Roosevelt Junior High School Baseball Team, 235

Rosenquist, James, 221

Rousseau, Henri, 89

sacramental loaves (*manii*), 47–48, 54–55

sacred space, waste with, 195–204

sacrifice, ape as, 29–30, 45

"Sailing to Byzantium" (Yeats), 84, 103–4, 105

Salinger, J. D., 293n31

students, 295n2; *House of Leaves* and
reaction of, 113–15, 141–44; as owners
of new spatial domains, 139; on
reading books in sun, 297n18; as
thinking differently today, 110; Web as
inhabitable space for today's, 109–10
style: art's influence on, 10; Danielewski,
Mark, and writing, 113, 115, 119; non,
281; questions of, 281–86; religion
within limits of, 272–81
sublimation: with alchemy, 16–17, 36;
Freud and, 17; gold, 17
Sufi chants, 241
sun, 129; birthday of, 42; as gold, 36;
reading books in, 141, 297n18; as
redemption, 36, 40, 43–44, 174; solar
economy and, 212
surgical technology, 75
surrealists, 177, 237, 300, 300n18
syphilis, 292n11

Taimur (fictional character): in solitude,
96–103; with time, 99–101. *See also
Plowing the Dark*
Tansey, Mark, 87
Taylor, Mark C., 10–11; baseball and,
185–91; De Lillo influencing, 248;
Earth Work and, *246–47*, 248–49
Taylor, Noel Alexander (father), 1; baseball
and, 185, *186*, *187*
technology: classroom teaching, 111–13,
295n2; Freud on, 71–73; Heidegger
on, 282–83; information, 5–6; Powers
with, 74–75, 81–82; psychological and
surgical, 75; virtual reality, 7, 75, 80, 81,
84–88, 104–5
teleconferencing, 111
"Terrified Heart," 147

terror, 126–27
theology: as anthropology, 19; art
influencing, 3, 4, 57–58; cosmological,
9–10, 252–53; eighteenth century and
changes in, 3–4; nominalist, 264–65;
ontological, 9–10, 250–53; originality
as issue of, 20
theory: developmental, 69; film, 113; game,
75, 299n11; literary, 118–19; quantum,
302n4; scientific, 7, 8
thing as nothing, in *House of Leaves*,
124–25, 127–29, 136–37, 150–51
thinking, as different today, 110
*This Is Not a Pipe* (Foucault), 112
Thomas Aquinas (saint), 10
Thomson, Bobby, baseball and, 182, 191,
194, 204–5, 232, 233
Thoreau, Henry David, 4
three, in *The Recognitions*, 47
*Three Farmers on Their Way to the Dance*
(Powers), 74, 75
Tillich, Paul, 302n1; with cosmological
theology, 9–10, 252–53; influence of,
9; with ontological theology, 9–10,
250–53
time: abolition of distance and, 123–24;
*Being and Time*, 121–22; in *Plowing the
Dark*, 98–101; solitude and, 99
*Time of Our Singing, The* (Powers),
75–76
transcendentalism, in U.S., 4
*Travels in Hyperreality* (Eco), 112
"Triumph of Death, The," 231, 233
Truman, Harry, 299n10
truth, 150; *Aletheia* and, 279–80; image's
relation to, 113; in *The Recognitions*,
13–14; self-negation of, 28–29; in
solitude, 106–8

*Truth in Painting, The* (Derrida), 136, 295n5

Turkey, 163–64

Turrell, James, 5, 139

"Two Types of Philosophy of Religion" (Tillich), 9

*Tympanum* (Derrida), 132, *133*, 134–35

uncanny, 121; Freud and, 67–69, 79, 89, 121–22; mother related to, 69, 79, 89

"'Uncanny,' The" (Freud), 67–68

unconcealment. *See Aletheia*

under erasure. *See sous rature*

*Underworld* (DeLillo), 8–9; Cold War in, 182; counternarratives in, 199–200; economy of waste and, 212–19; epilogue in, 180; with excessive production of waste, 220–29; with inner division of people and systems, 179–80; Part 1, 179–85; prologue, 156–78; title of, 179; waste, baseball and, 191–95; with waste as sacred space, 195–204; waste of desert as underworld in, 206–11

*unheimlich* (un-homelike): etymology of, 67–68; Freud and, 67–69, 121–22; Heidegger and, 121

un-homelike. *See unheimlich*

United States, transcendentalism in, 4

unity, of object and image, 59–60

University of Illinois, Chicago, 80–81

Unmoved Mover, 20. *See also* God

*Unterwelt* (film), 179

Upanishads, 249

Valentinus: Gnosticism and, 14–15, 32; on origin of art, 34

van der Rohe, Mies, 270

van Gogh, Vincent, 89

van Meegeren, Hans, 290n10

Venturi, Robert, 271–72, 281

video games, *Motel Réal: Las Vegas, Nevada*, 67

Vienna, modernism in, 269–70

Vienna Circle, 263–64, 270

Vinge, Vernor, 96

virtual reality, reality replaced by, 110

virtual reality technology: Baudrillard on, 104–5; influence of, 7, 75; origins, 80; in *Plowing the Dark*, 84–88; religion's ties to, 81

*Vorstellungen* (representations), 3, 275–76, 283

Wagner, Otto, 270

Wagner, Richard, 291n5

Waite, Terry, 82, 107

Warhol, Andy, 112, 221

waste: archaeology and, 196–97; baseball and, 191–95; containment of, 191, 202, 207; debt and, 222–23; desert as underworld with, 206–11; economy of, 212–19; excessive production of, 220–22; heterotopias and, 201–2; nuclear, 223, 299n4; radioactive, 168–69; religion with, 202–4; as sacred space, 195–204

Watts Towers, 163, 210

Web. *See* World Wide Web

web, dreams as subterranean, 197–98

webcast classes, 110

websites: Amazon.com, 63, 296n7; *Idiot's Guide to House of Leaves*, 143–44; miracles, 27; Real Fakes, 143; Singularity University, 95

Western tradition, devil in, 16

"What Is Metaphysics?" (Heidegger), 268

white: black and, 46, 150, 153–54, 201; light and, 46–47

Whitehead, Alfred North, 250

William of Ockham, 10

will to power, 10–11, 260

Wilson, David, 112

*wissenschaftlich* (scientific): changing meaning of, 3; philosophy as, 2

Wordsworth, William, 4, 151

World Wide Web, 8; browsers, 80–81; classes on, 110; *House of Leaves* as, 139; spatial domains of, 139, 142–43. *See also* websites

writers: Danielewski, Mark, on, 109; God and creative activity as one for, 4, 285–86; Kant influencing, 3–4; originality of, 22; in solitude, 83–84. *See also specific writers*

writing, 244–45; as black and white interplay, 150; Danielewski, Mark, and style of, 113, 115, 119; as different today, 110; of disaster, 127; in isolation, 83–84; as religious activity, 83

Yeats, William Butler, 84, 103–4, 105

*Young Westerwald Farmers on Their Way to the Dance*, 74

Yucca Mountain Development Act of 2002, 168, 299n4

Zampanò (fictional character): authorship of, 116–20. *See also House of Leaves*

Zwingli, Ulrich, 24

## BOOKS BY MARK C. TAYLOR

*Refiguring the Spiritual: Beuys, Barney, Turrell, Goldsworthy*
*Crisis on Campus: A Bold Plan for Reforming Our Colleges and*
    *Universities*
*Field Notes: Reflections on Dying and Living*
*After God*
*Mystic Bones*
*Confidence Games: Money and Markets in a World Without Redemption*
*The Moment of Complexity: Emerging Network Culture*
*Grave Matters* (with Christian Lammerts)
*About Religion: Economies of Faith in Virtual Culture*
*The Picture in Question: Mark Tansey and the Ends of Representation*
*Hiding*
*The Réal: Las Vegas, Nevada* (CD-ROM, with José Marquez)
*Imagologies: Media Philosophy* (with Esa Saarinen)
*Nots*
*Disfiguring: Art, Architecture, Religion*
*Double Negative*
*Tears*
*Altarity*
*Erring: A Postmodern A/theology*
*Deconstructing Theology*
*Journeys to Selfhood: Hegel and Kierkegaard*
*Religion and the Human Image* (with Carl Raschke and James Kirk)
*Kierkegaard's Pseudonymous Authorship: A Study of Time and the Self*

## BOOKS EDITED BY MARK C. TAYLOR

*Critical Terms for Religious Studies*
*Deconstruction in Context: Literature and Philosophy*
*Unfinished Essays in Honor of Ray L. Hart*